THE PRINCETON REVIEW
High School
Math III Review

THE PRINCETON REVIEW

High School Math III Review

BY DAVID S. KAHN

RANDOM HOUSE, INC.
New York 1998
www.randomhouse.com

Princeton Review Publishing, L.L.C.
2315 Broadway, 3rd Floor
New York, NY 10024
E-mail: info@review.com

Copyright © 1998 by Princeton Review Publishing, L.L.C.

All rights reserved under International and Pan-American Copyright Conventions. Published in the United States by Random House, Inc., New York, and simultaneously in Canada by Random House of Canada Limited, Toronto.

ISBN: 0-375-75075-4

Editor: Steve Schreiber
Production Editor: Amy Bryant
Designer: Illeny Maaza
Production Coordinator: Matt Reilly
Illustrations: Scott Harris, Adam Hurwitz, and Iam Williams

Manufactured in the United States of America on recycled paper.

9 8 7 6 5 4 3 2 1

First Edition

ACKNOWLEDGMENTS

First of all, I would like to thank Arnold Feingold and Peter B. Kahn for once again doing every problem, reading every word, and otherwise lending their invaluable assistance. I also want to thank my editor, Lesly Atlas, and my producer, Amy Bryant; and the rest of The Princeton Review for their assistance. Thanks also to Gary King, Nancy Schneider, and Blase Caruana, for reviewing all of the test problems. Thanks to Frank, without whose advice I probably wouldn't be doing this altogether, and to Carl, for reasons beyond counting. Thanks to Jeffrey and Miriam for moral support. Thanks Mom.

Finally, I would like to thank the people who really made all of this effort worthwhile—my students. Your support truly helped make this book possible, so thank you:

Aaron G., Aaron R., Abby B., Abby F., Aidan, Alex, Alex and Gabe, Alexandra, Alexes, Alexis, Ali, Alicia, Allison and Andrew S., Ally, Alyssa, Amanda B., Amanda C., Amanda M., Amelia,Andrea T., Andrea V., Andrew B., Andrew S., Andy and Allison, Anna L-W., Anna F., Anna M., April, Arthur, Arya, Asheley and Freddy, Ashley, Ashley and Lauren, Bethany and Lesley, Betsy and Jon, Blythe, Brett, Brian, Brooke, Butch, Caitlin, Caroline, Chad, Christine, Christine W., Chrissy, Claudia, Corinne, Courtney, Craig, Daniel, Danielle, Dara P., Dara M. Deborah, Devon, Dora, Eairinn, Elisa, Emily B., Emily C., Emily G., Emily L., Emily S., Emily T. and Erica H., Eric and Lauren, Erin, Frank, Gabby, Geoffrey, George, Gloria, Heather, Hilary, Holli, Holly G., Holly K., Ingrid, Jackson, Jaclyn, Jacob, Jan, Jason, Jason Q., Jay, Jenna, Jen, Jennifer B., Jennifer W., Jesse, Jessica, Jessica L., Jocelyn, Johanna, John, John and Dan, Jon, Jordan, Josh, Judie, Julia, Julie H., Julie and Dana, Kat, Kate D., Kate L., Kate S., Katie, Katrina, Kimberly, Kitty, Laura F., Laura G., Laura Z., Lauren R., Lauren T., Lauren W., Lee R., Lee S., Leigh, Lila, Lily, Lily Hayes, Lindsay F., Lindsay R., Lindsay, Lisa, Lizzy, Magnolia, Mara, Mariel, Marielle, Marietta, Marisa, Marsha, Mary M., Matt, Matt S., Matthew B., Matt B., Matthew F., Matt V., Maya and Rohit, Melissa, Meredith, Milton, Morgan, Nadia, Nathania, Nicole, Nikki,

Nora, Oliver, Omar, Oren, Paige, Pam, Peter, Rachel A., Rachel B., Rachel F., Rachel M., Rachel R., Ramit, Rayna, Rebecca, Ricky, Ruthie, Sally, Sam C., Sam L., Sam W., Samantha W., Samar, Samuel C., Sara, Sarah L., Sarah M-D., Sarah S., Sascha, Sasha, Saya, Sonja, Sonja and Talya, Sophia, Sophie, Stacy, Stacey, Stephanie, Stefanie, Tammy and Hayley, Taylor, Tenley, Terrence, Tracy, Tripp H., Tripp W., Waleed, and Zach.

If I forgot anyone, I apologize. I'll get you next time.

CONTENTS

Acknowledgments v

Introduction xi

Chapter 1: Rational and Radical Expressions 1

Chapter 2: Degrees and Radians 13

      Arc Length 15

      Sector Area 18

Chapter 3: Trigonometry 23

      Definitions of Trig Functions 23

      Special Angles 29

      More Special Angles 34

      Reference Angles 39

      How to Remember the Special Angles 46

      Trig Formulas 52

      Double Angle Formulas 67

      Trig Equations 74

      Trig Identities 79

      Sine and Cosine Graphs 83

Inverse Trig Functions 98
Applications of Trigonometry 108
Chapter 4: Complex Numbers 121
Chapter 5: Quadratic Equations 133
Chapter 6: Transformations 145
Chapter 7: Circle Rules 159
Chapter 8: Probability 175
Chapter 9: Statistics 185
Chapter 10: Logarithms 197
Chapter 11: Conic Sections 209
Chapter 12: Solutions to Practice Problems 221
Practice Exams 239
Practice Exam One 241
Practice Exam Two 253
About the Author 265

Introduction

Sequential Math III (which also goes by the name of Integrated Math III), is the last of the basic math courses for high school students. After Sequential III, students go into Precalculus and Calculus, or sometimes directly to Calculus. The course covers a wide range of topics, but its main emphasis is on Trigonometry, Transformations, and Circle Rules. It also covers some basic theory (which we call Algebra Theory), Rational Expressions, Complex Numbers (also known as *Imaginary Numbers*), Probability, Statistics, Sequences and Series, Logarithms, and (sometimes) Conic Sections. Depending on where you go to school, you will cover some of these topics in more depth than others.

We have written this book to serve as a study guide for the fundamentals of the topics covered in Sequential Math III. It is not intended to be a textbook, nor should you treat it as one. Instead, we have tried to teach you the basics of each topic, so that you can do the mechanics. We will leave it to your teachers and your textbook to go over the theory behind this stuff, and to go through the proofs. Our job is to help you get the questions right!

You will find that this course involves learning a lot of formulas. We try to show you some of the derivations of the formulas, not so much to understand them, but so that you can derive them yourself.

Why is this important? It is very difficult to keep all of these rules and formulas in your head. If you know where the formulas come from, and you can derive them on the fly, then you don't need to memorize them. For example, if you know the rule for the sine of the sum of two angles, then you can easily find the sine of a double angle (we'll show you how to do this in the appropriate chapter). Unfortunately, there are some things that you will have to memorize during this course. We try to point these out to you in the book so that you can get to work learning them.

A great deal of Sequential Math III involves trigonometry. In most courses, this occupies about half of the curriculum and we have devoted space to it accordingly. You will find that there are a lot of formulas to learn, but most of them can be derived pretty easily, so pay attention to where the formulas come from. We cover almost all of trigonometry, except for some of the graphs, so if you are taking a course in Advanced Algebra and Trigonometry, rather than Sequential Math III, you should find this very handy.

You will find that this book works best when you use it along with your textbook. When the teacher begins a topic, we suggest that you immediately read the corresponding chapter here in this book. You can work through most of the chapters in an hour or two, and that should carry you a long way through the classwork in the subject. Here we will go over the basic rules and the things that you need to know. We will also give you problems on the topic so that you know what to expect when the teacher covers it. You can also use the chapters to review a topic after the teacher has taught it to you, but we recommend that you read the stuff *before* you see it in school, not after. Many students run into trouble in courses like Sequential Math III because the teacher will spend the class time deriving something at the board and you won't understand why. Thus, you will be confused and not see a point to the exercise, rather than absorbing what the teacher shows you. If you already know what's coming, then you can pay attention to the teacher's lecture and flesh out what you learned from this book.

You will find that the chapters give both examples and practice problems. If you work through the examples carefully, you should be able to handle any of the practice problems. We tried to include a lot of examples so that you could teach yourself how to do the math.

All right, enough of the introduction. Let's get to work!

CHAPTER 1
Rational and Radical Expressions

RATIONAL EXPRESSIONS

Most of the expressions that you have seen are polynomials—that is, of the form $ax^n + bx^{n-1} + cx^{n-2} + \ldots$ where n is a nonnegative integer. Here we will learn how to manipulate *rational expressions*, which are in the form of fractions of polynomials, for example:

$$\frac{3x-5}{x^2+1}.$$

When we add fractions, we need to find a common denominator so that we can combine them. The same is true for rational expressions. Sometimes the denominators of the expressions are integers. Then, in order to combine them, we need to find a common denominator.

Example 1:

Combine $\dfrac{3x-5}{4} + \dfrac{2x+1}{3}$ *into a single expression.*

A common denominator for the two expressions is 12. We need to multiply the top and bottom of the expression on the left by 3, and the top and bottom of the expression on the right by 4. This gives us:

$$\frac{3x-5}{4} \cdot \frac{3}{3} + \frac{2x+1}{3} \cdot \frac{4}{4}$$

Now we get:

$$\frac{9x-15}{12} + \frac{8x+4}{12}.$$

If we add these two expressions together, we get:

$$\frac{9x-15+8x+4}{12} = \frac{17x-11}{12}.$$

Example 2:

Simplify $\dfrac{x^2-4x+1}{5} - \dfrac{3x+2x^2}{3} + \dfrac{7x^2+27x}{15}$.

A common denominator is 15. We need to multiply the top and bottom of the expression on the left by 3, and the top and bottom of the expression in the middle by 5. The expression on the right already has a denominator of 15, so we don't need to do anything to it. This gives us:

$$\frac{x^2-4x+1}{5} \cdot \frac{3}{3} - \frac{3x+2x^2}{3} \cdot \frac{5}{5} + \frac{7x^2+27x}{15}.$$

So the first term is: $\dfrac{3x^2-12x+3}{15}$.

The second term is: $-\dfrac{15x+10x^2}{15}$.

If we combine the three expressions, we get:

$$\frac{3x^2-12x+3}{15} - \frac{15x+10x^2}{15} + \frac{7x^2+27x}{15} =$$

$$\frac{3x^2-12x+3-15x-10x^2+7x^2+27x}{15} = \frac{3}{15} = \frac{1}{5}$$

(Notice that we distributed the minus sign in the second fraction.)

What if the rational expressions have polynomials on the bottom, instead of integers? We still have to find a common denominator in order to add them.

Example 3:

Simplify $\dfrac{4x-7}{x} + \dfrac{3x^2+1}{5}$.

Here, a common denominator is $5x$. We need to multiply the top and bottom of the expression on the left by 5, and the top and bottom of the expression on the right by x. This gives us:

$$\dfrac{4x-7}{x} \cdot \dfrac{5}{5} + \dfrac{3x^2+1}{5} \cdot \dfrac{x}{x}$$

The first term is: $\dfrac{20x-35}{5x}$.

The second term is: $\dfrac{3x^3+x}{5x}$.

Combining the two, we get: $\dfrac{20x-35+3x^3+x}{5x} = \dfrac{3x^3+21x-35}{5x}$.

Example 4:

Simplify $\dfrac{3}{x} - \dfrac{2x-5}{x-1}$.

Here, a common denominator is $x(x-1)$. Notice that we found this by multiplying the two denominators together, just as we would have had they been integers. We need to multiply the top and bottom of the first term by $(x-1)$, and the top and bottom of the second term by x. This gives us:

$$\dfrac{3}{x} \cdot \dfrac{(x-1)}{(x-1)} - \dfrac{2x-5}{x-1} \cdot \dfrac{x}{x}.$$

The first term is: $\dfrac{3x-3}{x(x-1)}$.

The second term is: $-\dfrac{2x^2 - 5x}{x(x-1)}$.

Combining the two expressions, we get:

$$\dfrac{3x - 3 - 2x^2 + 5x}{x(x-1)} = \dfrac{-2x^2 + 8x - 3}{x(x-1)}.$$

Example 5:

Simplify $\dfrac{5}{x} + \dfrac{3x-7}{x^2} - \dfrac{4x+1}{x+3}$.

Here, a common denominator is $x^2(x+3)$. We need to multiply the top and bottom of the first term by $x(x+3)$, the top and bottom of the second term by $(x+3)$, and the top and bottom of the third term by x^2. This gives us:

$$\dfrac{5}{x} \cdot \dfrac{x(x+3)}{x(x+3)} + \dfrac{3x-7}{x^2} \cdot \dfrac{(x+3)}{(x+3)} - \dfrac{4x+1}{x+3} \cdot \dfrac{x^2}{x^2}.$$

The first term is: $\dfrac{5x(x+3)}{x^2(x+3)}$,

which expands to: $\dfrac{(5x^2 + 15x)}{x^2(x+3)}$.

The second term is: $\dfrac{(3x-7)(x+3)}{x^2(x+3)}$,

which expands to: $\dfrac{(3x^2 + 2x - 21)}{x^2(x+3)}$.

The third term is: $-\dfrac{4x^3 + x^2}{x^2(x+3)}$.

Combining the three expressions, we get:

$$\dfrac{(5x^2 + 15x) + (3x^2 + 2x - 21) - 4x^3 - x^2}{x^2(x+3)} = \dfrac{-4x^3 + 7x^2 + 17x - 21}{x^2(x+3)}.$$

Wasn't that messy? Let's do one more.

Example 6:

Simplify $\dfrac{3}{x+2} + \dfrac{4}{x-1} + \dfrac{2}{x+3}$.

Here, a common denominator is $(x + 2)(x - 1)(x + 3)$. Notice that we got this by multiplying the three denominators together. We need to multiply the top and bottom of the first term by $(x - 1)(x + 3)$, the top and bottom of the second term by $(x + 2)(x + 3)$, and the top and bottom of the third term by $(x + 2)(x - 1)$. This gives us:

$$\dfrac{3}{x+2} \cdot \dfrac{(x-1)(x+3)}{(x-1)(x+3)} + \dfrac{4}{x-1} \cdot \dfrac{(x+2)(x+3)}{(x+2)(x+3)} + \dfrac{2}{x+3} \cdot \dfrac{(x+2)(x-1)}{(x+2)(x-1)}.$$

The first term is: $\dfrac{3(x-1)(x+3)}{(x+2)(x-1)(x+3)}$,

which simplifies to: $\dfrac{3x^2 + 6x - 9}{(x+2)(x-1)(x+3)}$.

The second term is: $\dfrac{4(x+2)(x+3)}{(x-1)(x+2)(x+3)}$,

which simplifies to: $\dfrac{4x^2 + 20x + 24}{(x-1)(x+2)(x+3)}$.

The third term is: $\dfrac{2(x+2)(x-1)}{(x+3)(x+2)(x-1)}$,

which simplifies to: $\dfrac{2x^2 + 2x - 4}{(x-1)(x+2)(x+3)}$.

Combining the three expressions, we get:

$$\dfrac{3x^2 + 6x - 9 + 4x^2 + 20x + 24 + 2x^2 + 2x - 4}{(x+2)(x-1)(x+3)} = \dfrac{9x^2 + 28x + 11}{(x+2)(x-1)(x+3)}.$$

RATIONAL EQUATIONS

Now, let's learn how to solve equations involving rational expressions. Whenever we solve a rational equation we must remember one very important thing:

If the solution makes the denominator zero, then we throw out the solution.

Why? Because the expression is undefined there.

For example, if the denominator of a rational equation is $x - 2$, and we get a solution to the equation of $x = 2$, then we have to throw out the solution.

This means that, whenever we solve a rational equation, we always check the answer to make sure that it is allowed.

Let's do a few examples.

Example 7:

Solve for x: $\dfrac{5}{x-3} + \dfrac{2}{x} = 0$.

There are several ways to solve this equation. We will do it by combining the expressions using a common denominator of $x(x-3)$.

We get: $\dfrac{5x}{x(x-3)} + \dfrac{2(x-3)}{x(x-3)} = 0$.

Combine the two expressions: $\dfrac{5x+2x-6}{x(x-3)} = \dfrac{7x-6}{x(x-3)} = 0$.

A fraction is zero when the numerator is zero (assuming the denominator is not also zero), so we can set the numerator equal to zero and solve. We get: $7x - 6 = 0$ and thus $x = \dfrac{6}{7}$.

Is the denominator equal to zero when $x = \dfrac{6}{7}$? No, so this is our solution.

Another technique to solving these equations is to multiply through by a common denominator, which will "clear" the denominator. This is usually faster than finding a common denominator and setting the numerator equal to zero.

Example 8:

Solve for x: $\dfrac{x}{x+1} + \dfrac{x+3}{5} = 0$.

Here, a common denominator $5(x + 1)$ is , so we will multiply through by $5(x + 1)$.

We get: $\dfrac{x}{x+1} \cdot 5(x+1) + \dfrac{x+3}{5} \cdot 5(x+1) = 0.$.

On the left, the denominator cancels, leaving us with: $5x$.

On the right, the denominator cancels, leaving us with: $(x+3)(x+1) = x^2 + 4x + 3$.

Now we are left with: $5x + (x^2 + 4x + 3) = 0$.

We can simplify this to: $x^2 + 9x + 3 = 0$.

We can solve this using the quadratic formula:

$x = \dfrac{-9 \pm \sqrt{81 - 12}}{2} = \dfrac{-9 \pm \sqrt{69}}{2}$.

Note that the denominator of the original equation is only equal to zero at $x = -1$, so we don't have to throw out the solutions.

Example 9:

Solve for x: $\dfrac{3}{x+2} + \dfrac{4}{x-1} + \dfrac{2}{x+3} = \dfrac{9x^2}{(x+2)(x-1)(x+3)}$

Here, a common denominator is $(x + 2)(x - 1)(x + 3)$, so we will multiply through by $(x + 2)(x - 1)(x + 3)$. On the left side of the equal sign, we get:

$\dfrac{3}{x+2} \cdot (x+2)(x-1)(x+3) + \dfrac{4}{x-1} \cdot (x+2)(x-1)(x+3) + \dfrac{2}{x+3} \cdot (x+2)(x-1)(x+3)$

On the left, the denominator cancels. We get:

$3(x-1)(x+3) = 3x^2 + 6x - 9$.

In the middle, the denominator cancels. We get:

$4(x+2)(x+3) = 4x^2 + 20x + 24$.

On the right, the denominator cancels. We get:

$2(x+2)(x-1) = 2x^2 + 2x - 4$.

When we multiply through by $(x + 2)(x - 1)(x + 3)$ on the right side of the equal sign, we get:

$$\frac{9x^2}{(x+2)(x-1)(x+3)} \cdot (x+2)(x-1)(x+3) = 9x^2.$$

Now, we can combine the three expressions on the left side of the equal sign, which gives us:

$3x^2 + 6x - 9 + 4x^2 + 20x + 24 + 2x^2 + 2x - 4 = 9x^2 + 28x + 11$

Setting this equal to the right side, we get:

$9x^2 + 28x + 11 = 9x^2$. We can subtract $9x^2$ from both sides, leaving us with $28x + 11 = 0$, and thus $x = -\frac{11}{28}$. (Notice that the denominator is not zero when $x = -\frac{11}{28}$.)

RADICAL EQUATIONS

Equations that involve a square root sign are called *radical* equations. As with rational equations, it is important to check that your solution does not make the original equation undefined. This happens when the *radicand* (the expression inside the radical), is negative. If we get a solution that makes the radicand negative, we throw it out—unless the problem allows for complex numbers.

The basic technique that we will use is to square both sides.

Example 10:

Solve for x: $\sqrt{x+3} = 8$.

If we square both sides, we get: $\left(\sqrt{x+3}\right)^2 = 8^2$.

When we square a square root, we are left with the radicand.

Here, we get: $x+3=64$.

We can solve this for x: $x=61$.

Always check the solution! Does $\sqrt{61+3}=8$? Yes.

Example 11:

Solve for x: $\sqrt{x^2-9}=4$.

If we square both sides, we get: $\left(\sqrt{x^2-9}\right)^2 = 4^2$.

This simplifies to: $x^2-9=16$.

Add 9 to both sides: $x^2=25$.

We solve for x by taking the square root of both sides. We get: $x=\pm 5$.

Check the solutions. Does $\sqrt{(5)^2-9}=4$? Yes

Does $\sqrt{(-5)^2-9}=4$? Yes.

Example 12:

Solve for x: $\sqrt{3x+7}=x+1$.

Square both sides: $3x+7=(x+1)^2$.

Expand: $3x+7=x^2+2x+1$.

$x^2-x-6=0$.

Factor the left side: $(x-3)(x+2)=0$.

The solutions are $x=3$ and $x=-2$.

Check the solutions.

Does $\sqrt{3(3)+7}=3+1$? Yes.

Does $\sqrt{3(-2)+7} = -2+1$? No! Throw this one out.

Note that a radical sign means that we take the **positive** square root. If we want the negative square root, we put a minus sign in front of the radical.

For example: $\sqrt{9} = 3$ and $-\sqrt{9} = -3$.

Therefore, the solution is $x = 3$.

Here is a more complicated radical equation.

Example 13:

Solve for x: $2 + \sqrt{x} = \sqrt{4+x}$.

Start out by squaring both sides: $\left(2+\sqrt{x}\right)^2 = \left(\sqrt{4+x}\right)^2$.

On the left side, we FOIL, which gives us: $4 + 4\sqrt{x} + x$.

On the right side, we are left with the radicand: $4 + x$.

This gives us: $4 + 4\sqrt{x} + x = 4 + x$

Now, simplify the expression by isolating the radical term on one side and putting all of the other terms on the other side:

$4 - 4 - x + x = 4\sqrt{x}$.

$0 = 4\sqrt{x}$.

Now, square both sides again: $0 = 16x$.

Therefore, $x = 0$.

Check the solution. Does $2 + \sqrt{0} = \sqrt{4+0}$? Yes.

Example 14:

Solve for x: $\sqrt{x+8} + 3 = \sqrt{x+35}$.

Start out by squaring both sides: $\left(\sqrt{x+8}+3\right)^2 = \left(\sqrt{x+35}\right)^2$.

On the left side, we FOIL, which gives us: $(x+8)+6\sqrt{x+8}+9$.

On the right side, we are left with the radicand: $x+35$.

This gives us: $x+8+6\sqrt{x+8}+9 = x+35$.

Now, simplify the expression by isolating the radical term on one side and putting all of the other terms on the other side:

$6\sqrt{x+8} = x+35-x-17$.

$6\sqrt{x+8} = 18$.

Now this looks like one of the simpler radical equations. We know what to do.

Divide through by 6: $\sqrt{x+8} = 3$.

Square both sides: $x+8 = 9$.

Solve for x: $x = 1$.

Does $\sqrt{1+8}+3 = \sqrt{1+35}$? Yes.

PROBLEMS

1. Express in simplest form: $\dfrac{1+\dfrac{x}{y}}{\dfrac{1}{x}+\dfrac{1}{y}}$

2. Express in simplest form: $\dfrac{\dfrac{3}{x}-\dfrac{x}{3}}{\dfrac{1}{3}+\dfrac{1}{x}}$

3. Solve for x: $\dfrac{5}{x-3} - \dfrac{30}{x^2-9} = 1$

4. Solve for x: $\dfrac{2x^2}{x^2-1} - \dfrac{3}{x+1} = \dfrac{x}{x-1}$

5. Solve for x: $\dfrac{2}{x^2-7x+10} = \dfrac{3}{x-5} - \dfrac{x}{x-2}$

6. Solve for x: $\sqrt{x+10} + 2 = 5$

7. Solve for x: $\dfrac{8}{x+1} = \dfrac{x}{x-1} + \dfrac{2}{x^2-1}$

8. Solve for x: $\sqrt{x+3} - 4 = 0$

9. Solve for x: $2\sqrt{x} = \sqrt{3x-11} + 2$

10. Solve for x: $x + \sqrt{4-3x} = -2$

CHAPTER 2
Degrees and Radians

In Sequential III, you are expected to know how to convert measurements from degrees to radians.

When graphing trig functions, always use radians.

The reason why we use radians instead of degrees won't matter until you are taking Calculus. Just know that you will be expected to do problems in both degrees and radians, and to be able to convert between the two.

Where do radians come from? (Well, first there has to be a mommy radian and a daddy radian.) But seriously, suppose you have a circle with a radius of 1 unit. This circle, by the way, is often called the *unit circle*. Then the circumference of the circle is $2\pi(1) = 2\pi$ units. There are also 360 degrees in a circle. We can set these equal to each other, which gives us:

$$2\pi \text{ radians} = 360°$$

If we divide through by 2π, we get $1 \text{ rad.} = \left(\dfrac{360}{2\pi}\right)°$.

If we reduce the fraction, we find that 1 radian is equal to $\left(\dfrac{180}{\pi}\right)°$.

(This means that 1 radian is approximately 57°).

If, instead, we divide through by 360°, we get: $\dfrac{2\pi}{360} \text{ rad.} = 1°$.

If we reduce, we get that 1 degree is equal to $\dfrac{\pi}{180}$ rad.

These equivalencies give us a relationship between the length of the arc of a circle (which is measured in radians) and the measure of the angle that generates that arc (which is measured in degrees).

It is conventional to leave off the units when an answer is in radians, and to use the degree symbol when an answer is in degrees.

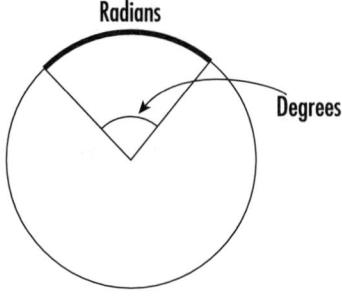

Let's do a couple of examples.

Example 1:

How many degrees are equivalent to $\dfrac{\pi}{4}$ radians?

As we saw above, 1 radian is equal to $\left(\dfrac{180}{\pi}\right)°$. All that we have to do is multiply the number of radians by $\left(\frac{180}{\pi}\right)^{\circ}$ in order to convert to degrees.

$$\frac{\pi}{4} \cdot \left(\frac{180}{\pi}\right)^{\circ} = \frac{180^{\circ}}{4} = 45^{\circ}$$

Therefore, $\frac{\pi}{4}$ radians equals 45 degrees.

Example 2:
How many radians are equivalent to 60°?

As we saw above, 1 degree is equal to $\frac{\pi}{180}$ radians. All that have to do is multiply the number of degrees by $\frac{\pi}{180}$ in order to convert to radians.

$$60 \cdot \frac{\pi}{180} = \frac{60\pi}{180} = \frac{\pi}{3}$$

Therefore, 60° equals $\frac{\pi}{3}$ radians.

ARC LENGTH OF A SECTOR

Using radians, it is easy to find the length of the arc of a circle, given its radius and central angle (or vice versa).

Suppose you have a circle with a central angle of θ measured in degrees and a radius of *r*, and the arc that is *subtended* (which means intercepted) by the angle is of length *s*.

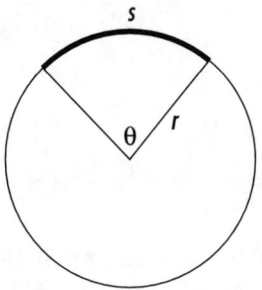

We can set up the following proportion:

$$\frac{\text{central angle}}{360°} = \frac{\text{arc length}}{\text{circumference}}$$

In other words,

$$\frac{\theta}{360°} = \frac{s}{2\pi r}$$

Let's do some examples.

Example 3:

If a circle has a central angle of 40° and a radius of 18, how long is the length of the arc subtended by the angle?

Just set up the proportion and solve.

$$\frac{40°}{360°} = \frac{s}{2\pi(18)}$$

$$\frac{1}{9} = \frac{s}{36\pi}$$

$$s = \frac{36\pi}{9} = 4\pi$$

Example 4:

If a circle has a central angle of 12° and the length of the arc subtended by the angle is 4π, find the radius of the circle.

Once again, set up the proportion.

$$\frac{12°}{360°} = \frac{4\pi}{2\pi r}$$

$$\frac{1}{30} = \frac{2}{r}$$

$$r = 60$$

Example 5:

A circle with a radius of 10 has a central angle of θ. The length of the arc subtended by the angle is 8π. Find θ.

Set up the proportion.

$$\frac{\theta}{360°} = \frac{8\pi}{2\pi(10)}$$

$$\frac{\theta}{360°} = \frac{2}{5}$$

$$\theta = \frac{2(360°)}{5} = 144°$$

Now, suppose that instead of being given the angle in degrees, we are given the angle in radians. You might want to convert the angle from radians to degrees and then use the proportion above, but there is a much simpler formula for you to learn.

Let's go back to our proportion $\frac{\theta}{360°} = \frac{s}{2\pi r}$. Suppose that we were given θ in radians rather than in degrees. Now, given that 2π rad $= 360°$, we can substitute and we get: $\frac{\theta}{2\pi} = \frac{s}{2\pi r}$. This can be simplified to $\theta = \frac{s}{r}$. Often, the formula is written as:

$$s = r\theta$$

Remember, θ has to be in radians, not degrees, for this formula to work!

Let's do some examples.

Example 6:

If a circle has a central angle of $\frac{\pi}{6}$ and a radius of 12, how long is the length of the arc subtended by the angle?

Just use the formula

$s = r\theta$.

$s = 12 \cdot \frac{\pi}{6} = 2\pi$.

Example 7:

If a circle has a central angle of $\frac{5\pi}{4}$ and the length of the arc subtended by the angle is 20π, find the radius of the circle.

Just use the formula

$s = r\theta$.

$20\pi = r \cdot \dfrac{5\pi}{4}$

$r = \dfrac{80\pi}{5\pi} = 16$

Example 8:

A circle with a radius of 15 has a central angle of θ. The length of the arc subtended by the angle is 3. Find θ in radians.

Just use the formula

$s = r\theta$.

$3 = 15\theta$

$\theta = \dfrac{3}{15} = \dfrac{1}{5}$ radians.

AREA OF A SECTOR

Let's go back to the picture that helped us find arc length. This time, instead of finding the length of the arc, we want to find the area of the sector. This is very handy if you want to know how much pizza is in a slice. Let's call this area a.

We can set up the following proportion:

$$\frac{\text{central angle}}{360°} = \frac{\text{sector}}{\text{area of the circle}}$$

In other words,

$$\frac{\theta}{360°} = \frac{a}{\pi r^2}$$

Let's do some examples using the same numbers as in the previous examples.

Example 9:

If a circle has a central angle of 40° and a radius of 18, how large is the area of the sector created by the angle?

Just set up the proportion and solve.

$$\frac{40°}{360°} = \frac{a}{\pi(18)^2}$$

$$\frac{1}{9} = \frac{a}{324\pi}$$

$$a = \frac{324\pi}{9} = 36\pi$$

Example 10:

If a circle has a central angle of 12° and the area of the sector created by the angle is 4π, find the radius of the circle.

Once again, set up the proportion.

$$\frac{12°}{360°} = \frac{4\pi}{\pi r^2}$$

$$\frac{1}{30} = \frac{4}{r^2}$$

$$r^2 = 120$$

$$r = \sqrt{120}$$

(Obviously we can ignore the negative answer $r = -\sqrt{120}$, because areas have to be positive.)

Example 11:

A circle with a radius of 10 has a central angle of θ. The area of the sector created by the angle is 8π. Find θ.

Set up the proportion.

$$\frac{\theta}{360°} = \frac{8\pi}{\pi(10)^2}$$

$$\frac{\theta}{360°} = \frac{8}{100} = \frac{2}{25}$$

$$\theta = \frac{2(360°)}{25} = \frac{144°}{5} \text{ or } 28.8°$$

Now, suppose that instead of being given the angle in degrees, we are given the angle in radians. Once again, you might want to convert the angle from radians to degrees and then use the proportion above, but there is a much simpler formula for you to learn.

Let's go back to our proportion $\frac{\theta}{360°} = \frac{a}{\pi r^2}$. Suppose that we were given θ in radians rather than in degrees. Now, given that 2π rad = 360°, we can substitute to get: $\frac{\theta}{2\pi} = \frac{a}{\pi r^2}$. This can be simplified to $\frac{\theta}{2} = \frac{a}{r^2}$. Often, the formula is written as:

$$a = \frac{1}{2} r^2 \theta$$

Remember, θ has to be in radians, not degrees, for this formula to work!

Let's do some examples using the same numbers as in the previous examples.

Example 12:

If a circle has a central angle of $\frac{\pi}{6}$ and a radius of 12, how large is the area of the sector created by the angle?

Just use the formula

$a = \frac{1}{2} r^2 \theta$.

$a = \frac{1}{2}(12^2)\frac{\pi}{6} = 12\pi$

Example 13:

If a circle has a central angle of $\dfrac{5\pi}{4}$ and the area of the sector created by the angle is 20π, find the radius of the circle.

Just use the formula.

$$20\pi = \frac{1}{2}r^2 \frac{5\pi}{4}$$

$$r^2 = \frac{160\pi}{5\pi} = 32$$

$$r = \sqrt{32} = 4\sqrt{2}$$

Example 14:

A circle with a radius of 15 has a central angle of θ. The area of the sector created by the angle is 3. Find θ in radians.

Just use the formula.

$$3 = \frac{1}{2}15^2\theta$$

$$\theta = \frac{6}{225} = \frac{2}{75}$$

Problems

1. How many degrees are equivalent to $\frac{2\pi}{3}$ radians?
2. How many degrees are equivalent to $\frac{\pi}{6}$ radians?
3. How many degrees are equivalent to $\frac{7\pi}{4}$ radians?
4. How many degrees are equivalent to 4 radians?
5. How many radians are equivalent to 210°?
6. How many radians are equivalent to 90°?
7. How many radians are equivalent to 216°?
8. How many radians are equivalent to 40°?
9. In a circle of radius 9, find the number of radians in a central angle that intercepts an arc of 18.
10. In a circle of radius 8 and a central angle of $\frac{\pi}{3}$ radians, find: (a) the measure of the intercepted arc formed by the central angle; and (b) the area of the sector formed by the central angle.
11. In a circle of radius 6 and a central angle of 40°, find: (a) the measure of the intercepted arc formed by the central angle; and (b) the area of the sector formed by the central angle.
12. In a circle of radius 4, find the number of degrees in a central angle that intercepts an arc of 2π.

CHAPTER 3
Trigonometry

The most important aspect of trigonometry that students tend to avoid is memorization. There are some parts of trig that you just have to learn and stick in your memory. Or, you'll have to know how to derive the values and be able to do it quickly. Your calculator won't help you because the **form** of the answer won't be calculator friendly. For example, the answer will be $\frac{\sqrt{3}}{3}$ and your teacher might not accept a decimal approximation. So if you use your calculator and come up with 0.577, and you don't know that this is $\frac{\sqrt{3}}{3}$, you won't be able to get the right answer.

DEFINITIONS OF THE TRIG FUNCTIONS

The trig functions are all ratios of the sides of a right triangle. First, let's draw a right triangle and label it.

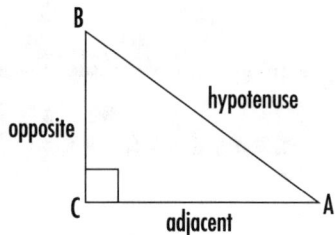

Notice that the side that we label *opposite* is the side **opposite angle A**, and the side that we label *adjacent* is the side **next to angle A** (other than the hypotenuse). It is **very important** to remember that what we call opposite and adjacent depend on which angle we pick. If we were to pick the other angle, the two sides would be switched.

When we find trig ratios, we divide the **length** of a particular side of the triangle by the **length** of another side.

Now let's define the basic trig ratios.

- The *sine* of angle A is $\frac{opposite}{hypotenuse}$. This is usually abbreviated $\sin A$.

- The *cosine* of angle A is $\frac{adjacent}{hypotenuse}$. This is usually abbreviated $\cos A$.

- The *tangent* of angle A is $\frac{opposite}{adjacent}$. This is usually abbreviated $\tan A$.

A good way to remember these is with the mnemonic **SOHCAHTOA**, which stands for: *Sine is Opposite over Hypotenuse, Cosine is Adjacent over Hypotenuse, Tangent is Opposite over Adjacent.*

Note that the sides of a right triangle can never be bigger than the hypotenuse, so sine and cosine can never be bigger than 1.

Suppose we have the following right triangle:

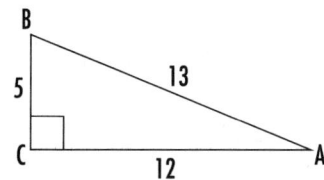

24 HIGH SCHOOL MATH III REVIEW

Then the three trig ratios with respect to angle A are:

$$\sin A = \frac{5}{13} \qquad \cos A = \frac{12}{13} \qquad \tan A = \frac{5}{12}$$

That wasn't too hard, was it?

Remember what we said about the sides depending on which angle you pick? Notice that the side of length 5 is the one opposite angle A. Well, it is also the side *adjacent* to angle B. Similarly, the side of length 12 is the one adjacent to angle A. It is also the side *opposite* angle B. Therefore, the three trig ratios with respect to angle B are:

$$\sin B = \frac{12}{13} \qquad \cos B = \frac{5}{13} \qquad \tan B = \frac{12}{5}$$

What about angle C you ask? For now, we will ignore the right angle of the triangle and just deal with the other two angles.

Did you notice that $\sin A = \cos B$ and $\cos A = \sin B$? In a right triangle, the sum of the two acute angles is 90°, so one acute angle is equal to 90 degrees minus the other angle. In other words, $B = (90° - A)$ and $A = (90° - B)$.

This leads us to a very important rule:

$$\sin A = \cos(90° - A)$$

$$\cos A = \sin(90° - A)$$

Let's do a couple of examples.

Example 1:

If $\sin(x + 12) = \cos(4x + 3)$, solve for x.

Using the rule above, $(x + 12) = 90 - (4x + 3)$.

$x + 12 = 90 - 4x - 3$

$5x = 90 - 12 - 3 = 75$

$x = 15$

Example 2:

If $\sin(4x + 1) = \cos(3x - 30)$, solve for x.

Using the rule above, $4x + 1 = 90 - (3x - 30)$.

$4x + 1 = 90 - 3x + 30$

TRIGONOMETRY **25**

$7x = 90 + 30 - 1 = 119$

$x = 17$

In addition to the three basic trig ratios (sometimes called the *circular functions*—which you will learn more about later), there are three more to learn. These are sometimes called the *reciprocal functions*).

These three functions are the *cotangent, secant,* and *cosecant,* and are defined as:

- The *cotangent* of angle A is $\frac{adjacent}{opposite}$. This is usually abbreviated $\cot A$.

- The *secant* of angle A is $\frac{hypotenuse}{adjacent}$. This is usually abbreviated $\sec A$.

- The *cosecant* of angle A is $\frac{hypotenuse}{opposite}$. This is usually abbreviated $\csc A$.

Notice that $\cot A = \frac{1}{\tan A}$, $\sec A = \frac{1}{\cos A}$, and $\csc A = \frac{1}{\sin A}$. This is why these are sometimes called the *reciprocal functions*. In other words, if you turn the *sine* of an angle upside down, you get the *cosecant* (and vice versa). If you turn the *cosine* of an angle upside down, you get the secant (and vice versa). Likewise for *tangent* and *cotangent*.

There is another relationship that you might not have noticed:

- $\tan A = \frac{\sin A}{\cos A}$; and $\cot A = \frac{\cos A}{\sin A}$.

These are the basic identities that you will be expected to know. Let's review them:

$$\cot A = \frac{1}{\tan A} \qquad \sec A = \frac{1}{\cos A}$$

$$\csc A = \frac{1}{\sin A} \qquad \tan A = \frac{\sin A}{\cos A}$$

Notice that this gives us the following rules:

$\tan A = \cot(90° - A)$ $\qquad\qquad$ $\cot A = \tan(90° - A)$

$\sec A = \csc(90° - A)$ $\qquad\qquad$ $\csc A = \sec(90° - A)$

Functions that obey these relationships are called *cofunctions*. That is, the cofunction of *sine* is *cosine*, the cofunction of *cosine* is *sine*, the cofunction of *tangent* is *cotangent*, the cofunction of *cotangent* is *tangent*, and so on.

Example 3:

Find the six trig ratios for angles A and B in the triangle below.

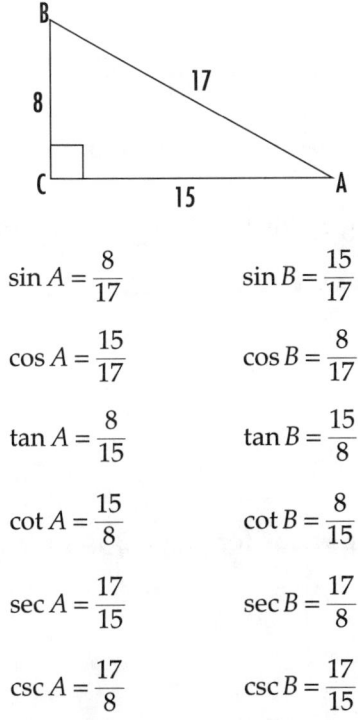

$\sin A = \dfrac{8}{17}$ $\qquad\qquad$ $\sin B = \dfrac{15}{17}$

$\cos A = \dfrac{15}{17}$ $\qquad\qquad$ $\cos B = \dfrac{8}{17}$

$\tan A = \dfrac{8}{15}$ $\qquad\qquad$ $\tan B = \dfrac{15}{8}$

$\cot A = \dfrac{15}{8}$ $\qquad\qquad$ $\cot B = \dfrac{8}{15}$

$\sec A = \dfrac{17}{15}$ $\qquad\qquad$ $\sec B = \dfrac{17}{8}$

$\csc A = \dfrac{17}{8}$ $\qquad\qquad$ $\csc B = \dfrac{17}{15}$

Now that we have learned what the six trig ratios are, and how they are related, let's learn trig ratios for specific angles. These are called "special angles" and they are used **all the time** in trigonometry. You will be expected to know these by heart, or to derive them easily. Think of them as your "times tables of trig."

PROBLEMS

1. Find the six trig ratios for angle A in the triangle below.

   [Right triangle with right angle at C, BC = 5, CA = 12, BA = 13]

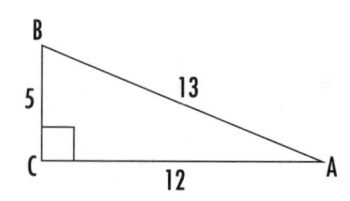

2. Find the six trig ratios for angle B in the triangle in Example 1.

3. Find the six trig ratios for angle A in the triangle below.

   [Right triangle with right angle at C, BC = 7, CA = 24, BA = 25]

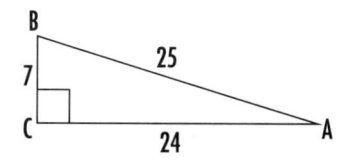

4. Find the six trig ratios for angle B in the triangle in Example 3.

5. Find the six trig ratios for angle A in the triangle below.

   [Right triangle with right angle at C, BC = 4, CA = 7, BA = $\sqrt{65}$]

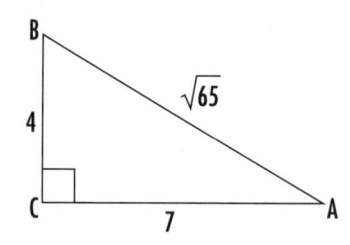

6. Find the six trig ratios for angle B in the triangle in Example 5.

SPECIAL ANGLES

Do you remember the Pythagorean Theorem? It says that, given a right triangle with legs of length a and b, and a hypotenuse of length c, then:

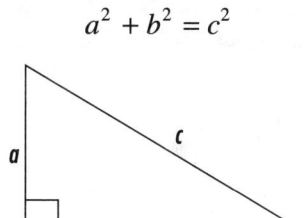

$$a^2 + b^2 = c^2$$

There is a special triangle that is made by cutting a square in half along the diagonal. It's called an *isosceles right triangle*. Because its legs are the sides of a square, they are the same length. Let's call the length of each leg x, and the length of the hypotenuse h.

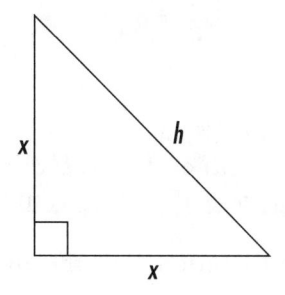

Now, we can use the Pythagorean Theorem to find h.

$$x^2 + x^2 = h^2$$
$$2x^2 = h^2$$
$$x\sqrt{2} = h$$

Thus we can re-label the triangle as follows:

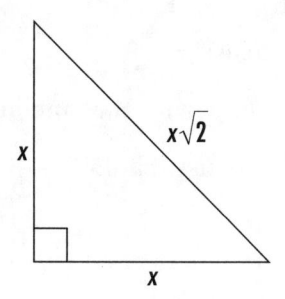

By the way, how do we know that the two acute angles have measures of 45° each? Because the diagonal of the square cuts the angles in half, and they were right angles to begin with, so $\frac{90°}{2} = 45°$.

Okay. Now we have our special triangle, so let's find the trig ratios for the angles. Because the angles are both 45°, we only have to do this once.

$$\sin 45° = \frac{x}{x\sqrt{2}} = \frac{1}{\sqrt{2}}$$

$$\cos 45° = \frac{x}{x\sqrt{2}} = \frac{1}{\sqrt{2}}$$

$$\tan 45° = \frac{x}{x} = 1$$

$$\cot 45° = \frac{x}{x} = 1$$

$$\sec 45° = \frac{x\sqrt{2}}{x} = \sqrt{2}$$

$$\csc 45° = \frac{x\sqrt{2}}{x} = \sqrt{2}$$

Notice that sin 45° = cos 45°, tan 45° = cot 45°, and sec 45° = csc 45°.

Notice also that the length of the sides doesn't matter because, as long as the triangle is a 45° – 45° – 90° triangle, the **ratios** will stay the same.

Many teachers like to rationalize the denominator of the trig functions. If we multiply the top and bottom of $\sin 45° = \frac{1}{\sqrt{2}}$ by $\sqrt{2}$, we get:

$$\sin 45° = \frac{1}{\sqrt{2}} \cdot \frac{\sqrt{2}}{\sqrt{2}} = \frac{\sqrt{2}}{2}.$$

If we do the same for cosine, we get:

$$\cos 45° = \frac{1}{\sqrt{2}} \cdot \frac{\sqrt{2}}{\sqrt{2}} = \frac{\sqrt{2}}{2}$$

You should get used to seeing the sine and cosine written both ways. Some books like to use $\sin 45° = \frac{1}{\sqrt{2}}$ and some like to use $\sin 45° = \frac{\sqrt{2}}{2}$.

In most Trigonometry classes, you usually see $\sin 45° = \frac{\sqrt{2}}{2}$.

On the other hand, when you take Calculus, you usually see $\sin 45° = \frac{1}{\sqrt{2}}$. Therefore, get used to knowing them both ways.

The same for $\cos 45° = \frac{\sqrt{2}}{2}$ and $\cos 45° = \frac{1}{\sqrt{2}}$.

The other special triangle is made by cutting an equilateral triangle in half along the altitude and is called a 30°–60°–90° triangle. This is because the altitude makes a right angle with the base and bisects the vertex angle of the equilateral triangle. (You do know that all three of the angles of an equilateral triangle are 60°, don't you?)

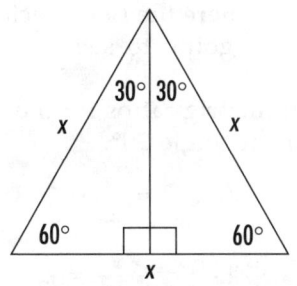

You should also know that the altitude of an equilateral triangle cuts the base in half, so the side opposite the 30° angle is half of the hypotenuse of the 30°–60°–90° triangle. Therefore, we can label the side opposite the 30° angle, as x, and the hypotenuse, as $2x$.

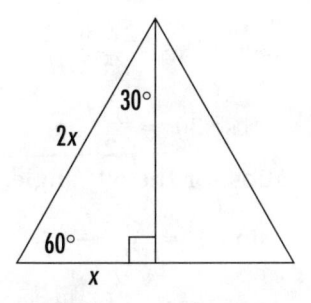

Now, let's figure out the length of the third side. We'll call it y for now. Using the Pythagorean Theorem, we know that $x^2 + y^2 = (2x)^2$. If we solve for y, we get:

$$x^2 + y^2 = (2x)^2$$
$$x^2 + y^2 = 4x^2$$

TRIGONOMETRY **31**

$$y^2 = 3x^2$$
$$y = x\sqrt{3}$$

Thus we can re-label the triangle as follows:

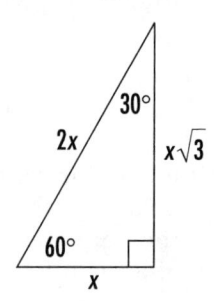

[Triangle with 30° at top, 60° at bottom-left, right angle at bottom-right; hypotenuse $2x$, vertical side $x\sqrt{3}$, horizontal side x]

Did you ever wonder where the two special triangles came from? Now you know. You are going to see these again and again and again!

Now let's figure out the trig ratios for the two acute angles. First, let's find the ratios for the angle 30°.

$$\sin 30° = \frac{x}{2x} = \frac{1}{2}$$

$$\cos 30° = \frac{x\sqrt{3}}{2x} = \frac{\sqrt{3}}{2}$$

$$\tan 30° = \frac{x}{x\sqrt{3}} = \frac{1}{\sqrt{3}}$$

$$\cot 30° = \frac{x\sqrt{3}}{x} = \sqrt{3}$$

$$\sec 30° = \frac{2x}{x\sqrt{3}} = \frac{2}{\sqrt{3}}$$

$$\csc 30° = \frac{2x}{2} = 2$$

Now let's find the ratios for the 60° angle.

$$\sin 60° = \frac{x\sqrt{3}}{2x} = \frac{\sqrt{3}}{2}$$

$$\cos 60° = \frac{x}{2x} = \frac{1}{2}$$

$$\tan 60° = \frac{x\sqrt{3}}{x} = \sqrt{3}$$

$$\cot 60° = \frac{x}{x\sqrt{3}} = \frac{1}{\sqrt{3}}$$

$$\sec 60° = \frac{2x}{2} = 2$$

$$\csc 60° = \frac{2x}{x\sqrt{3}} = \frac{2}{\sqrt{3}}$$

Notice that sin 30° = cos 60°, sin 60° = cos 30°, tan 30° = cot 60°.

As with sin 45°, many teachers like to rationalize tan 30°. If we multiply the top and bottom of tan 30° by $\sqrt{3}$, we get:

$$\tan 30° = \frac{1}{\sqrt{3}} \cdot \frac{\sqrt{3}}{\sqrt{3}} = \frac{\sqrt{3}}{3}$$

which, of course, is also the value for cot 60°.

For some reason, it's traditional *not* to rationalize the denominator for sec 30° and csc 60°. We have no idea why.

You should, however, get used to seeing tan 30° and cot 60° written both ways. Some books like to use $\tan 30° = \frac{1}{\sqrt{3}}$ and some like to use $\tan 30° = \frac{\sqrt{3}}{3}$.

In most Trigonometry classes, you usually see $\tan 30° = \frac{\sqrt{3}}{3}$.

On the other hand, when you take Calculus, you usually see $\tan 30° = \frac{1}{\sqrt{3}}$. Therefore, get used to knowing them both ways.

The same for $\cot 60° = \frac{\sqrt{3}}{3}$ and $\cot 60° = \frac{1}{\sqrt{3}}$.

By the way, you should know the trig ratios for the angles if you are given them either in degrees or in radians. You will usually use radians for graphing and in Calculus. You will usually use degrees for trig stuff other than graphing and before Calculus. If you look back at the chapter on Degrees and Radians, you will see that we have already found the radian values of the special angles. They are:

$$30° = \frac{\pi}{6} \text{ radians} \qquad 45° = \frac{\pi}{4} \text{ radians} \qquad 60° = \frac{\pi}{3} \text{ radians}$$

Confused? We're not surprised.

Let's recap and make a table of the trig values for these special angles.

TRIGONOMETRY

Deg	Rad	sin	cos	tan	cot	sec	csc
30	$\frac{\pi}{6}$	$\frac{1}{2}$	$\frac{\sqrt{3}}{2}$	$\frac{\sqrt{3}}{3}$ or $\frac{1}{\sqrt{3}}$	$\sqrt{3}$	$\frac{2}{\sqrt{3}}$	2
45	$\frac{\pi}{4}$	$\frac{\sqrt{2}}{2}$ or $\frac{1}{\sqrt{2}}$	$\frac{\sqrt{2}}{2}$ or $\frac{1}{\sqrt{2}}$	1	1	$\sqrt{2}$	$\sqrt{2}$
60	$\frac{\pi}{3}$	$\frac{\sqrt{3}}{2}$	$\frac{1}{2}$	$\sqrt{3}$	$\frac{\sqrt{3}}{3}$ or $\frac{1}{\sqrt{3}}$	2	$\sqrt{2}$

MORE SPECIAL ANGLES

Sometimes you will hear the trig functions referred to as *circular functions* (or, less often, *wrapping functions*). Let's learn why.

Suppose that you have a circle with a radius of one unit, centered at the origin, which we call a *unit circle*.

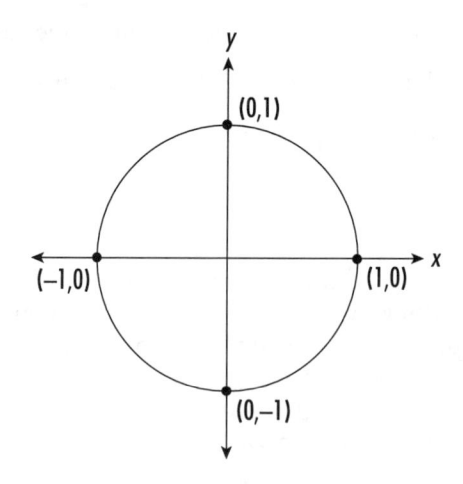

Now, if we draw a radius and label the point where it intersects the circle (x,y) and call the angle that the radius makes with the x-axis θ, we can find the values of the coordinates using trigonometry.

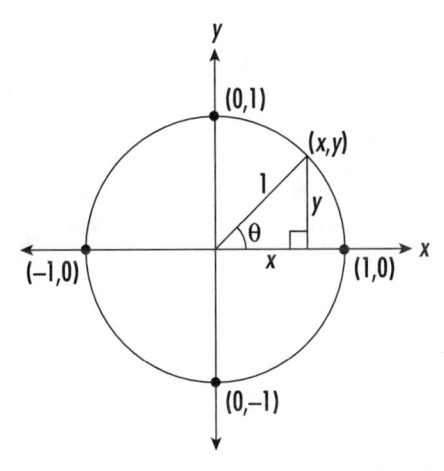

The coordinates of any point on the circle (x, y) can be found by figuring out the distance x and the distance y. Let's use trig to find the two distances.

Remember that cosine is adjacent over hypotenuse. Thus, $\cos\theta = \dfrac{x}{1} = x$.

Similarly, sine is opposite over hypotenuse. Thus, $\sin\theta = \dfrac{y}{1} = y$.

In other words, if we measure the angle θ between the radius and the x-axis for a point on the unit circle, the coordinates of that point are $(\cos\theta, \sin\theta)$.

The tangent of angle θ is opposite over adjacent, so $\tan\theta = \dfrac{y}{x}$. This happens to be the slope of the line segment made by the radius.

Let's recap. You pick a point on a unit circle and you draw the radius from the origin to that point. Next you find the angle θ between the radius and the x-axis. Then:

- the coordinates of that point are $(\cos\theta, \sin\theta)$ and
- the slope of the radius is $\tan\theta$.

Let's generalize this concept to a circle with any radius, r.

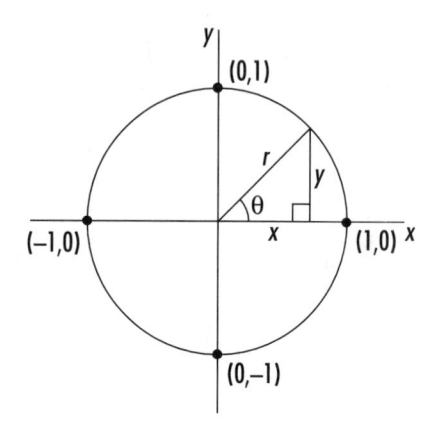

We find the trig ratios the same way as before, and now we get:

$$\cos\theta = \frac{x}{r}, \text{ so } x = r\cos\theta$$

$$\sin\theta = \frac{y}{r}, \text{ so } y = r\sin\theta$$

$$\tan\theta = \frac{y}{x}$$

So, the coordinates of any point on the circle are $(r\cos\theta, r\sin\theta)$ and the slope is $\tan\theta$.

Example 1:

Given a circle with a radius of 5, find the coordinates of point P if the radius makes an angle of 30° with the positive x-axis.

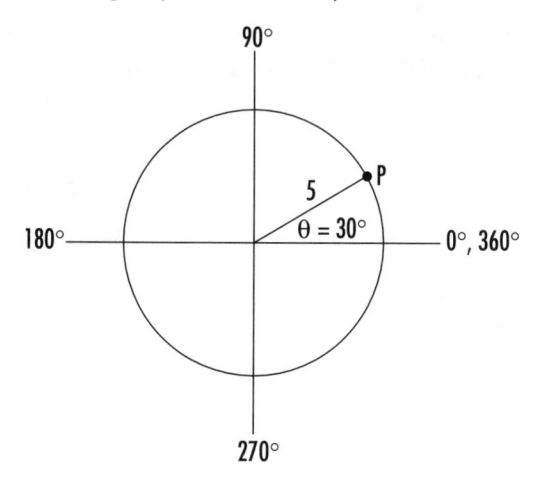

Using the rule above, the coordinates of P are

$$\left(5\cos 30°, 5\sin 30°\right) = \left(\frac{5\sqrt{3}}{2}, \frac{5}{2}\right).$$

Now, let's use this rule to find the sine and cosine of some special angles (the whole point of this section).

When we draw the unit circle, the positive x-axis is considered to be at $0°$, and all other degrees are found by moving counterclockwise around the circle. This means that the positive y-axis is at $90°$, the negative x-axis is at $180°$, the negative y-axis is $270°$, and, going around one complete cycle, the positive x-axis is also at $360°$.

The coordinates of a point on the circle are $(\cos\theta, \sin\theta)$, so we can now easily find the trig ratios for the four points where the unit circle crosses the coordinate axes.

At $0°$, the coordinates of the point of intersection are $(1, 0)$, therefore $\cos 0° = 1$ and $\sin 0° = 0$.

At $90°$, the coordinates of the point of intersection are $(0, 1)$, therefore $\cos 90° = 0$ and $\sin 90° = 1$.

At $180°$, the coordinates of the point of intersection are $(-1, 0)$, therefore $\cos 180° = -1$ and $\sin 180° = 0$.

At $270°$, the coordinates of the point of intersection are $(0, -1)$, therefore $\cos 270° = 0$ and $\sin 270° = -1$.

Now we can use the trig identities that we have already learned to find the other four trig ratios at each of these points.

Remember that $\tan\theta = \dfrac{\sin\theta}{\cos\theta}$.

$$\tan 0° = \frac{\sin 0°}{\cos 0°} = \frac{0}{1} = 0.$$

$$\tan 90° = \frac{\sin 90°}{\cos 90°} = \frac{1}{0} = \text{undefined}.$$

$$\tan 180° = \frac{\sin 180°}{\cos 180°} = \frac{0}{-1} = 0$$

$$\tan 270° = \frac{\sin 270°}{\cos 270°} = \frac{-1}{0} = \text{undefined}.$$

Notice how some of the trig ratios are "undefined." This occurs when the denominator of the ratio is zero. Sine and cosine are never undefined, tangent and secant are undefined wherever cosine is zero, and cotangent and cosecant are undefined wherever sine is zero.

Let's do the rest of the trig ratios.

Remember that $\cot\theta = \frac{\cos\theta}{\sin\theta}$

$$\cot 0° = \frac{\cos 0°}{\sin 0°} = \frac{1}{0} = \text{undefined} \quad \cot 90° = \frac{\cos 90°}{\sin 90°} = \frac{0}{1} = 0$$

$$\cot 180° = \frac{\cos 180°}{\sin 180°} = \frac{-1}{0} = \text{undefined} \quad \cot 270° = \frac{\cos 270°}{\sin 270°} = \frac{0}{-1} = 0$$

Remember that $\sec\theta = \frac{1}{\cos\theta}$

$$\sec 0° = \frac{1}{\cos 0°} = \frac{1}{1} = 1 \quad \sec 90° = \frac{1}{\cos 90°} = \frac{1}{0} = \text{undefined}$$

$$\sec 180° = \frac{1}{\cos 180°} = \frac{1}{-1} = -1 \quad \sec 270° = \frac{1}{\cos 270°} = \frac{1}{0} = \text{undefined}$$

Remember that $\csc\theta = \frac{1}{\sin\theta}$

$$\csc 0° = \frac{1}{\sin 0°} = \frac{1}{0} = \text{undefined} \quad \csc 90° = \frac{1}{\sin 90°} = \frac{1}{1} = 1$$

$$\csc 180° = \frac{1}{\sin 180°} = \frac{1}{0} = \text{undefined} \quad \csc 270° = \frac{1}{\sin 270°} = \frac{1}{-1} = -1$$

Let's recap and make a table of the trig values for these special angles.

Degree	Radian	sine	cosine	tangent	cotangent	secant	cosecant
0	0	0	1	0	undefined	1	undefined
90	$\frac{\pi}{2}$	1	0	undefined	0	undefined	1
180	π	0	-1	0	undefined	-1	undefined
270	$\frac{3\pi}{2}$	-1	0	undefined	0	undefined	-1

There is one last important point about special angles that we need to learn and that relates to finding the trig values in different quadrants. We do this using *reference angles*.

REFERENCE ANGLES

Suppose that we draw two radii — one at 30° and one at 150°, then drop perpendiculars to the x-axis to create triangles.

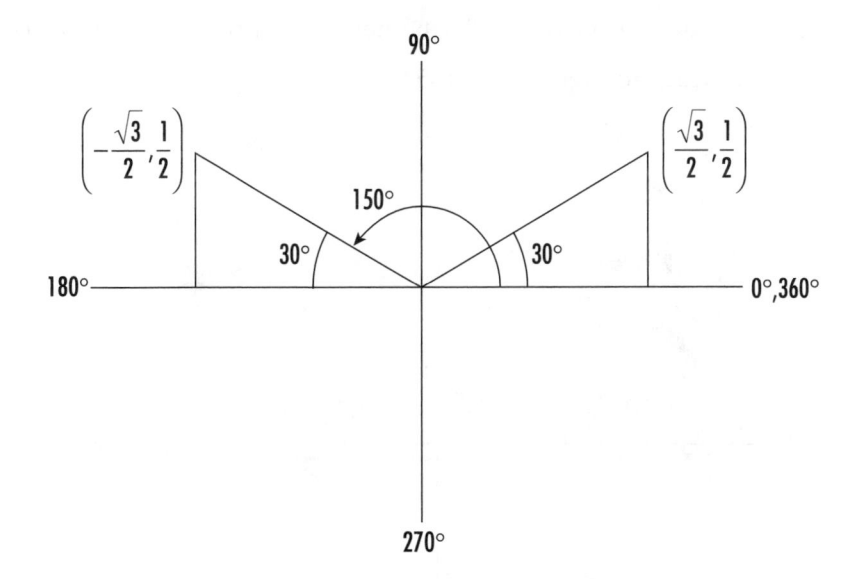

Notice that the two triangles are congruent except that one is in quadrant I and one is in quadrant II. Because the triangle that is formed by the 150° angle is congruent to the triangle formed by the 30° angle, we say that the *reference* angle for 150° is 30°. Let's see how this affects the trig ratios.

The coordinates of the point in quadrant I are $\left(\frac{\sqrt{3}}{2}, \frac{1}{2}\right)$ and the coordinates of the point in quadrant II are $\left(-\frac{\sqrt{3}}{2}, \frac{1}{2}\right)$. Since the coordinates of the points are $(\cos\theta, \sin\theta)$, any trig ratio for the triangle in quadrant I that involves *sine* only will be the same for the triangle in quadrant II. These are sine and cosecant. But trig ratio for the triangle in quadrant I that involves *cosine* will become negative in quadrant II because any point in quadrant II has coordinates $(-x,y)$. These are cosine, secant, tangent, and cotangent.

Thus, we get the following:

$$\sin 150° = \frac{1}{2} \text{ and } \csc 150° = 2 \text{ (the same ratios as for 30°).}$$

$$\cos 150° = -\frac{\sqrt{3}}{2} \quad \sec 150° = -\frac{2}{\sqrt{3}} \text{ (the negative of the ratios for 30°)}$$

$$\tan 150° = -\frac{\sqrt{3}}{3} \quad \cot 150° = -\sqrt{3} \text{ (the negative of the ratios for 30°)}$$

Let's repeat the exercise for 135°.

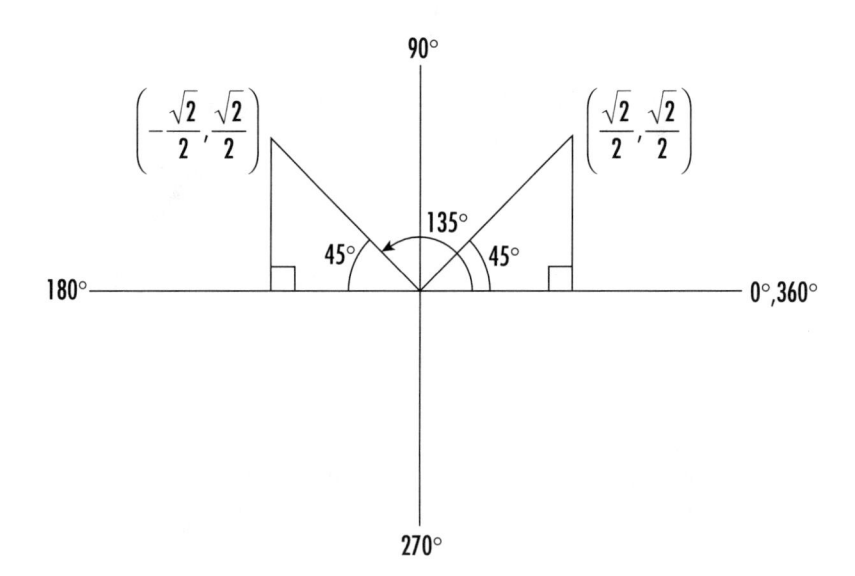

Here, the reference angle for 135° is 45°. Once again we are in quadrant II, so the trig ratios for 135° will be the same as for 45° except that the values will be negative for cosine, secant, tangent, and cotangent.

Notice that reference angles are always acute, and are always measured with respect to the *x*-axis.

Thus we get:

$\sin 135° = \dfrac{\sqrt{2}}{2}$ $\csc 135° = \sqrt{2}$ (the same ratios as for 45°).

$\cos 135° = -\dfrac{\sqrt{2}}{2}$ $\sec 135° = \sqrt{2}$ (the negative of the ratios for 45°)

$\tan 135° = -1$ $\cot 135° = -1$ (the negative of the ratios for 45°)

Now let's do 300°.

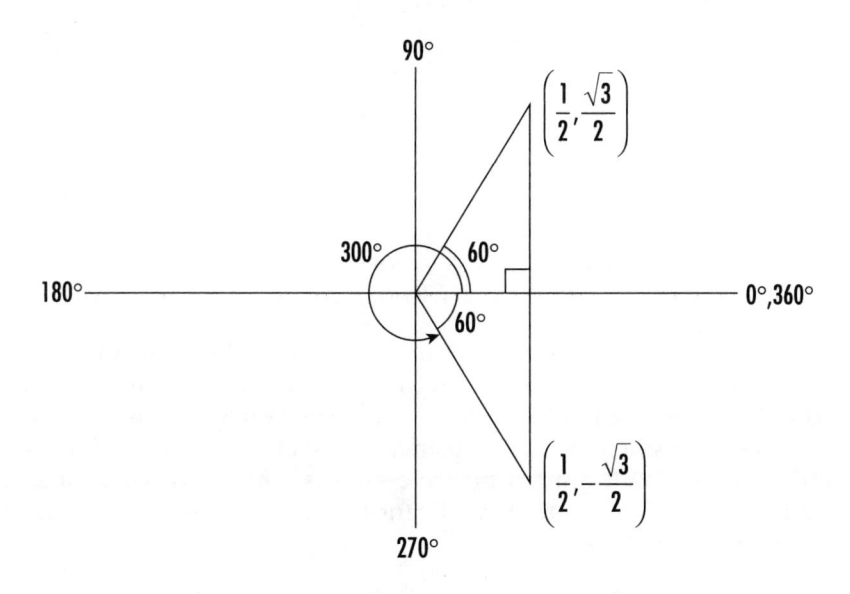

Now we are in quadrant IV. Here, the *y*-coordinate has become negative but the *x*-coordinate has stayed the same. This means that any trig ratio for the triangle in quadrant I that involves *cosine* only will be the same for the triangle in quadrant IV. These are cosine and secant. Any trig ratio for the triangle in quadrant I that involves *sine* will become negative in quadrant IV. These are sine, cosecant, tangent, and cotangent.

$\cos 300° = \dfrac{1}{2}$ $\sec 300° = 2$ (the same ratios as for 60°).

$\sin 300° = -\dfrac{\sqrt{3}}{2}$ $\csc 300° = -\dfrac{2}{\sqrt{3}}$ (the negative of the ratios for 60°)

$\tan 300° = -\sqrt{3}$ $\cot 300° = -\dfrac{\sqrt{3}}{3}$ (the negative of the ratios for 60°)

Are you getting the hang of this? Let's do this one more time, this time for 210°.

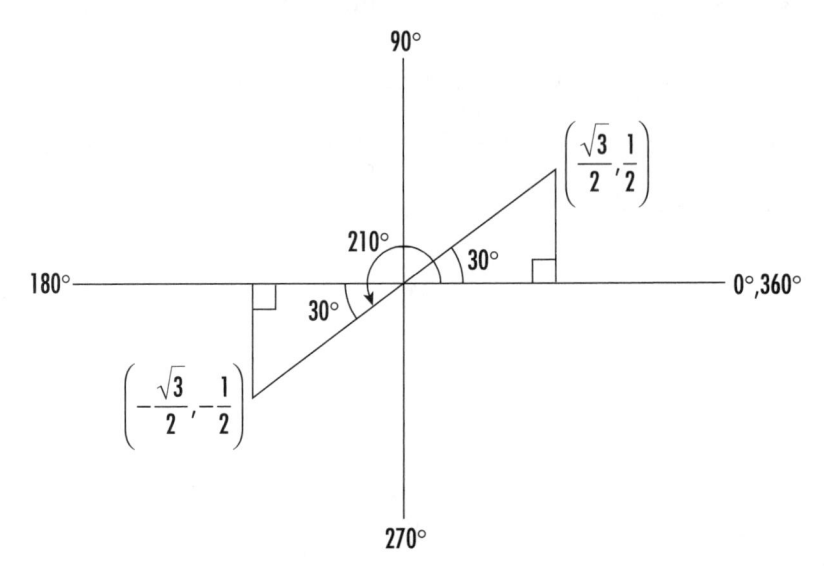

Here the reference angle is 30°, but *both* of the coordinates are negative. This means that any trig ratio for the triangle in quadrant I that involves *sine or cosine* alone will become negative in quadrant III. These are sine, cosecant, cosine, and secant. However, tangent, and cotangent will remain positive because they involve both sine *and* cosine, so the negatives will cancel each other out and the ratio will remain positive.

$\tan 210° = \dfrac{\sqrt{3}}{3}$ $\cot 210° = \sqrt{3}$ (the same ratios as for 30°).

$\sin 210° = -\dfrac{1}{2}$ $\csc 210° = -2$ (the negative of the ratios for 30°)

$\cos 210° = -\dfrac{\sqrt{3}}{2}$ $\sec 210° = -\dfrac{2}{\sqrt{3}}$ (the negative of the ratios for 30°)

Now we have found trig ratios of special angles in all four quadrants. The effect of the quadrants is very simple and the way to remember the quadrant rules is with the mnemonic

All Students Take Calculus

(which, of course, isn't true, but it's a good mnemonic and that's what counts!)

It stands for:

All trig ratios are positive in quadrant I.

Sine and cosecant are positive in quadrant II. (The rest are negative.)

Tangent and cotangent are positive in quadrant III. (The rest are negative.)

Cosine and cosecant are positive in quadrant IV. (The rest are negative.)

What if we are given a *negative* angle? Simple. We do the same process as we did for a positive angle, but we go clockwise (down) from the x-axis instead of counterclockwise. For example, find $\sin(-210°)$.

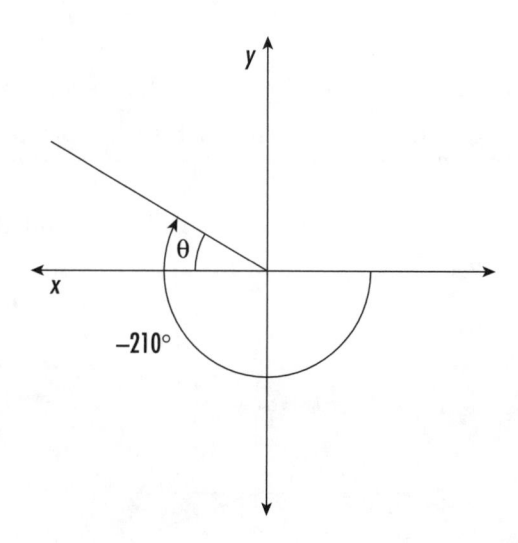

Notice that the angle between the line and the x-axis is $30°$ and the reference angle is thus $30°$ and $\sin 30° = \dfrac{1}{2}$.

What if we are given an angle that is greater than 360°? Then we go around the axes more than once. For example, find $\sin(495°)$. This means that we go around the axes once (which equals 360°) and continue for another 495° − 360° = 135°.

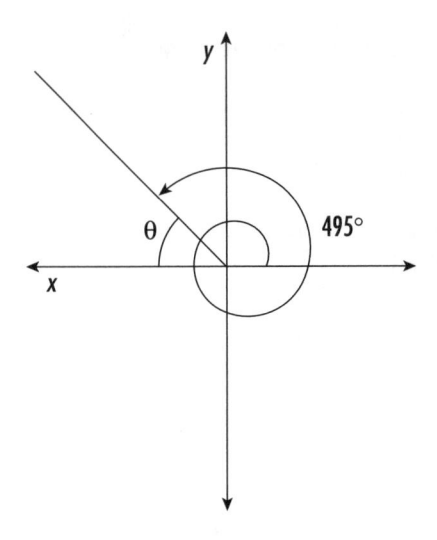

This has a reference angle of 45°, and thus $\sin 45° = \frac{\sqrt{2}}{2}$.

Naturally, we can combine the last two concepts. Let's find $\sin(-750°)$.

This means that we will proceed *clockwise* around the axes *twice* (which equals −720°) and continue for another −30°.

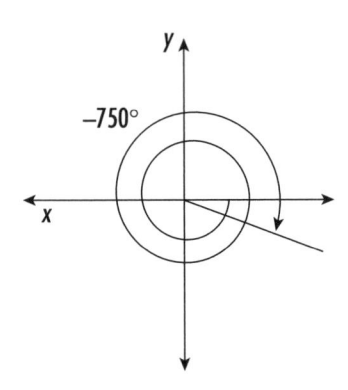

This has a reference angle of 30° and thus $\sin 30° = \frac{1}{2}$. BUT, because we are in quadrant IV, the answer is negative. Therefore, $\sin(-750°) = -\frac{1}{2}$.

Got it?

We will leave it up to you to figure out all of the remaining reference angles for the special angles. You should get the following:

	120° $\frac{2\pi}{3}$	225° $\frac{5\pi}{4}$	240° $\frac{4\pi}{3}$	315° $\frac{7\pi}{4}$	330° $\frac{11\pi}{6}$
sine	$\frac{\sqrt{3}}{2}$	$-\frac{\sqrt{2}}{2}$	$-\frac{\sqrt{3}}{2}$	$-\frac{\sqrt{2}}{2}$	$-\frac{1}{2}$
cosine	$-\frac{1}{2}$	$-\frac{\sqrt{2}}{2}$	$-\frac{1}{2}$	$\frac{\sqrt{2}}{2}$	$\frac{\sqrt{3}}{2}$
tangent	$-\sqrt{3}$	1	$\sqrt{3}$	-1	$-\frac{\sqrt{3}}{3}$
cotangent	$-\frac{\sqrt{3}}{3}$	1	$\frac{\sqrt{3}}{3}$	-1	$-\sqrt{3}$
secant	-2	$-\sqrt{2}$	-2	$\sqrt{2}$	$\frac{2}{\sqrt{3}}$
cosecant	$\frac{2}{\sqrt{3}}$	$-\sqrt{2}$	$-\frac{2}{\sqrt{3}}$	$-\sqrt{2}$	-2

If you have an angle, θ, in quadrant II, its reference angle is:
$$180° - θ.$$
If you have an angle, θ, in quadrant III, its reference angle is:
$$θ - 180°.$$
If you have an angle, θ, in quadrant IV, its reference angle is:
$$360° - θ.$$

HOW TO REMEMBER THE SPECIAL ANGLES

You're probably thinking "You must be joking if you think that I can memorize all of these?!" Well, the good news is that you don't have to know all of them. In fact, if you memorize just a few things, then you can **easily** figure out all of the rest. Here's what you need to memorize:

First, memorize these sines and cosines:

$$\sin 30° = \frac{1}{2} \qquad \sin 45° = \frac{\sqrt{2}}{2} \qquad \sin 60° = \frac{\sqrt{3}}{2}$$

$$\cos 30° = \frac{\sqrt{3}}{2} \qquad \cos 45° = \frac{\sqrt{2}}{2} \qquad \cos 60° = \frac{1}{2}$$

See how the two follow the same pattern, but in reverse?

Now we'll learn how to derive the rest of the trig ratios from just these ratios.

Remember that $\tan\theta = \frac{\sin\theta}{\cos\theta}$. This means that we can find the tangents of these angles by dividing the appropriate sine by the appropriate cosine.

$$\tan 30° = \frac{\sin 30°}{\cos 30°} = \frac{\frac{1}{2}}{\frac{\sqrt{3}}{2}} = \frac{1}{\sqrt{3}}$$

$$\tan 45° = \frac{\sin 45°}{\cos 45°} = \frac{\frac{\sqrt{2}}{2}}{\frac{\sqrt{2}}{2}} = 1$$

$$\tan 60° = \frac{\sin 60°}{\cos 60°} = \frac{\frac{\sqrt{3}}{2}}{\frac{1}{2}} = \sqrt{3}$$

Now to find the other three ratios, you just turn its corresponding ratio upside down.

$\cot\theta = \dfrac{1}{\tan\theta}$ so $\cot 30° = \sqrt{3}$ $\cot 45° = 1$ $\cot 60° = \dfrac{1}{\sqrt{3}}$

$\sec\theta = \dfrac{1}{\cos\theta}$ so $\sec 30° = \dfrac{2}{\sqrt{3}}$ $\sec 45° = \sqrt{2}$ $\sec 60° = 2$

$\csc\theta = \dfrac{1}{\sin\theta}$ so $\sin 30° = 2$ $\csc 45° = \sqrt{2}$ $\csc 60° = \dfrac{2}{\sqrt{3}}$

See how easy it is to derive the other ratios once you know the sines and cosines?

Now here is the second set to memorize:

$\sin 0° = 0$	$\sin 90° = 1$	$\sin 180° = 0$	$\sin 270° = -1$
$\cos 0° = 1$	$\cos 90° = 0$	$\cos 180° = -1$	$\cos 270° = 0$

Once again we can derive the rest of the trig ratios from just these.

Using the identities, we get:

$\tan 0° = 0$ $\tan 90° = und.$ $\tan 180° = 0$ $\tan 270° = und.$

$\cot 0° = und.$ $\cot 90° = 0$ $\cot 180° = und.$ $\cot 270° = 0$

$\sec 0° = 1$ $\sec 90° = und.$ $\sec 180° = -1$ $\sec 270° = und.$

$\csc 0° = und.$ $\csc 90° = 1$ $\csc 180° = und.$ $\csc 270° = -1$

Now you can see that, just by knowing the sines and cosines of seven angles — 0°, 30°, 45°, 60°, 90°, 180°, 270° — you can find all of the rest.

The last step to memorizing the special angles is to learn the mnemonic for the quadrants:

All **S**tudents **T**ake **C**alculus

which stands for:

All trig ratios are positive in quadrant I.

Sine and cosecant are positive in quadrant II. (The rest are negative.)

Tangent and cotangent are positive in quadrant III. (The rest are negative.)

Cosine and secant are positive in quadrant IV. (The rest are negative.)

Now, once you are given an angle, just figure out the reference angle and then use the appropriate trig ratio from above.

Example 1:

Find csc 330°.

First, draw a little picture to help figure out the reference angle.

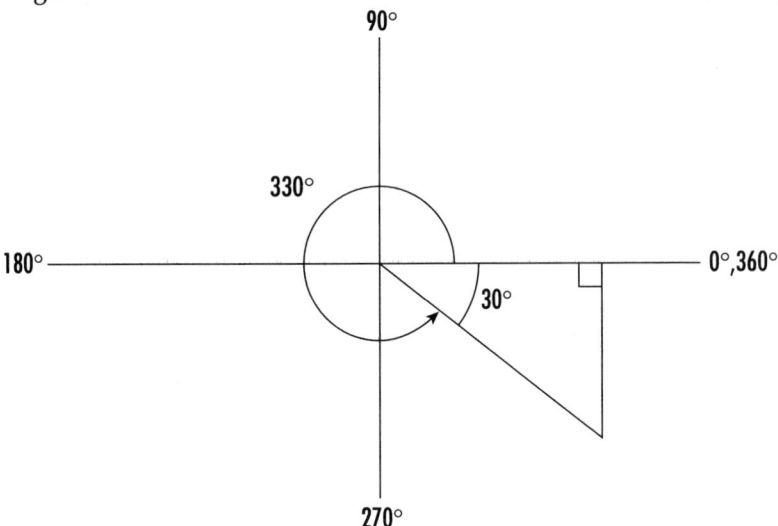

Now that we know that the reference angle is 30°, we remember that $\sin 30° = \frac{1}{2}$, which means that $\csc 30° = 2$. In quadrant

IV, cosine and secant are positive, and the rest are negative, so $\csc 330° = -2$.

Example 2:

Find $\cot 225°$.

First, draw a little picture to help figure out the reference angle.

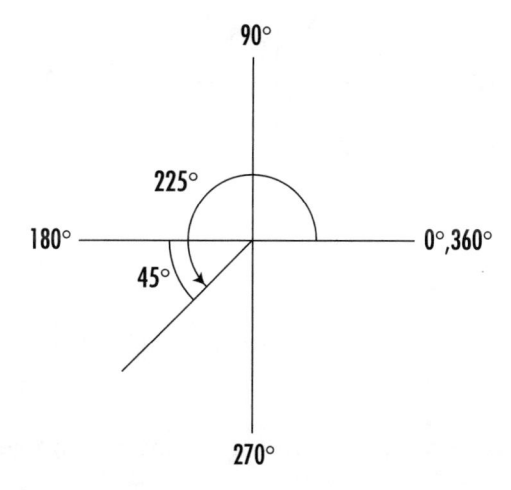

Now that we know that the reference angle is $45°$, we remember that $\sin 45° = \cos 45° = \frac{\sqrt{2}}{2}$, which means that $\tan 45° = 1$ and thus $\cot 45° = 1$. In quadrant III, tangent and cotangent are positive, so $\cot 225° = 1$.

Example 3:

Find $\sec 120°$.

First, draw a little picture to help figure out the reference angle.

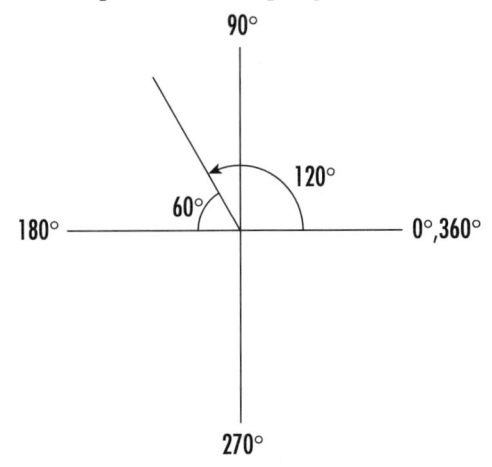

```
          90°
           |
       \   |
        \  |
      60° \| 120°
180° ------+------ 0°, 360°
           |
           |
          270°
```

Now that we know that the reference angle is 60°, we remember that $\cos 60° = \frac{1}{2}$, which means that $\sec 60° = 2$. In quadrant II, sine and cosecant are positive, and the rest are negative, so $\sec 120° = -2$

Now for a slightly harder one.

Example 4:

Find $\tan 495°$.

First, draw a little picture to help figure out the reference angle.

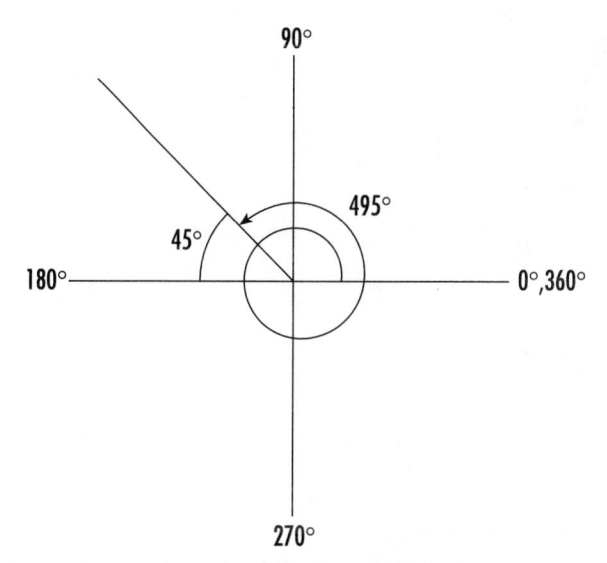

Notice that the angle is bigger than 360° so, as we go around the coordinate axes, we continue past 360° and go around a second time. This is allowed! In fact, you can keep going around as many times as you want!

Now that we know that the reference angle is 45°, we remember that $\sin 45° = \cos 45° = \frac{\sqrt{2}}{2}$, which means that $\tan 45° = 1$. In quadrant II, sine and cosecant are positive, and the rest are negative, so $\tan 495° = -1$.

PROBLEMS

1) Find $\sin 300°$.

2) Find $\cos 210°$.

3) Find $\tan 120°$.

4) Find $\sec 330°$.

5) Find $\csc 150°$.

6) Find $\cot 225°$.

7) Find $\sin 750°$.

8) Find $\cos 585°$.

9) Find $\tan \dfrac{7\pi}{4}$.

10) Find $\sin \dfrac{11\pi}{6}$.

TRIG FORMULAS

There are a bunch of trig formulas that you will need to learn for Sequential III. The first set is derived from something called the *Pythagorean Theorem of Trigonometry*.

Remember the unit circle? It is centered at the origin and has a radius of one. We can determine the coordinates of each point on the unit circle if we measure the angle between the radius and the positive *x*-axis. If we call that angle θ, then $\cos\theta$ is the *x*-coordinate and $\sin\theta$ is the *y*-coordinate.

The formula for a circle, centered at the origin, with a radius of one, is $x^2 + y^2 = 1$. If we substitute $\cos\theta$ for *x*, and $\sin\theta$ for *y*, we get:

$$\sin^2\theta + \cos^2\theta = 1$$

This is the *Pythagorean Theorem of Trigonometry*. As long as the sine and cosine are taken of the same angle, this is always true. Let's check it to see for ourselves. Suppose $\theta = 60°$. Is $\sin^2 60° + \cos^2 60° = 1$?

$$\sin 60° = \frac{\sqrt{3}}{2} \text{ and } \cos 60° = \frac{1}{2}, \text{ so } \sin^2 60° + \cos^2 60° = \left(\frac{\sqrt{3}}{2}\right)^2 + \left(\frac{1}{2}\right)^2.$$

We simplify and we get:

$$\left(\frac{\sqrt{3}}{2}\right)^2 + \left(\frac{1}{2}\right)^2 = \frac{3}{4} + \frac{1}{4} = 1.$$

Look at that. It works!

This is a very handy formula to know for several types of problems. Let's do some examples.

Example 1:

If $\sin\theta = \frac{8}{17}$, and θ is in quadrant I, find $\cos\theta$.

Using the formula, we know that $\left(\frac{8}{17}\right)^2 + \cos^2\theta = 1$. Now, we can solve for $\cos\theta$.

$\frac{64}{289} + \cos^2\theta = 1$,

so $\cos^2\theta = 1 - \frac{64}{289} = \frac{225}{289}$.

Therefore, $\cos\theta = \pm\frac{15}{17}$.

How do we know whether to use the positive or negative value of $\cos\theta$? We were told that θ is in quadrant I, and ALL trig functions are positive in quadrant I, so the answer must be $\cos\theta = \frac{15}{17}$. If we had been told that θ was in quadrant II, then we know that $\cos\theta$ is negative there (remember the mnemonic?), so the answer would have been $\cos\theta = -\frac{15}{17}$.

There is another way to get the right answer to the above triangle, which many people prefer to just using the formula. We were given that $\sin\theta = \frac{8}{17}$, and θ is in quadrant I, and we know that the sine of an angle is $\frac{opposite}{hypotenuse}$ (remember the mnemonic?), so we could construct a triangle with this information.

TRIGONOMETRY **53**

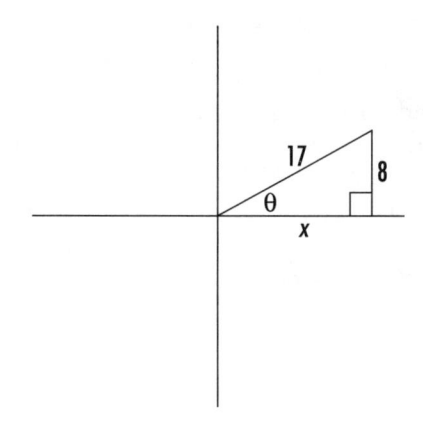

We have labeled the third side (the *adjacent* one) of the triangle x, and we can now use the Pythagorean Theorem to find the third side. $x^2 + 8^2 = 17^2$, and thus

$x = \pm 15$.

Because x is on the positive x-axis, we know that $x = 15$.

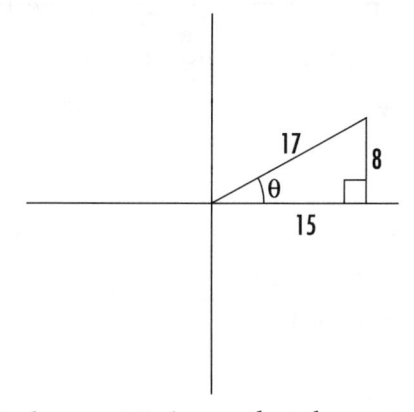

Now we can find $\cos\theta$. We know that the cosine of an angle is $\frac{adjacent}{hypotenuse}$, so $\cos\theta = \frac{15}{17}$.

Example 2:

If $\cos\theta = \frac{8}{11}$, and θ is in quadrant IV, find $\sin\theta$.

Using the formula, we know that $\sin^2\theta + \left(\frac{8}{11}\right)^2 = 1$.

Now, we can solve for $\sin\theta$.

We get: $\sin^2\theta + \frac{64}{121} = 1$

$\sin^2\theta = 1 - \frac{64}{121} = \frac{57}{121}$

$\sin\theta = \pm\sqrt{\frac{57}{121}} = \pm\frac{\sqrt{57}}{11}$

Since θ is in quadrant IV, we know that $\sin\theta$ is negative, so $\sin\theta = -\frac{\sqrt{57}}{11}$.

Let's do it again, this time by drawing a picture.

We were given that $\cos\theta = \frac{8}{11}$, and θ is in quadrant IV, so our picture looks like this:

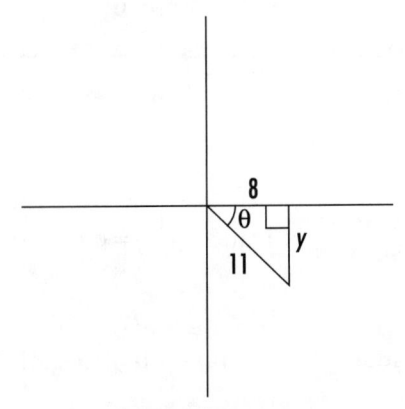

We can use the Pythagorean Theorem to solve for y. We get:

$8^2 + y^2 = 11^2$

$y^2 = 11^2 - 8^2 = 57$

$$y = \pm\sqrt{57}$$

Because y is in quadrant IV, we use $y = -\sqrt{57}$. Therefore,

$$\sin\theta = -\frac{\sqrt{57}}{11}.$$

As you can see, both methods are pretty efficient, so the choice of which one to use is up to you. By the way, can you see why this formula is called the *Pythagorean Theorem of Trigonometry*?

Now, let's derive a couple of other formulas from this one. First of all, it should be obvious that, since $\sin^2\theta + \cos^2\theta = 1$, we know that $\sin^2\theta = 1 - \cos^2\theta$ and that $\cos^2\theta = 1 - \sin^2\theta$.

If we take $\sin^2\theta + \cos^2\theta = 1$ and divide each term by $\cos^2\theta$, we get:

$$\frac{\sin^2\theta}{\cos^2\theta} + \frac{\cos^2\theta}{\cos^2\theta} = \frac{1}{\cos^2\theta}.$$

Next, because $\frac{\sin\theta}{\cos\theta} = \tan\theta$ and $\frac{1}{\cos\theta} = \sec\theta$, we can rewrite this as:

$$\tan^2\theta + 1 = \sec^2\theta,$$

which it is customary to write as $1 + \tan^2\theta = \sec^2\theta$.

Similarly, if we instead divide each term by $\sin^2\theta$, we get:

$$\frac{\sin^2\theta}{\sin^2\theta} + \frac{\cos^2\theta}{\sin^2\theta} = \frac{1}{\sin^2\theta}$$

Next, because $\frac{\cos\theta}{\sin\theta} = \cot\theta$ and $\frac{1}{\sin\theta} = \csc\theta$, we can rewrite this as:

$$1 + \cot^2\theta = \csc^2\theta$$

Thus, our three main Pythagorean Identities of Trigonometry are:

$$\sin^2\theta + \cos^2\theta = 1$$

$$1 + \tan^2\theta = \sec^2\theta$$

$$1 + \cot^2\theta = \csc^2\theta$$

Let's do some examples.

Example 3:

If $\tan A = \dfrac{7}{12}$ and A is in quadrant I, find $\sec A$.

Using the formula, $1 + \tan^2 \theta = \sec^2 \theta$, we get:

$$1 + \left(\dfrac{7}{12}\right)^2 = \sec^2 \theta.$$

$$1 + \dfrac{49}{144} = \dfrac{193}{144} = \sec^2 A$$

$$\sec A = \pm \dfrac{\sqrt{193}}{12}.$$

Because A is in quadrant I, the answer is $\sec A = \dfrac{\sqrt{193}}{12}$.

Again, we could have drawn a triangle.

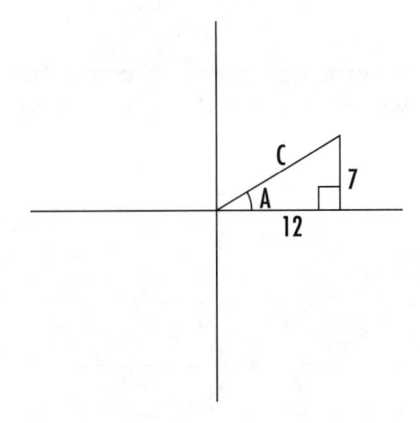

From the Pythagorean Theorem, we know that $7^2 + 12^2 = C^2$, so $C^2 = 49 + 144 = 193$, and thus $C = \sqrt{193}$.

This leads to $\sec A = \dfrac{\sqrt{193}}{12}$.

Example 4:

If $\csc\theta = \dfrac{15}{8}$, and $\tan\theta < 0$, find $\cot\theta$.

Using the formula, we get: $1 + \cot^2\theta = \left(\dfrac{15}{8}\right)^2 = \dfrac{225}{64}$.

$\cot^2\theta = \dfrac{225}{64} - 1 = \dfrac{161}{64}$.

$\cot\theta = \pm\dfrac{\sqrt{161}}{8}$.

Now why were we told that $\tan\theta < 0$? Because the only quadrant where cosecant is positive and tangent is negative is quadrant II, (and cotangent is also negative there because tangent and cotangent always have the same sign), so $\cot\theta = -\dfrac{\sqrt{161}}{8}$.

If we were to draw a triangle, we would first have had to figure out that we were in quadrant II. Then we would have gotten:

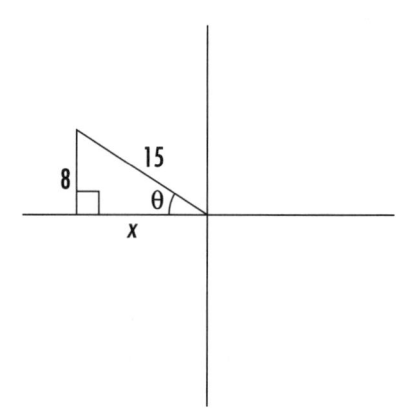

$$x^2 + 8^2 = 15$$

$$x^2 = 15^2 - 8^2 = 161$$

$$x = \pm\sqrt{161}$$

Then, because we were on the negative x-axis, the answer would be $\cot\theta = \dfrac{-\sqrt{161}}{8}$.

MORE TRIG FORMULAS

The second set of formulas that you need to know for Sequential III involve the sum and difference of two angles. We will dispense with the derivation of these formulas and just tell them to you.

> If we are given angles A and B, then
> $\sin(A+B) = \sin A \cos B + \cos A \sin B$.

For example, suppose that we are asked to find $\sin 75°$ without a calculator (your teacher might ask for the *exact* value of $\sin 75°$, which means that she doesn't want a decimal answer).

We know that $75° = 30° + 45°$, so $\sin 75° = \sin(30° + 45°)$. Then, using the formula that we just learned,

$\sin(30° + 45°) = \sin 30° \cos 45° + \cos 30° \sin 45°$.

We know from our special angles that $\sin 30° = \dfrac{1}{2}$, $\cos 30° = \dfrac{\sqrt{3}}{2}$, and $\sin 45° = \cos 45° = \dfrac{\sqrt{2}}{2}$, so we can substitute and get:

$\left(\dfrac{1}{2}\right)\left(\dfrac{\sqrt{2}}{2}\right) + \left(\dfrac{\sqrt{3}}{2}\right)\left(\dfrac{\sqrt{2}}{2}\right)$, which simplifies to $\left(\dfrac{\sqrt{2}}{4}\right) + \left(\dfrac{\sqrt{6}}{4}\right) = \dfrac{\sqrt{2}+\sqrt{6}}{4}$.

Check this with a calculator. $\sin 75° \approx 0.9659$ and $\dfrac{\sqrt{2}+\sqrt{6}}{4} \approx 0.9659$

The formula for the difference of two angles is almost the same, but instead of adding the terms, we subtract them. Thus, the formula is:

> If we are given angles A and B, then
>
> $$\sin(A - B) = \sin A \cos B - \cos A \sin B.$$

Suppose that we want to find the exact value of $\sin 15°$. We know that $15° = 45° - 30°$, so $\sin 15° = \sin(45° - 30°)$. Now, using the formula above, $\sin(45° - 30°) = \sin 45° \cos 30° - \cos 45° \sin 30°$.

We know from our special angles that $\sin 30° = \frac{1}{2}$, $\cos 30° = \frac{\sqrt{3}}{2}$, and $\sin 45° = \cos 45° = \frac{\sqrt{2}}{2}$, so we can substitute and get:

$\left(\frac{\sqrt{2}}{2}\right)\left(\frac{\sqrt{3}}{2}\right) - \left(\frac{\sqrt{2}}{2}\right)\left(\frac{1}{2}\right)$, which simplifies to $\left(\frac{\sqrt{6}}{4}\right) - \left(\frac{\sqrt{2}}{4}\right) = \frac{\sqrt{6} - \sqrt{2}}{4}$.

Check this with a calculator.

$\sin 15° \approx 0.2588$ and $\frac{\sqrt{6} - \sqrt{2}}{4} \approx 0.2588$

What if we want to find the cosine of the sum of two angles? Now the formula is:

> If we are given angles A and B, then
>
> $$\cos(A + B) = \cos A \cos B - \sin A \sin B.$$

For example, if we want to find the exact value of $\cos 75°$.

We know that $75° = 30° + 45°$, so $\cos 75° = \cos(30° + 45°)$. Using the formula above, $\cos(30° + 45°) = \cos 30° \cos 45° - \sin 30° \sin 45°$.

As before, we know from our special angles that $\sin 30° = \frac{1}{2}$, $\cos 30° = \frac{\sqrt{3}}{2}$, and $\sin 45° = \cos 45° = \frac{\sqrt{2}}{2}$, so we can substitute and get:

$\left(\frac{\sqrt{3}}{2}\right)\left(\frac{\sqrt{2}}{2}\right) - \left(\frac{1}{2}\right)\left(\frac{\sqrt{2}}{2}\right)$, which simplifies to $\left(\frac{\sqrt{6}}{4}\right) - \left(\frac{\sqrt{2}}{4}\right) = \frac{\sqrt{6} - \sqrt{2}}{4}$.

Check this with a calculator. $\cos 75° \approx 0.2588$ and $\dfrac{\sqrt{6}-\sqrt{2}}{4} \approx 0.2588$

(By the way, this is the same as $\sin 15°$, but you should have expected that!)

Finally, the formula for the cosine of the difference of two angles is:

> If we are given angles A and B, then
>
> $\cos(A-B) = \cos A \cos B + \sin A \sin B.$

Let's find the exact value of $\cos 15°$. We know that $15° = 45° - 30°$, so $\cos 15° = \cos(45° - 30°)$. Using the formula above,

$\cos(45° - 30°) = \cos 45° \cos 30° + \sin 45° \sin 30°.$

We know from our special angles that $\sin 30° = \dfrac{1}{2}$, $\cos 30° = \dfrac{\sqrt{3}}{2}$, and $\sin 45° = \cos 45° = \dfrac{\sqrt{2}}{2}$, so we can substitute and get:

$\left(\dfrac{\sqrt{2}}{2}\right)\left(\dfrac{\sqrt{3}}{2}\right) + \left(\dfrac{\sqrt{2}}{2}\right)\left(\dfrac{1}{2}\right)$, which simplifies to $\left(\dfrac{\sqrt{6}}{4}\right) + \left(\dfrac{\sqrt{2}}{4}\right) = \dfrac{\sqrt{6}+\sqrt{2}}{4}.$

Check this with a calculator. $\cos 15° \approx 0.9659$ and $\dfrac{\sqrt{6}+\sqrt{2}}{4} \approx 0.9659$

Let's put the four formulas in one place so that you can learn them easily.

If we are given angles A and B, then:

> $\sin(A+B) = \sin A \cos B + \cos A \sin B$
>
> $\sin(A-B) = \sin A \cos B - \cos A \sin B$
>
> $\cos(A+B) = \cos A \cos B - \sin A \sin B$
>
> $\cos(A-B) = \cos A \cos B + \sin A \sin B.$

Naturally, if you learn the formulas for the sum of two angles, it is easy to figure out the formulas for the difference of two angles. Let's do a little more practice.

Example 1:

Using the angles $60°$ and $90°$, and the formula for the cosine of the sum of two angles, verify that $\cos 150° = -\frac{\sqrt{3}}{2}$.

Since $60° + 90° = 150°$, $\cos 150°$ can be found by evaluating $\cos(60° + 90°)$.

Using the formula above, we get:

$$\cos(60° + 90°) = \cos 60° \cos 90° - \sin 60° \sin 90°.$$

We know from our special angles that $\cos 60° = \frac{1}{2}$, $\sin 60° = \frac{\sqrt{3}}{2}$, $\cos 90° = 0$, and $\sin 90° = 1$, so we can substitute into the formula, giving us:

$$\left(\frac{1}{2}\right)(0) - \left(\frac{\sqrt{3}}{2}\right)(1) = -\frac{\sqrt{3}}{2}.$$

Example 2:

Use special angles to verify that $\sin(A + 180°) = -\sin A$.

Our formula says that

$$\sin(A + 180°) = \sin A \cos 180° + \cos A \sin 180°.$$

We know from our special angles that $\sin 180° = 0$ and $\cos 180° = -1$,

so $\sin A \cos 180° + \cos A \sin 180° = \sin A(-1) + \cos A(0) = -\sin A$.

Example 3:

Find the exact value of $\cos 105°$.

Using 60° and 45°, and the formula

$$\cos(A+B) = \cos A \cos B - \sin A \sin B,$$

we can evaluate $\cos(60° + 45°) = \cos 60° \cos 45° - \sin 60° \sin 45°$.

We know from our special angles that $\cos 60° = \frac{1}{2}$, $\sin 60° = \frac{\sqrt{3}}{2}$ and $\sin 45° = \cos 45° = \frac{\sqrt{2}}{2}$.

Substituting into the formula, we get

$$\cos 60° \cos 45° - \sin 60° \sin 45° = \left(\frac{1}{2}\right)\left(\frac{\sqrt{2}}{2}\right) - \left(\frac{\sqrt{3}}{2}\right)\left(\frac{\sqrt{2}}{2}\right)$$

This can be simplified to $\frac{\sqrt{2}}{4} - \frac{\sqrt{6}}{4} = \frac{\sqrt{2} - \sqrt{6}}{4}$.

What about the formulas for the tangent of the sum or difference of two angles? First of all, you can always use the rule that the tangent of an angle is the sine of that angle divided by the cosine. In other words, $\tan(A+B) = \frac{\sin(A+B)}{\cos(A+B)}$. Thus, if you are asked to find $\tan 75°$, you could find $\tan(30° + 45°) = \frac{\sin(30° + 45°)}{\cos(30° + 45°)}$. We found above that $\sin 75° = \frac{\sqrt{2} + \sqrt{6}}{4}$ and that $\cos 75° = \frac{\sqrt{6} - \sqrt{2}}{4}$. Therefore,

$$\tan 75° = \frac{\frac{\sqrt{2} + \sqrt{6}}{4}}{\frac{\sqrt{6} - \sqrt{2}}{4}} = \frac{\sqrt{6} + \sqrt{2}}{\sqrt{6} - \sqrt{2}}.$$

There is another way to find the tangent of the sum or difference of two angles. If you take $\frac{\sin(A+B)}{\cos(A+B)} = \frac{\sin A \cos B + \cos A \sin B}{\cos A \cos B - \sin A \sin B}$, and do a little algebra, you get:

$$\tan(A+B) = \frac{\tan A + \tan B}{1 - \tan A \tan B}$$

(We are omitting the derivation here, but see if you can do it on your own).

We can find $\tan 75°$ using this formula and we get:

$$\tan 75° = \tan(30° + 45°) = \frac{\tan 30° + \tan 45°}{1 - \tan 30° \tan 45°} = \frac{\frac{\sqrt{3}}{3} + 1}{1 - \left(\frac{\sqrt{3}}{3}\right)(1)}.$$

Let's simplify this by multiplying the top and bottom by 3, which gives us: $\frac{3+\sqrt{3}}{3-\sqrt{3}}$.

This doesn't look the same as the result that we got when we divided the sine by the cosine, but if you check the values with your calculator, they both give you approximately 3.732. (Of course, you could always do some algebra, but we will leave that up to you. It should be a good test of your abilities.)

What we just learned for $\tan(A+B)$ **also holds true for** $\tan(A-B)$**. That is, you can either find** $\sin(A-B)$ **and** $\cos(A-B)$ **and divide, or you can use a formula.**

The formula for the tangent of the difference of two angles is:

$$\tan(A-B) = \frac{\tan A - \tan B}{1 + \tan A \tan B}$$

Suppose that we wanted to find $\tan 15°$. We know that $\sin 15° = \frac{\sqrt{6}-\sqrt{2}}{4}$ and that $\cos 15° = \frac{\sqrt{6}+\sqrt{2}}{4}$. If we divide the former by the latter, we get: $\tan 15° = \frac{\sin 15°}{\cos 15°} = \frac{\frac{\sqrt{6}-\sqrt{2}}{4}}{\frac{\sqrt{6}+\sqrt{2}}{4}} = \frac{\sqrt{6}-\sqrt{2}}{\sqrt{6}+\sqrt{2}}.$

If we use the formula for the tangent of the difference between two angles, we get:

$$\tan 15° = \tan(45° - 30°) = \frac{\tan 45° - \tan 30°}{1 + \tan 45° \tan 30°} = \frac{1 - \frac{\sqrt{3}}{3}}{1 + (1)\left(\frac{\sqrt{3}}{3}\right)} = \frac{3 - \sqrt{3}}{3 + \sqrt{3}}.$$

Convince yourself that these are the same.

Once again, the formulas for the sum and difference of two angles are:

$$\sin(A + B) = \sin A \cos B + \cos A \sin B$$

$$\sin(A - B) = \sin A \cos B - \cos A \sin B$$

$$\cos(A + B) = \cos A \cos B - \sin A \sin B$$

$$\cos(A - B) = \cos A \cos B + \sin A \sin B.$$

$$\tan(A - B) = \frac{\tan A - \tan B}{1 + \tan A \tan B}$$

$$\tan(A + B) = \frac{\tan A + \tan B}{1 - \tan A \tan B}$$

PROBLEMS

1) If $\sin A = \frac{11}{15}$ and $\tan A < 0$, find $\cos A$.

2) If $\tan A = \frac{24}{7}$ and $\sec A < 0$, find $\sin A$.

3) If $\csc A = \frac{8}{3}$ and $\cot A > 0$, find $\cos A$.

4) If $\cos A = \frac{5}{11}$ and $\tan A < 0$, find $\csc A$.

5) Find the exact value of $\tan 165°$.

6) Find the exact value of $\sin 105°$.

7) Find the exact value of $\cos\left(\dfrac{2\pi}{3} + \dfrac{\pi}{6}\right)$.

8) Find the exact value of $\sin\left(\dfrac{5\pi}{12}\right)$.

9) Evaluate the expression $\cos 96° \cos 6° + \sin 96° \sin 6°$.

10) Evaluate the expression $\sin 290° \cos 20° - \cos 290° \sin 20°$.

11) Evaluate the expression $\dfrac{\tan 65° - \tan 20°}{1 + \tan 65° \tan 20°}$.

12) Evaluate the expression $\cos\dfrac{7\pi}{12}\cos\dfrac{5\pi}{12} - \sin\dfrac{7\pi}{12}\sin\dfrac{5\pi}{12}$.

13) If $\sin A = \dfrac{4}{5}$ and $\sin B = \dfrac{5}{13}$, and A and B are both in quadrant I, find the value of:

   (a) $\sin(A+B)$

   (b) $\cos(A+B)$

   (c) $\tan(A-B)$

14) If $\cos x = \dfrac{1}{3}$ and $\cos y = \dfrac{\sqrt{5}}{3}$, and x and y are in quadrant IV, find the value of:

   (a) $\sin(x-y)$

   (b) $\cos(x+y)$

   (c) $\tan(x+y)$

15) Prove that $\sin(A+B)\sin(A-B) = \sin^2 A - \sin^2 B$.

DOUBLE ANGLE FORMULAS

The next formulas that you need to learn are called the "Double Angle Formulas" and are all derived from the formulas that we just learned. It's not necessary to memorize these, but you will use them a lot, so learn to recognize them.

First, let's learn the double angle formula for sine. Suppose that you are given an angle A. How do we find $\sin 2A$? You might think that it is simply twice $\sin A$, but you would be wrong. Let's look again at the formula for the sine of the sum of two angles. It is: $\sin(A+B) = \sin A \cos B + \cos A \sin B$.

If we let $B = A$, then $\sin(A+A) = \sin 2A$, which is what we are trying to find. Thus, if we substitute $B = A$ into the formula, we get: $\sin 2A = \sin A \cos A + \cos A \sin A$. This can be simplified to:

$$\sin 2A = 2 \sin A \cos A$$

This is called the Double Angle Formula for sine. We are often asked to use the formula in problems and identities. Let's do some examples.

Example 1:

Use the Double Angle formula and $\sin 30° = \dfrac{1}{2}$ *and* $\cos 30° = \dfrac{\sqrt{3}}{2}$ *to find* $\sin 60°$.

If we use the formula above, we get:

$\sin 2(30°) = \sin 60° = 2 \sin 30° \cos 30°$. Substituting in $\sin 30° = \dfrac{1}{2}$ and $\cos 30° = \dfrac{\sqrt{3}}{2}$, we get: $\sin 60° = 2\left(\dfrac{1}{2}\right)\left(\dfrac{\sqrt{3}}{2}\right) = \dfrac{\sqrt{3}}{2}$; which is what we expected.

Example 2:

If $\sin 45° = \dfrac{\sqrt{2}}{2}$, *use the Double Angle formula to find* $\sin 90°$.

Using the formula above, $\sin 2(45°) = \sin 90° = 2 \sin 45° \cos 45°$.

We know that $\cos 45° = \dfrac{\sqrt{2}}{2}$, so we get:

$$\sin 90° = 2\sin 45° \cos 45° = 2\left(\dfrac{\sqrt{2}}{2}\right)\left(\dfrac{\sqrt{2}}{2}\right) = 1;$$

which, once again, is what we expected.

Now, let's find the Double Angle Formula for cosine.

Recall that $\cos(A+B) = \cos A \cos B - \sin A \sin B$. If we let $B = A$, then $\cos(A+A) = \cos 2A$, which is what we are trying to find. Thus, if we substitute $B = A$ into the formula, we get:

$\cos 2A = \cos A \cos A - \sin A \sin A$. This can be simplified to:

$$\cos 2A = \cos^2 A - \sin^2 A$$

Let's do some examples:

Example 3:

Use the Double Angle formula and $\sin 30° = \dfrac{1}{2}$ and $\cos 30° = \dfrac{\sqrt{3}}{2}$ to find $\cos 60°$.

If we use the formula above, we get:

$\cos 2(30°) = \cos^2 30° - \sin^2 30°$. Substituting in $\sin 30° = \dfrac{1}{2}$ and $\cos 30° = \dfrac{\sqrt{3}}{2}$, we get: $\cos 60° = \left(\dfrac{\sqrt{3}}{2}\right)^2 - \left(\dfrac{1}{2}\right)^2 = \dfrac{3}{4} - \dfrac{1}{4} = \dfrac{1}{2}$; which is what we expected.

Example 4:

If $\cos 45° = \dfrac{\sqrt{2}}{2}$, use the Double Angle formula to find $\cos 90°$.

Using the formula above, $\cos 2(45°) = \cos^2 45° - \sin^2 45°$. We know that $\sin 45° = \frac{\sqrt{2}}{2}$, so we get: $\cos 90° = \left(\frac{\sqrt{2}}{2}\right)^2 - \left(\frac{\sqrt{2}}{2}\right)^2 = 0$; which, once again, is what we expected.

One interesting aspect of the double angle formula for cosine is that there is more than one way to write the formula. If you recall from the Pythagorean Identities, $\sin^2 A + \cos^2 A = 1$, we can rewrite this as $\sin^2 A = 1 - \cos^2 A$. If we then substitute this into the double angle formula, we get:

$$\cos 2A = \cos^2 A - \left(1 - \cos^2 A\right) = 2\cos^2 A - 1.$$

Similarly, we could rewrite the Pythagorean Identity as $\cos^2 A = 1 - \sin^2 A$, and substitute it into the double angle formula. We get: $\cos 2A = \left(1 - \sin^2 A\right) - \sin^2 A = 1 - 2\sin^2 A$

Let's recapitulate the double angle formulas so far:

$$\sin 2A = 2\sin A \cos A$$

$$\cos 2A = \cos^2 A - \sin^2 A$$

$$\cos 2A = 2\cos^2 A - 1$$

$$\cos 2A = 1 - 2\sin^2 A$$

Why would we want to write the double angle formula for cosine three different ways? Suppose that you were given the following.

Example 4:

If $\sin A = \frac{3}{7}$, find $\cos 2A$.

We could use the fact that $\sin A = \frac{3}{7}$ to find $\cos A$ (we could either draw a triangle and find the missing side or use the Pythagorean Identity), and plug it into the first of the three double angle formulas, or we could simply use the third formula.

$$\cos 2A = 1 - 2\sin^2 A = 1 - 2\left(\frac{3}{7}\right)^2 = 1 - 2\left(\frac{9}{49}\right) = 1 - \frac{18}{49} = \frac{31}{49}.$$

Wasn't that easier?

Example 5:

If $\cos A = \frac{8}{15}$, find $\cos 2A$.

Again, we could use the fact that $\cos A = \frac{8}{15}$ to find $\sin A$ and plug it into the first of the three double angle formulas, or we could simply use the second formula.

$$\cos 2A = 2\cos^2 A - 1 = 2\left(\frac{8}{15}\right)^2 - 1 = 2\left(\frac{64}{225}\right) - 1 = \frac{128}{225} - 1 = -\frac{97}{225}.$$

Now let's learn the Double Angle Formula for tangent. As with sine and cosine, we start with the formula for the tangent of the sum of two angles. $\tan(A+B) = \frac{\tan A + \tan B}{1 - \tan A \tan B}$. Now, we let $B = A$ and we get: $\tan(A+A) = \tan 2A = \frac{\tan A + \tan A}{1 - \tan A \tan A}$. This can be simplified to:

$$\tan 2A = \frac{2\tan A}{1 - \tan^2 A}$$

Of course, we can also find $\tan 2A$ by finding the quotient of $\sin 2A$ and $\cos 2A$.

Let's do some examples.

Example 6:

If $\tan 30° = \frac{\sqrt{3}}{3}$, find $\tan 60°$.

Using the formula above, we get:

$$\tan 2(30°) = \tan 60° = \frac{2\tan 30°}{1-\tan^2 30°}.$$

Substituting in $\tan 30° = \frac{\sqrt{3}}{3}$, we get:

$$\tan 60° = \frac{2\left(\frac{\sqrt{3}}{3}\right)}{1-\left(\frac{\sqrt{3}}{3}\right)^2} = \frac{\frac{2\sqrt{3}}{3}}{1-\frac{1}{3}} = \frac{\frac{2\sqrt{3}}{3}}{\frac{2}{3}} = \sqrt{3};$$

which is what we expected.

Example 7:

If $\sin A = \frac{15}{17}$, and A is in quadrant I, find $\tan 2A$.

First, we need to find $\tan A$. Using the identity $\sin^2 A + \cos^2 A = 1$, we have $\left(\frac{15}{17}\right)^2 + \cos^2 A = 1$. Solving for $\cos A$, we get: $\cos^2 A = 1 - \left(\frac{15}{17}\right)^2 = 1 - \frac{225}{289} = \frac{64}{289}$ and thus $\cos A = \pm\frac{8}{17}$. Because A is in quadrant I, where all trig functions have positive values, $\cos A = \frac{8}{17}$. Now that we know $\sin A$ and $\cos A$, we can find $\tan A$.

$$\tan A = \frac{\frac{15}{17}}{\frac{8}{17}} = \frac{15}{8}.$$

Thus, $\tan 2A = \dfrac{2\left(\frac{15}{8}\right)}{1-\left(\frac{15}{8}\right)^2} = \dfrac{\frac{15}{4}}{-\frac{161}{64}} = -\dfrac{240}{161}.$

Now for a cumulative example.

Example 8:

If $\sin A = \dfrac{6}{11}$, and A is in quadrant II, find $\sin 2A$, $\cos 2A$, and $\tan 2A$.

First, let's use the Pythagorean Identity to find $\cos A$.

$\left(\dfrac{6}{11}\right)^2 + \cos^2 A = 1$, so $\cos^2 A = 1 - \left(\dfrac{6}{11}\right)^2 = 1 - \dfrac{36}{121} = \dfrac{85}{121}$, and thus $\cos A = \pm\dfrac{\sqrt{85}}{11}$. Because A is in quadrant II, and cosine is negative in quadrant II, we get $\cos A = -\dfrac{\sqrt{85}}{11}$.

Now we can use the double angle formulas.

$$\sin 2A = 2\sin A \cos A = 2\left(\dfrac{6}{11}\right)\left(-\dfrac{\sqrt{85}}{11}\right) = -\dfrac{12\sqrt{85}}{121}$$

$$\cos 2A = \cos^2 A - \sin^2 A = \left(-\dfrac{\sqrt{85}}{11}\right)^2 - \left(\dfrac{6}{11}\right)^2 = \dfrac{85}{121} - \dfrac{36}{121} = \dfrac{49}{121}.$$

Another way to find $\cos 2A$, would be to use one of the alternate formulas:

$$\cos 2A = 1 - 2\sin^2 A = 1 - 2\left(\dfrac{6}{11}\right)^2 = 1 - \dfrac{72}{121} = \dfrac{49}{121}$$

(Whew! Same result!)

Now, we can find $\tan 2A$ by using $\sin A$ and $\cos A$ to find $\tan A$ and plugging into the formula, but it is simpler to divide $\sin 2A$ by $\cos 2A$. We get:

$$\tan 2A = \frac{\sin 2A}{\cos 2A} = \frac{-\frac{12\sqrt{85}}{121}}{\frac{49}{121}} = -\frac{12\sqrt{85}}{49}.$$

Once again, the Double Angle Formulas are:

$$\sin 2A = 2\sin A \cos A$$

$$\cos 2A = \cos^2 A - \sin^2 A$$

$$\cos 2A = 2\cos^2 A - 1$$

$$\cos 2A = 1 - 2\sin^2 A$$

$$\tan 2A = \frac{2\tan A}{1 - \tan^2 A}$$

You don't need to memorize any of these formulas. They are all simple to derive from the formulas for the sum of two angles A and B by letting $A = B$.

PROBLEMS

1) Given $\sin \theta = \frac{1}{5}$, find $\cos 2\theta$.

2) Given $\tan A = \frac{\sqrt{7}}{2}$, find $\sin 2A$.

3) Given $\sin \theta = \frac{1}{2}$, and $90° \leq \theta \leq 180°$, find $\tan 2\theta$.

4) Given $\cos \theta = -\frac{4}{5}$, and $90° \leq \theta \leq 180°$, find $\sin 2\theta$.

5) Given $\cos \theta = \frac{\sqrt{10}}{10}$, and $270° \leq \theta \leq 360°$, find $\sin 2\theta$.

6) Evaluate $2\cos^2 15° - 1$.

7) Evaluate $2\sin \frac{11\pi}{12} \cos \frac{11\pi}{12}$.

8) Evaluate $\dfrac{2\tan\dfrac{5\pi}{12}}{1-\tan^2\dfrac{5\pi}{12}}$.

9) Evaluate $\cos^2 75° - \sin^2 75°$.

10) Evaluate $1 - 2\sin^2 105°$.

11) If $\sin A = \dfrac{2}{3}$, find $\cos 4A$.

12) Show that $\cos A = \pm\sqrt{\dfrac{1+\cos 2A}{2}}$.

TRIG EQUATIONS

In Algebra, we learned to find the solution (or solutions) to equations that were in terms of a variable, usually x. For example, $2x - 1 = 0$. In this unit, we will learn to find the solution (or solutions) to equations that are in terms of a trig function. We will go about solving the problem exactly as if it were an algebraic equation in terms of x, and then find the angle (or angles) that satisfy the trig equation. This is easier to understand with an example.

Example 1:

Find the solutions to $2\sin x - 1 = 0$, where $0 \leq x < 2\pi$.

This looks just like the equation $2x - 1 = 0$. If we were to solve that equation, we would first add 1 to both sides, giving us $2x = 1$. Then, we would divide by 2, giving us $x = \dfrac{1}{2}$.

Similarly, we take the equation $2\sin x - 1 = 0$ and add 1 to both sides, giving us $2\sin x = 1$. Then, we divide by 2, giving us $\sin x = \dfrac{1}{2}$. Now, we need to know what values of x in the domain satisfy this equation.

We recall from special angles that $\sin x = \dfrac{1}{2}$ when $x = \dfrac{\pi}{6}$ and $x = \dfrac{5\pi}{6}$. These are the solutions to the equation.

Notice that there are actually an infinite number of values of

x for which $\sin x = \frac{1}{2}$, but the domain is restricted to $0 \leq x < 2\pi$. Thus, the solution to trig equations will *always* depend on the domain of x. **(That was important! Did you pay attention to what we just said?)** If the domain had been $0° \leq x < 360°$, the answers would have been $x = 30°$ and $x = 150°$. Or, if the domain had been $0 \leq x < 4\pi$, the answers would have been $x = \frac{\pi}{6}$, $x = \frac{5\pi}{6}$, $x = \frac{13\pi}{6}$, and $x = \frac{17\pi}{6}$.

Example 2:

Find the solutions to $3\tan\theta + \sqrt{3} = 0$, where $0° \leq \theta < 360°$.

First, subtract $\sqrt{3}$ from both sides, which gives us $3\tan\theta = -\sqrt{3}$. Then, divide both sides by 3, which gives us $\tan\theta = -\frac{\sqrt{3}}{3}$.

We know from special angles that $\tan\theta = -\frac{\sqrt{3}}{3}$ when $\theta = 150°$ and $\theta = 330°$. These are the solutions to the equation.

Example 3:

Find the solutions to $2\cos^2 x - 1 = 0$, where $0 \leq x < 2\pi$.

First, add 1 to both sides. We get: $2\cos^2 x = 1$.

Next, divide both sides by 2. We get: $\cos^2 x = \frac{1}{2}$.

Finally, take the square root of both sides. We get: $\cos x = \pm\frac{1}{\sqrt{2}}$. (Note the $\pm$ sign!)

For what values of x is $\cos x = \pm\frac{1}{\sqrt{2}}$? (Remember that $\frac{1}{\sqrt{2}}$ is the same thing as $\frac{\sqrt{2}}{2}$.) From special angles, we know that the solutions are $x = \frac{\pi}{4}, \frac{3\pi}{4}, \frac{5\pi}{4}$, and $\frac{7\pi}{4}$.

Example 4:

Find the solutions to $\sin^2 x + 2\sin x - 3 = 0$, where $0 \le x < 2\pi$. Notice that this equation has the form of the quadratic $x^2 + 2x - 3 = 0$. We could factor that quadratic into $(x+3)(x-1) = 0$. Similarly, we can factor the given equation into $(\sin x + 3)(\sin x - 1) = 0$. This means that $\sin x = -3$ or $\sin x = 1$.

For what values of x does $\sin x = -3$? None! This is because $-1 \le \sin x \le 1$ for all values of x. (Remember this).

For what values of x does $\sin x = 1$? When $x = \frac{\pi}{2}$. Thus, the solution to the equation is only $x = \frac{\pi}{2}$.

Example 5:

Find the solutions to $\sin 2\theta + \sin \theta = 0$, *where* $0° \le \theta < 360°$.

First of all, use the Double Angle Formula $\sin 2\theta = 2\sin\theta\cos\theta$ to rewrite the equation as $2\sin\theta\cos\theta + \sin\theta = 0$.

Next, factor out $\sin\theta$ to get $\sin\theta(2\cos\theta + 1) = 0$.

This means that $\sin\theta = 0$ or $2\cos\theta + 1 = 0$.

The solution to the first of these equations is $\theta = 0°$ or $180°$.

The second equation can be rearranged into $\cos\theta = -\frac{1}{2}$, and its solutions are $\theta = 120°$ or $240°$.

Example 6:

Find the solutions to $3\sin^2\theta - 2 = 0$, *where* $0° \le \theta < 360°$.

First, add 2 to both sides. This gives us $3\sin^2\theta = 2$.

Next, divide through by 3. This give us $\sin^2\theta = \frac{2}{3}$.

Finally, take the square root of both sides. This gives us $\sin\theta = \pm\sqrt{\frac{2}{3}}$.

Now we have a small problem. The solutions to this equation are not special angles. So, let's use the calculator to find the values of θ. We need to use the $\sin^{-1}$ function on the calculator, which is usually found by pushing **2nd sin** or **Inv sin**.

If we push **2nd sin** $\left(\sqrt{\frac{2}{3}}\right)$, we get approximately 54.7° (Did you remember to put the calculator in **Degree** mode?) Let's round this to 55°. The other values of θ will be the angles in the other three quadrants that have a reference angle of 55°. They are: 125°, 235°, and 305°.

There is one last type of trig equation that you need to learn how to handle. This is the equation where, instead of being in terms of x or θ, it is in terms of a multiple of one of those variables. It's easiest to learn how to deal with these by doing a couple of examples.

Example 7:

Find the solutions of $2\cos 2\theta - 1 = 0$, where $0° \leq \theta < 360°$.

First, add 1 to both sides, which gives us $2\cos 2\theta = 1$.

Next, divide both sides by 2, which gives us $\cos 2\theta = \frac{1}{2}$.

Now, we find the values of 2θ that satisfy this equation. They are $2\theta = 60°$ and $2\theta = 300°$. BUT, because we are looking for values of 2θ, not θ, we find additional values by adding 360° to each of these solutions, which gives us $2\theta = 420°$ and $2\theta = 660°$ (we'll explain why in a moment). Then, we divide each of the solutions by 2, which gives us:

θ = 30°, 150°, 210°, 330°. These are the solutions to the equation.

Notice what we did. Because the equation was in terms of 2θ, we added 360° to each of the answers, which equates to a second revolution about the x-axis for each of the reference angles — once for $0° \leq \theta < 360°$ and once for $360° \leq \theta < 720°$. Then we divided each of the answers by 2, which gave us our solutions for θ. If the equation had been in terms of 3θ, we would have added 360° to each of the answers, for a second revolution about the x-axis, and then added 360° again for a third revolution. Then we would have divided each of the answers by 3.

> In general, when an equation is in terms of nθ, we find the answers between $0° \leq \theta < 360°$ and then add 360° to each answer $n-1$ times. Then we divide each answer by n. Naturally, we do the same with 2π if the problem is in radians.

Confused? We do this because, if $0 \leq \theta < 360°$, then $0 \leq n\theta < n \cdot 360°$.

Let's do an example.

Example 8:

Find the solutions of $5\tan 3\theta + 2 = 0$, where $0° \leq \theta < 360°$.
First, subtract 2 from both sides, which gives us $5\tan 3\theta = -2$.

Next, divide through by 5, which gives us $\tan 3\theta = -\frac{2}{5}$.

Using a calculator, we get that $\tan 3\theta = -\frac{2}{5}$ when $3\theta \approx -22°$. We need to find the angles between $0° \leq \theta < 360°$ where this is true. Using 22° as a reference angle, we get $3\theta = 158°$ and $3\theta = 338°$.

Next, we add 360° to each answer to give us 3θ = 518° and 3θ = 698°.

Now, we add 360° again, to give us 3θ = 878° and 3θ = 1058°.

Finally, we divide each of the answers by 3 and we get:
θ ≈ 53°, 113°, 173°, 233°, 293°, and 353°.

PROBLEMS

If $0° \leq x < 360°$, solve for x to the nearest degree.

1) $\cos x - 2\cos x \sin x = 0$.
2) $2\cos^2 x = \cos x$.
3) $\sin^2 x = 1 - \cos 2x$.
4) $7\cos x + 1 = 6\sec x$.
5) $\sin 2x = \sqrt{3} \cos x$.
6) $5\sin 2x + \frac{1}{2}\cos x = 0$.
7) $8\sin x \cos x = 2\sqrt{3}$.
8) $\sin^2 3x - \sin 3x = 0$.
9) $2\cos^2 4x - \cos 4x = 0$; $0° \leq x \leq 180°$.
10) $\tan^2 3x + \tan 3x = 0$; $0° \leq x \leq 180°$.

TRIGONOMETRIC IDENTITIES

This is one of the more confusing topics in Trigonometry. Here, you will be doing algebra, using the relationships between the various trig functions. You will be asked to prove that something is true, and you will manipulate one or both of the sides to prove the identity. *But,* you are **never** allowed to move something from one side of the equal sign to the other.

Let's do an easy example.

Example 1:

Prove that $\dfrac{\sin 2x}{2\sin x} = \cos x$.

If we use the Double Angle Formula, we can rewrite $\sin 2x$ as $2\sin x \cos x$. This gives us: $\dfrac{2\sin x \cos x}{2\sin x} = \cos x$. Now, if we reduce the left-hand side, we get: $\cos x = \cos x$, and we have proved the identity.

Is that all there is to trig identities? Yes. The tough part is to find the relationships and to figure out what to plug in.

Generally, you should follow the following steps.

First, convert any double angles to single angles, using the double angle formulas.

Second, put everything in terms of sine and cosine.

Third, if there are fractions, combine them with common denominators.

Fourth, look to simplify things by canceling like terms or by using other identities.

Example 2:

Prove that $\tan x + \cot x = \csc x \sec x$.

First, rewrite both sides in terms of sines and cosines:

$$\frac{\sin x}{\cos x} + \frac{\cos x}{\sin x} = \left(\frac{1}{\sin x}\right)\left(\frac{1}{\cos x}\right).$$

Next, combine the fractions on the left side using a common denominator:

$$\frac{\sin x}{\cos x}\left(\frac{\sin x}{\sin x}\right) + \frac{\cos x}{\sin x}\left(\frac{\cos x}{\cos x}\right) = \left(\frac{1}{\sin x}\right)\left(\frac{1}{\cos x}\right)$$

$$\frac{\sin^2 x}{\sin x \cos x} + \frac{\cos^2 x}{\sin x \cos x} = \left(\frac{1}{\sin x}\right)\left(\frac{1}{\cos x}\right)$$

$$\frac{\sin^2 x + \cos^2 x}{\sin x \cos x} = \left(\frac{1}{\sin x}\right)\left(\frac{1}{\cos x}\right)$$

Finally, use the Pythagorean Identity $\sin^2 x + \cos^2 x = 1$ to get:

$\frac{1}{\sin x \cos x} = \left(\frac{1}{\sin x}\right)\left(\frac{1}{\cos x}\right)$. Multiply the two terms on the right, and we have proved the identity.

Example 3:

Prove that $\sec x + \tan x = \frac{\cos x}{1 - \sin x}$.

First, rewrite the left side in terms of sines and cosines: $\frac{1}{\cos x} + \frac{\sin x}{\cos x} = \frac{\cos x}{1 - \sin x}$

Next, combine the fractions on the left side: $\frac{1 + \sin x}{\cos x} = \frac{\cos x}{1 - \sin x}$.

Now, multiply the top and bottom of the left side by $1 - \sin x$:

$$\frac{1 + \sin x}{\cos x}\left(\frac{1 - \sin x}{1 - \sin x}\right) = \frac{\cos x}{1 - \sin x}.$$

The left side can now be written as: $\frac{1 - \sin^2 x}{\cos x(1 - \sin x)} = \frac{\cos x}{1 - \sin x}$.

Next, we know from the Pythagorean Identity that $\sin^2 x + \cos^2 x = 1$, so we can rewrite $1 - \sin^2 x$ as $\cos^2 x$.

This gives us: $\frac{\cos^2 x}{\cos x(1 - \sin x)} = \frac{\cos x}{1 - \sin x}$.

Finally, we can cancel $\cos x$ from the top and bottom of the left side, and we have proved the identity:

$$\frac{\cos x}{(1 - \sin x)} = \frac{\cos x}{1 - \sin x}.$$

You will find that there is often more than one way to prove an identity. The only rule that you can't violate is that you must work with the two sides separately. That is, no cross-multiplying or multiplying through.

Example 4:

Prove that $\cot x = \dfrac{\cos 2x + 1}{\sin 2x}$.

First, use the Double Angle Formulas to rewrite $\cos 2x$ and $\sin 2x$: $\cot x = \dfrac{\cos^2 x - \sin^2 x + 1}{2\sin x \cos x}$.

Next, use the Pythagorean Identity to replace 1 with $\sin^2 x + \cos^2 x$: $\cot x = \dfrac{\cos^2 x - \sin^2 x + \sin^2 x + \cos^2 x}{2\sin x \cos x}$.

The numerator of the right side can be simplified to: $\cot x = \dfrac{2\cos^2 x}{2\sin x \cos x}$.

Cancel like terms on the right side to get: $\cot x = \dfrac{\cos x}{\sin x}$.

Finally, we can rewrite $\dfrac{\cos x}{\sin x}$ as $\cot x$, and we have proved the identity: $\cot x = \cot x$.

PROBLEMS

1) $\dfrac{\tan A + \cot A}{\csc A} = \sec A$

2) $\dfrac{\tan \theta}{\sec \theta + 1} = \dfrac{1 - \cos \theta}{\sin \theta}$

3) $\dfrac{\cos \theta + \cot \theta}{\cos \theta \cot \theta} = \tan \theta + \sec \theta$

4) $\dfrac{\cos x}{\sin 2x} = \dfrac{\csc x}{2}$

5) $\sin 2x = \dfrac{2\tan x}{1+\tan^2 x}$

6) $\cot x = \dfrac{\cos 2x + \cos x + 1}{\sin 2x + \sin x}$

7) $\sin 2x \sec^2 x = 2\tan x$

8) $\dfrac{\cos 2\theta}{\sin \theta} + \sin \theta = \dfrac{1}{\sin \theta} - \sin \theta$

9) $\dfrac{(\cos x + \sin x)^2}{1 + 2\sin x \cos x} = \cos x \tan x \csc x$

10) $\cos 2A = \dfrac{1-\tan^2 A}{1+\tan^2 A}$

SINE AND COSINE GRAPHS

BASIC SINE AND COSINE CURVES

One of the more difficult topics in Trigonometry is learning how to graph the trig functions. The basic graphs are not that hard, and you should become familiar with their shapes, but you will usually be asked to transform the graphs, which is not easy.

By the way, when graphing trig functions, we usually use radians instead of degrees, and it is customary to use θ for degrees and x for radians.

First, let's learn to graph the sine function. That is, we are going to graph $y = \sin x$. We know from our special angles, that sine has the following values:

x	0	$\dfrac{\pi}{6}$	$\dfrac{\pi}{4}$	$\dfrac{\pi}{3}$	$\dfrac{\pi}{2}$	$\dfrac{2\pi}{3}$	$\dfrac{3\pi}{4}$	$\dfrac{5\pi}{6}$	π
$y = \sin x$	0	$\dfrac{1}{2}$	$\dfrac{\sqrt{2}}{2}$	$\dfrac{\sqrt{3}}{2}$	1	$\dfrac{\sqrt{3}}{2}$	$\dfrac{\sqrt{2}}{2}$	$\dfrac{1}{2}$	0

x	$\dfrac{7\pi}{6}$	$\dfrac{5\pi}{4}$	$\dfrac{4\pi}{3}$	$\dfrac{3\pi}{2}$	$\dfrac{5\pi}{3}$	$\dfrac{7\pi}{4}$	$\dfrac{11\pi}{6}$	2π
$y = \sin x$	$-\dfrac{1}{2}$	$-\dfrac{\sqrt{2}}{2}$	$-\dfrac{\sqrt{3}}{2}$	-1	$-\dfrac{\sqrt{3}}{2}$	$-\dfrac{\sqrt{2}}{2}$	$-\dfrac{1}{2}$	0

If we plot these points on the coordinate axes and connect them, we will get the following graph:

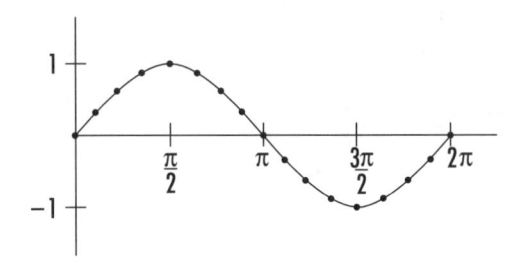

This is the basic sine graph and you should become familiar with its shape. See how it looks like a wave. This is why these graphs are frequently called *sine waves*. They are used throughout math and physics and there are many uses for them. **Note:**

It is customary to draw one wavelength of the graph from 0 to 2π.

The sine curve is traditionally drawn beginning at the origin and proceeding to the right for a period of 2π.

The cosine curve is traditionally drawn beginning at the point $(0,1)$ and proceeding to the right for a period of 2π.

IMPORTANT:

There is one thing about which there might be some confusion. Sine and cosine graphs repeat infinitely, so there is no real starting or ending point of a graph. When we refer to the *starting point* of a sine or cosine graph, we mean the following:

A sine graph has a *starting point* at the origin, which means that it proceeds from the origin up and to the right, toward its maximum.

A cosine has a *starting point* at the point $(0,1)$, which means that it proceeds from the y-axis down and to the right, toward the x-axis.

Therefore, when we say that a graph *begins* at a particular point, we mean that a sine curve proceeds up toward its maximum from that point, and a cosine curve proceeds down toward the x-axis from that point.

Notice that:

(1) the maximum is 1 and the minimum is -1;

(2) one wavelength stretches from the origin to 2π;

(3) the graph "begins" at $x = 0$ and $y = 0$; and

(4) the center line is the x-axis.

These are four important aspects of the graph that will be very important when we learn to transform the graphs.

The distance from the x-axis to the maximum (or minimum) height of the curve is called the *amplitude*. It is found by $\frac{|\text{max} - \text{min}|}{2}$. Here, the amplitude is 1.

The length of one wavelength is called the *period*. Here the period is 2π.

The distance from the y-axis to the starting point of the graph is called the *horizontal* or *phase shift*. Here, the horizontal shift is 0.

The distance from the x-axis to the center line is called the *vertical shift*. Here, the vertical shift is 0. By the way, the center line is the line that runs horizontally through the middle of the graph and is equidistant from the maximum and the minimum.

We will come back to these aspects of graphing sine curves in a little bit, but first, let's look at the graph for cosine.

Now we are going to graph $y = \cos x$. We know from our special angles, that cosine has the following values:

x	0	$\frac{\pi}{6}$	$\frac{\pi}{4}$	$\frac{\pi}{3}$	$\frac{\pi}{2}$	$\frac{2\pi}{3}$	$\frac{3\pi}{4}$	$\frac{5\pi}{6}$	π
$y = \cos x$	1	$\frac{\sqrt{3}}{2}$	$\frac{\sqrt{2}}{2}$	$\frac{1}{2}$	0	$-\frac{1}{2}$	$-\frac{\sqrt{2}}{2}$	$-\frac{\sqrt{3}}{2}$	-1

x	$\frac{7\pi}{6}$	$\frac{5\pi}{4}$	$\frac{4\pi}{3}$	$\frac{3\pi}{2}$	$\frac{5\pi}{3}$	$\frac{7\pi}{4}$	$\frac{11\pi}{6}$	2π
$y = \cos x$	$-\frac{\sqrt{3}}{2}$	$-\frac{\sqrt{2}}{2}$	$-\frac{1}{2}$	0	$\frac{1}{2}$	$\frac{\sqrt{2}}{2}$	$\frac{\sqrt{3}}{2}$	1

If we plot these points on the coordinate axes and connect them, we will get the following graph:

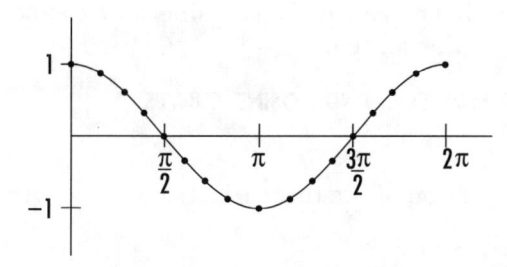

We use the same terminology for the cosine graph as for the sine graph. Thus:

- the amplitude is 1;
- the period is 2π;

- the horizontal shift is 0;
- the vertical shift is 0.

Notice that the four aspects of the graph of cosine are the same as the four aspects of the graph of sine. In fact, they have the same shape except that the cosine graph starts and finishes at a different point than the sine graph. You should have expected this because sine and cosine take on the same values, but at different angles. Let's look at the two graphs on the same axis:

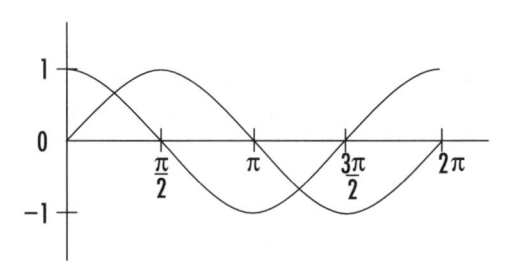

See how the sine graph hits exactly the same values as the cosine graph, but shifted by an amount of $\frac{\pi}{2}$. This means that they are the same curve, with a phase shift of $\frac{\pi}{2}$. In other words, if you shifted the cosine curve $\frac{\pi}{2}$ to the right, you would get the sine curve. Similarly, if you shifted the sine curve $\frac{\pi}{2}$ to the left, you would get the cosine curve. We'll learn how to write the equation for this in a little bit.

Now that we have seen the basic sine and cosine curves, let's learn how to transform them.

TRANSFORMATIONS OF SINE AND COSINE CURVES

Amplitude

If we have an equation of the form $y = A\sin x$ or $y = A\cos x$, then the amplitude of the graph is $|A|$.

For example, the graph of $y = 3\sin x$ has an amplitude of 3, the graph of $y = \frac{1}{2}\cos x$ has an amplitude of $\frac{1}{2}$, and the graph of $y = -2\sin x$ has an amplitude of 2 (*not* negative 2).

The effect of the amplitude on the graph is quite simple. It determines how high and low the graph goes. On a regular sine or cosine graph, we usually mark the highest, middle, and lowest y-coordinates of the graph. Let's do some examples.

Example 1:

Graph $y = 3\sin x$ for $0 \le x \le 2\pi$.

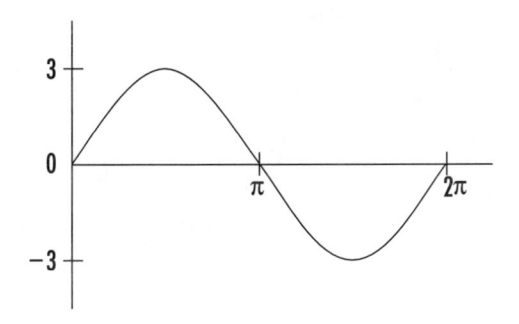

Notice that the curve looks just like a regular sine curve, except that, because it has an amplitude of 3, it reaches a maximum value of 3 at $x = \frac{\pi}{2}$ and a minimum value of -3 at $x = \frac{3\pi}{2}$.

Example 2:

Graph $y = 2\cos x$ for $0 \le x \le 2\pi$.

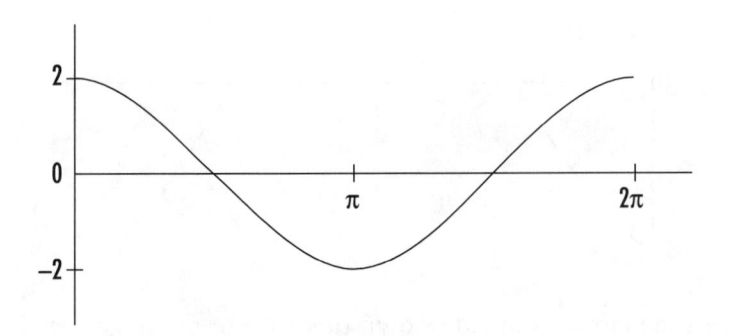

Notice that the curve looks just like a regular cosine curve, except that, because it has an amplitude of 2, it reaches a maximum value of 2 at $x = 0$ and $x = 2\pi$, and a minimum value of -2 at $x = \pi$.

Example 3:

Graph $y = \frac{1}{2}\sin x$ for $0 \leq x \leq 2\pi$.

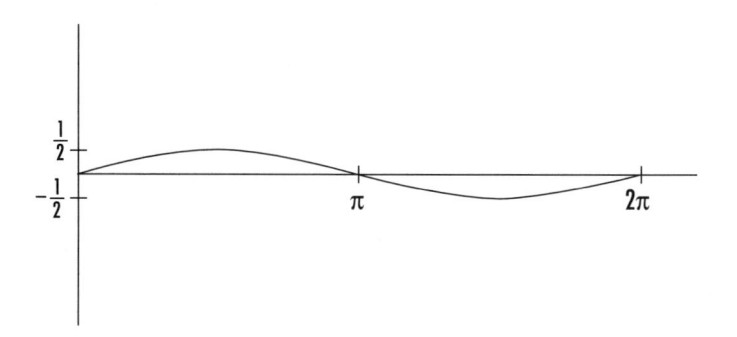

Here the curve has an amplitude of $\frac{1}{2}$, reaches a maximum value of $\frac{1}{2}$ at $x = \frac{\pi}{2}$ and a minimum value of $-\frac{1}{2}$ at $x = \frac{3\pi}{2}$.

Example 4:

Graph $y = -4\cos x$ for $0 \leq x \leq 2\pi$.

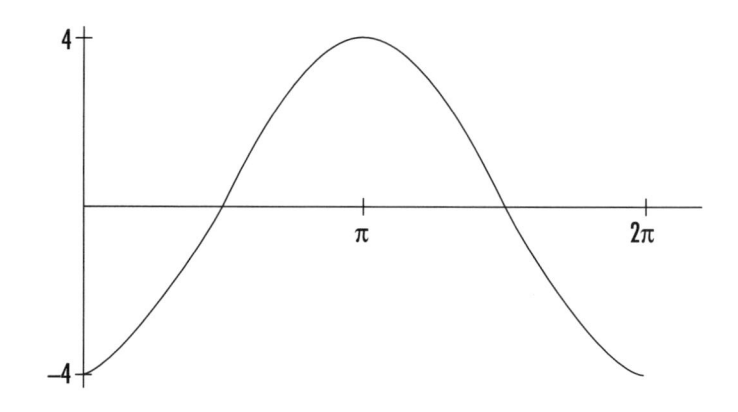

Here the curve is upside down (because of the negative sign) and has an amplitude of 4, so it reaches a minimum value of -4 at $x = 0$ and $x = 2\pi$, and a maximum value of 4 at $x = \pi$.

Now let's learn how to transform the period of a sine or cosine curve.

Period

If we have an equation of the form $y = A \sin Bx$ or $y = A \cos Bx$, then the period of the graph is $\frac{2\pi}{B}$. (If the angle is being measured in degrees rather than radians, the period is $\frac{360°}{B}$.)

For example, the graph of $y = \sin 3x$ has a period of $\frac{2\pi}{3}$, the graph of $y = \cos \frac{\pi}{2} x$ has a period of 4, and the graph of $y = \sin \frac{1}{2} x$ has a period of 4π.

The effect of the period on the graph is quite simple. It determines how long one wavelength of the graph is. Essentially what happens is this. On a regular sine curve, $y = \sin x$, there are five x-coordinates that we usually mark — the starting point, the maximum, the middle of the curve, the minimum, and the ending point. These points are $0, \frac{\pi}{2}, \pi, \frac{3\pi}{2}, 2\pi$. Similarly, on a regular cosine curve, $y = \cos x$, there are five x-coordinates that we usually mark — the starting (maximum) point, the first place where it crosses its horizontal axis, the minimum, the second point where it crosses its horizontal axis, and the ending point (again a maximum). These points are also $0, \frac{\pi}{2}, \pi, \frac{3\pi}{2}, 2\pi$.

For the general curves $y = A \sin Bx$ and $y = A \cos Bx$, we divide each of these points by the value B. Let's do some examples.

Example 5:

Graph $y = \cos 2x$ for one period beginning at $x = 0$.

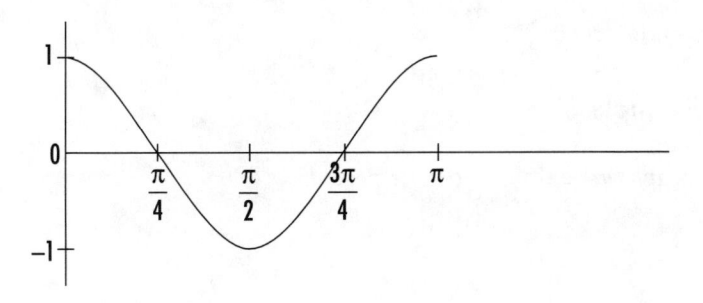

Here the curve has a period of $\frac{2\pi}{2} = \pi$. Thus, the marks on the x-axis are $0, \frac{\pi}{4}, \frac{\pi}{2}, \frac{3\pi}{4}, \pi$.

Example 6:

Graph $y = \sin\frac{1}{2}x$ for one period beginning at $x = 0$.

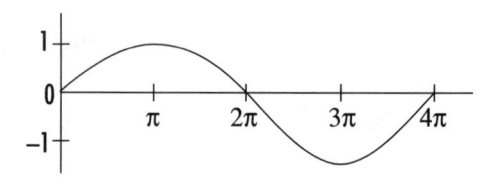

Here the curve has a period of $\frac{2\pi}{\frac{1}{2}} = 4\pi$. Thus, the marks on the x-axis are $0, \pi, 2\pi, 3\pi, 4\pi$.

Example 7:

Graph $y = \sin \pi x$ for one period.

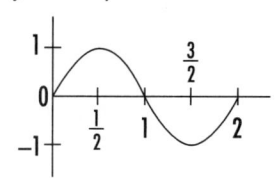

Here the curve has a period of $\frac{2\pi}{\pi} = 2$. Thus, the marks on the x-axis are $0, \frac{1}{2}, 1, \frac{3}{2}, 2$.

Example 8:

Graph $y = 2\sin\frac{1}{3}x$ for one period.

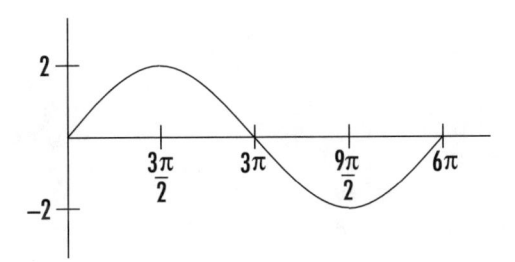

Here the curve has a period of $\frac{2\pi}{\frac{1}{3}} = 6\pi$ and the amplitude is 2.

Thus, the marks on the x-axis are $0, \frac{3\pi}{2}, 3\pi, \frac{9\pi}{2}, 6\pi$ and the marks on the y-axis are $2, 0, -2$.

Horizontal Shift

If we have an equation of the form $y = \sin(x \pm C)$ or $y = \cos(x \pm C)$, then we shift the graph C units to the left, if C is added; or we shift the graph C units to the right, if C is subtracted. A horizontal shift is often called a *phase shift*.

For example, the graph of $y = \sin\left(x - \frac{\pi}{6}\right)$ is shifted $\frac{\pi}{6}$ units to the right, and the graph of $y = \cos(x + 1)$ is shifted 1 unit to the left.

The effect of the shift is that we add the value of C to, or subtract the value of C from, each of the five x-coordinates that we usually mark on the x-axis. Let's do some examples.

Example 9:

Graph $y = \sin\left(x - \frac{\pi}{3}\right)$ for one period beginning at $x = \frac{\pi}{3}$.

This means that we are going to add $\frac{\pi}{3}$ to each of the five x-coordinates. Thus, the curve will "start" at $0 + \frac{\pi}{3} = \frac{\pi}{3}$, reach a maximum at $\frac{\pi}{2} + \frac{\pi}{3} = \frac{5\pi}{6}$, cross the x-axis at $\pi + \frac{\pi}{3} = \frac{4\pi}{3}$, reach a minimum at $\frac{3\pi}{2} + \frac{\pi}{3} = \frac{11\pi}{6}$, and "end" at $2\pi + \frac{\pi}{3} = \frac{7\pi}{3}$ (Remember what we said earlier about where a graph begins or ends.).

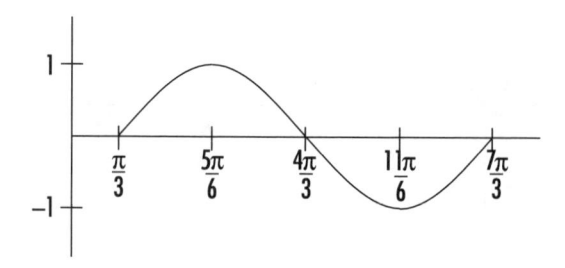

Example 10:

Graph $y = \cos\left(x + \dfrac{\pi}{6}\right)$ for one period beginning at $x = -\dfrac{\pi}{6}$.

This means that we are going to subtract $\dfrac{\pi}{6}$ from each of the five x-coordinates. Thus, the curve will start at $0 - \dfrac{\pi}{6} = -\dfrac{\pi}{6}$, cross the x-axis at $\dfrac{\pi}{2} - \dfrac{\pi}{6} = \dfrac{\pi}{3}$, reach a minimum at $\pi - \dfrac{\pi}{6} = \dfrac{5\pi}{6}$, cross the x-axis again at $\dfrac{3\pi}{2} - \dfrac{\pi}{6} = \dfrac{4\pi}{3}$, and end at $2\pi - \dfrac{\pi}{6} = \dfrac{11\pi}{6}$

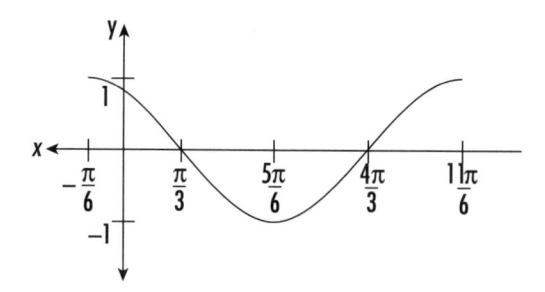

Example 11:

Graph $y = \cos \pi(x - 1)$ for one period beginning at $x = 1$.

First of all, note that the period is $\dfrac{2\pi}{\pi} = 2$. So, if there weren't a horizontal shift, the five x-coordinates would be $0, \dfrac{1}{2}, 1, \dfrac{3}{2}, 2$. But, the horizontal shift of 1 unit to the right means that we are to add 1 to each of the five x-coordinates. Thus, the curve will start at 1, cross the x-axis at $\frac{3}{2}$, reach a minimum at 2, cross the x-axis again at $\frac{5}{2}$, and end at 3

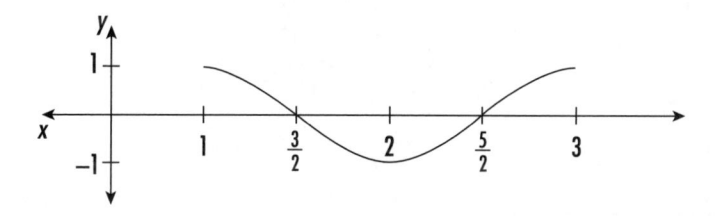

Example 12:

Graph $y = 2\sin\frac{1}{3}(x+\pi)$ for one period beginning at $x = -\pi$.

First of all, note that the period is $\frac{2\pi}{\frac{1}{3}} = 6\pi$. So, if there weren't a horizontal shift, the five x-coordinates would be $0, \frac{3\pi}{2}, 3\pi, \frac{9\pi}{2}, 6\pi$. But, the horizontal shift of π units to the left means that we are to subtract π from each of the five x-coordinates. Thus, the curve will start at $-\pi$, reach a maximum at $\frac{\pi}{2}$, cross the x-axis at 2π, reach a minimum at $\frac{7\pi}{2}$, and end at 5π. Finally, the curve has an amplitude of 2.

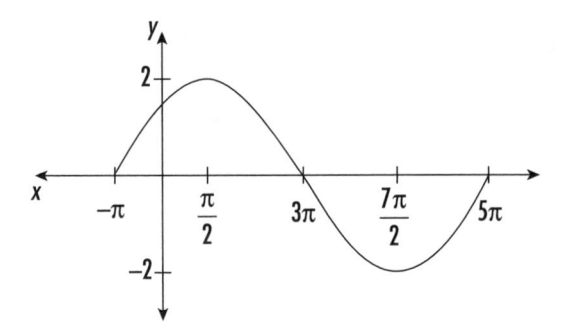

VERTICAL SHIFT

If we have an equation of the form $y = \sin x \pm D$ or $y = \cos x \pm D$, then we shift the graph D units up, if D is added; or we shift the graph D units down, if D is subtracted.

For example, the graph of $y = \sin x + 3$ is shifted 3 units up, and the graph of $y = \cos x - 4$ is shifted 4 units down.

The effect of the shift is that we add the value of D to, or subtract the value of D from, each of the three y-coordinates that we usually mark on the y-axis. Usually, we draw a dotted horizontal line to represent where the new center line of the graph is. Let's do some examples.

Example 13:

Graph $y = \sin x + 2$ for one period beginning at $x = 0$.

Here, we are shifting the graph up 2 units. This means that the maximum will be at $y = 1 + 2 = 3$, the center line will run through $y = 0 + 2 = 2$, and the minimum will be at $y = -1 + 2 = 1$

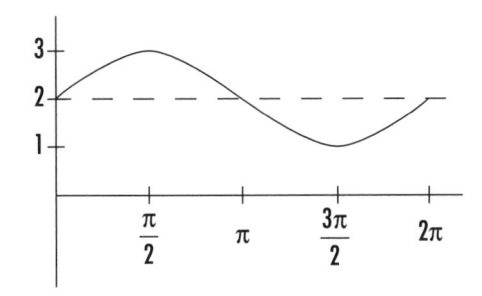

Example 14:

Graph $y = 2\cos x - 1$ for one period beginning at $x = 0$.

First of all, note that the amplitude is 2. So, if there weren't a vertical shift, the three y-coordinates would be $-2, 0, 2$. But, the vertical shift of 1 unit down means that we are to subtract 1 from each of the three y-coordinates. Thus, the curve will reach a maximum at 1, its center line will run through -1, and it will reach a minimum at -3.

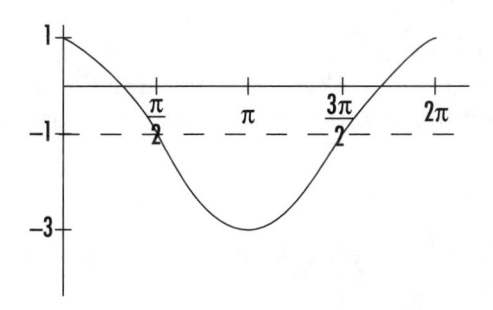

Are you ready to do **all four** transformations?

Example 15:

Graph $y = 2\sin\frac{\pi}{4}(x+1) + 1$ *for one period beginning at* $x = -1$.

Let's take care of the x-axis stuff first. *Always* do the period first and the horizontal shift second.

The period is 8. So, if there weren't a horizontal shift, the five x-coordinates would be $0, 2, 4, 6, 8$.

The horizontal shift of 1 unit to the left means that we are to subtract 1 from each of the five x-coordinates. Thus, the five x-coordinates are $-1, 1, 3, 5, 7$.

Now let's do the y-axis stuff. *Always* do the amplitude first and the vertical shift second.

The curve has an amplitude of 2. If there weren't a vertical shift, the three y-coordinates would be $-2, 0, 2$.

The vertical shift is up 1 unit. Therefore, the three y-coordinates are $-1, 1, 3$

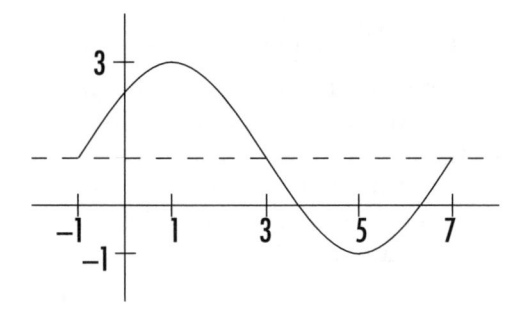

[Graph showing a sine-like curve with values marked at -1, 1, 3, 5, 7 on x-axis and -1, 3 on y-axis]

If you can do *this* last example, you can graph *any* sine or cosine function. Remember to do the transformations in this order: period, horizontal shift, amplitude, vertical shift.

Example 16:

Graph $y = -4\cos\frac{1}{4}\left(x + \frac{\pi}{2}\right) - 2$ *for one period beginning at* $x = -\frac{\pi}{2}$.

The period is $\frac{2\pi}{\frac{1}{4}} = 8\pi$. So, if there weren't a horizontal shift, the five x-coordinates would be $0, 2\pi, 4\pi, 6\pi, 8\pi$.

The horizontal shift of $\frac{\pi}{2}$ units to the left means that we are to subtract $\frac{\pi}{2}$ from each of the five x-coordinates. Thus, the five x-coordinates are $-\frac{\pi}{2}, \frac{3\pi}{2}, \frac{7\pi}{2}, \frac{11\pi}{2}, \frac{15\pi}{2}$.

The curve has an amplitude of 4. If there weren't a vertical shift, the three y-coordinates would be $-4, 0, 4$. Furthermore, because the *A* value is -4, the curve is inverted, so it will start at its minimum value instead of its maximum value.

The vertical shift is down 2 units. Therefore, the three y-coordinates are $-6, -2, 2$

[Graph showing a curve with x-axis markings at $-\frac{\pi}{2}$, $\frac{3\pi}{2}$, $\frac{7\pi}{2}$, $\frac{11\pi}{2}$, $\frac{15\pi}{2}$ and y-axis values 2 and -6]

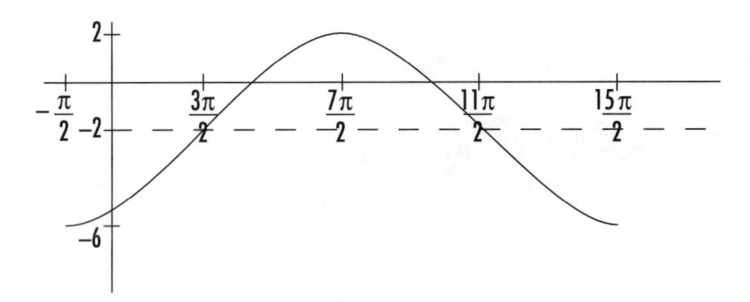

Let's recapitulate.

> If we are given a curve of the form or $y = A \sin B(x \pm C) \pm D$ or $y = A \cos B(x \pm C) \pm D$, then we have the following four transformations.
>
> The amplitude is A. (And if A is negative, turn the curve upside down.)
>
> The period is $\frac{2\pi}{B}$.
>
> The horizontal shift is C units to the right, if C is added; and C units to the left, if C is subtracted.
>
> The vertical shift is D units up, if D is added; and D units down, if D is subtracted.

PROBLEMS

Graph one complete period of each of the following equations.

1) $y = 3 \sin x$

2) $y = 2 \cos x + 3$

3) $y = -\frac{1}{2} \cos 2x$

4) $y = 4 \sin 4x$

5) $y = \cos\left(x + \frac{\pi}{2}\right)$

6) $y = \cos \frac{\pi}{4}(x + 1)$

7) $y = 3 \cos 2\left(x + \frac{\pi}{4}\right)$

TRIGONOMETRY **97**

8) $y = \sin 2\left(x - \dfrac{\pi}{6}\right)$

9) $y = -2\cos 3\left(x - \dfrac{\pi}{8}\right) + 1$

10) $y = 4\sin \dfrac{\pi}{6}(x+2) - 1$

INVERSE TRIG FUNCTIONS

Sometimes, we are given a value for a trig function and are asked to find the angle for which this is true. For example, find the value of x for which $\sin x = \dfrac{1}{2}$. We know from our special angles that one answer is $x = \dfrac{\pi}{6}$, but there are an infinite number of answers that will satisfy the above equation. We will use inverse trig functions to find these values.

The inverse of the sine function is either written as $\sin^{-1} x$ or as $\arcsin x$ (which is sometimes called an *arc function*). Some books use one notation, some use the other.

The inverse of the cosine function is either written as $\cos^{-1} x$ or as $\arccos x$.

And so on.

(By the way, we generally don't work with the inverse functions for the three reciprocal trig functions, but all of the rules apply to them in the same way.)

Notice how we write these functions in lower case letters. There is actually a significance to this, and a difference between $\sin^{-1} x$ and $\mathrm{Sin}^{-1} x$, or between $\arcsin x$ and $\mathrm{Arcsin}\, x$. We will get to the difference in a little bit.

Finding inverse trig functions of special angles is easy. Just work backwards. You already know the values of the special angles, or how to find them, so it shouldn't be very hard. For example, $\mathrm{Sin}^{-1} \dfrac{\sqrt{2}}{2} = \dfrac{\pi}{4}$ or $\mathrm{Tan}^{-1} \sqrt{3} = \dfrac{\pi}{3}$. But, as we pointed out above, there are an infinite number of solutions to these equations. How do we know which one to use?

If we want our trig functions to be "functions," then they must conform to the definition of a function. That is, among other things, they must be *one-to-one*. Remember, this means that for each x, there is one and only one y.

If we don't restrict the domain of the trig functions then, because there are an infinite number of solutions, they are not functions.

Therefore, $y = \sin x$ is restricted to $-\frac{\pi}{2} \leq x \leq \frac{\pi}{2}$ (that is, quadrants I and IV), which means that $y = \text{Sin}^{-1} x$ has a range from $-\frac{\pi}{2} \leq y \leq \frac{\pi}{2}$.

Similarly, $y = \cos x$ is restricted to $0 \leq x \leq \pi$, (that is, quadrants I and II), which means that $y = \text{Cos}^{-1} x$ is restricted to $0 \leq y \leq \pi$.

Finally, $y = \tan x$ is restricted to $-\frac{\pi}{2} \leq x \leq \frac{\pi}{2}$ (that is, quadrants I and IV), which means that $y = \text{Tan}^{-1} x$ is restricted to

$$-\frac{\pi}{2} \leq y \leq \frac{\pi}{2}.$$

When we use the uppercase , we refer to the *function* and thus the restrictions, and when we use the lowercase, we refer to *all* values for which the equation is true.

For example,

$$\text{Sin}^{-1} \frac{1}{2} = \frac{\pi}{6}, \text{ but } \sin^{-1} \frac{1}{2} = \frac{\pi}{6}, \frac{5\pi}{6}, \frac{13\pi}{6}, \frac{17\pi}{6}, \ldots .$$

The way to remember the restrictions is as follows:

> If the inverse function is of a *positive* number, the answer is *always* in quadrant I.
>
> If the inverse function is of a *negative* number, the answer is in quadrant IV, if the function is Sin^{-1} or Tan^{-1};
>
> and in quadrant II if the function is Cos^{-1}.

Example 1:

Find $\text{Sin}^{-1}\left(-\frac{\sqrt{3}}{2}\right)$

This means: what angle in quadrant IV has a sine equal to

$-\frac{\sqrt{3}}{2}$?

We know from special angles that the answer is the 60° reference angle in quadrant IV, or 300°. In radians, the answer is $\frac{5\pi}{3}$.

Example 2:

Find $\sin^{-1}\left(-\frac{\sqrt{3}}{2}\right) = \theta$, where $0° \leq \theta < 360°$.

Now, we will have multiple answers. We know from special angles that the answers are the 60° reference angles in quadrants III and IV, or 240° and 300°.

Let's try to understand the inverse trig functions a little more. Remember that the inverse of a function can be found by reflecting its graph over the line $y = x$. Let's take the graph of $y = \sin x$ and reflect it.

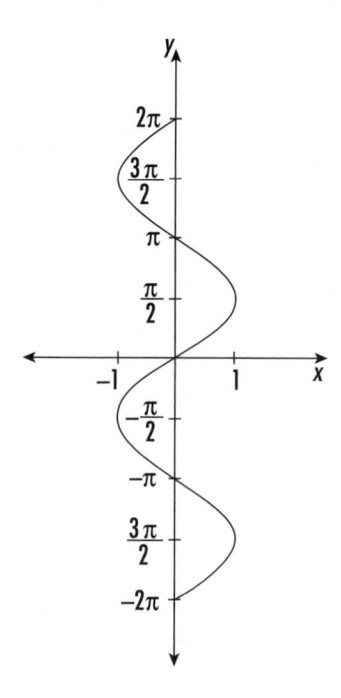

Notice that this graph will fail the *vertical line test*. That is, a vertical line can be drawn that will intersect the graph more than once. In fact, as we can see below, we can cut the graph an infinite number of times.

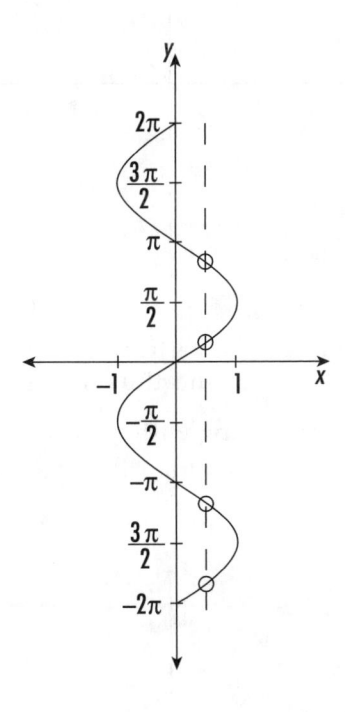

But, if we restrict the graph to a range of $-\frac{\pi}{2} \leq y \leq \frac{\pi}{2}$, then the graph looks like this:

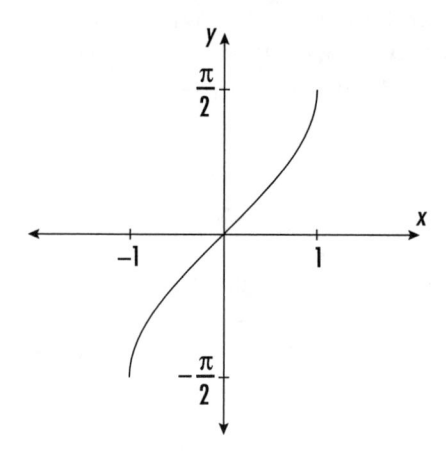

Now, we cannot draw a vertical line that will intersect the graph more than once, and thus this is a function.

We can do the same thing with $y = \text{Cos}^{-1}x$. If we restrict the range to $0 \leq y \leq \pi$, we will get a graph that looks like this:

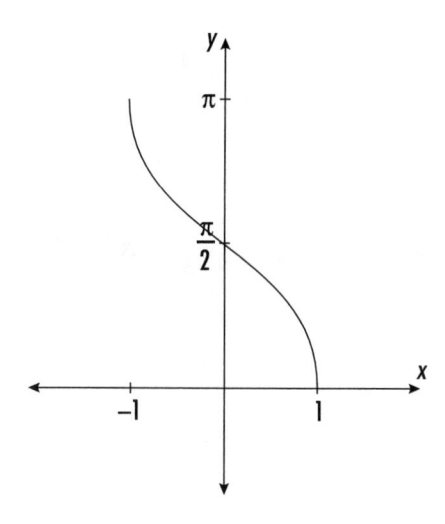

Notice again that this graph passes the vertical line test.

Finally, the graph of $y = \text{Tan}^{-1}x$ is restricted to $-\dfrac{\pi}{2} \leq y \leq \dfrac{\pi}{2}$ and looks like this:

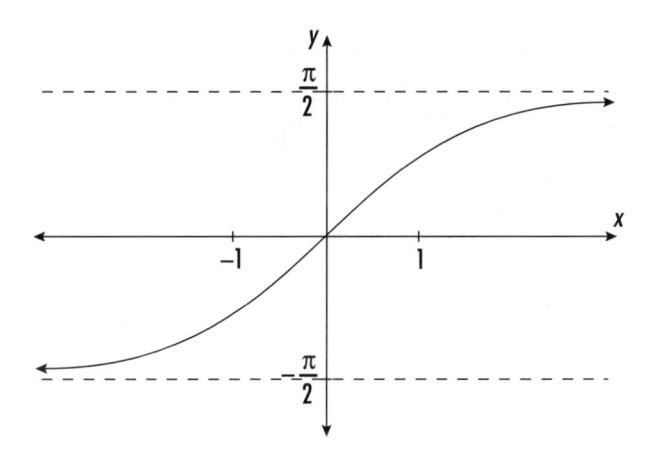

When we find the inverse trig function of a value, we get an angle. Suppose we then wanted to use that angle in a trig function. What do we do?

Example 3:

Find $\sin\left(\text{Tan}^{-1} \frac{\sqrt{3}}{3}\right)$.

First, let's find $\text{Tan}^{-1} \frac{\sqrt{3}}{3}$. Because the function is of a positive value, we use the angle in quadrant I (this comes from the domain restriction of the trig function). From special angles, we know that $\tan \frac{\pi}{6} = \frac{\sqrt{3}}{3}$, so $\text{Tan}^{-1} \frac{\sqrt{3}}{3} = \frac{\pi}{6}$.

Next, we find $\sin\left(\frac{\pi}{6}\right)$, which we know is $\frac{1}{2}$.

Example 4:

Find $\sin\left(\text{Cos}^{-1} \frac{4}{5}\right)$.

First, let's find $\text{Cos}^{-1} \frac{4}{5}$. We don't know what angle has a cosine of $\frac{4}{5}$, so we draw a triangle that represents the cosine.

The function is of a positive value, so we will draw the triangle in quadrant I. And, we know that cosine is $\frac{adjacent}{hypotenuse}$, so we can label two of the sides of the triangle.

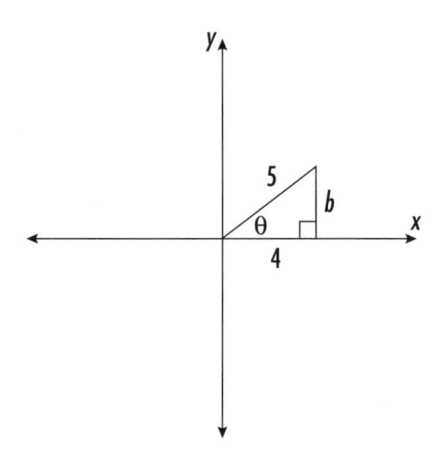

Thus $\text{Cos}^{-1}\frac{4}{5}$ is the angle θ. In order to find $\sin\theta$, we will need the *opposite* side, which we can find with the Pythagorean Theorem. We have labeled this side b, so $4^2 + b^2 = 5^2$, and if we solve this for b, we get $b = 3$. (Did you recognize that this was a 3,4,5 triangle?)

Therefore, $\sin\theta = \frac{3}{5}$.

Example 5:

Find $\tan\left(\text{Sin}^{-1} -\frac{3}{7}\right)$.

We don't know what angle has a sine of $-\frac{3}{7}$, so we will draw a triangle. The function is of a negative value, so we will draw the triangle in quadrant IV.

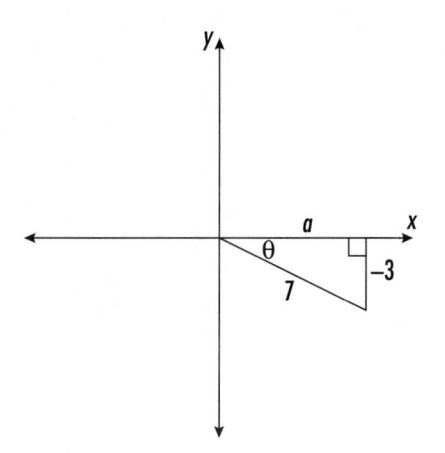

[Diagram: coordinate axes with a triangle in quadrant IV. The hypotenuse of length 7 goes from origin into quadrant IV, with angle θ at origin, horizontal leg labeled a, and vertical leg labeled −3.]

The angle θ stands for $\operatorname{Sin}^{-1} -\frac{3}{7}$, so we are looking for $\tan\theta$.

Using the Pythagorean Theorem, we can find the missing side, which we have labeled a. $a^2 + (-3)^2 = 7^2$. If we solve this for a, we get $a = \sqrt{40}$. Therefore, $\tan\theta = -\frac{3}{\sqrt{40}}$.

Example 6:

Find $\sec\left(\operatorname{Tan}^{-1} -\frac{5}{11}\right)$.

Let's draw a triangle. The function is of a negative value, so we will draw the triangle in quadrant IV.

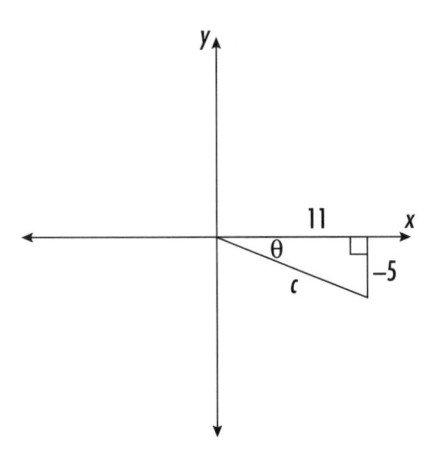

The angle θ stands for $\text{Tan}^{-1} -\frac{5}{11}$, so we are looking for $\sec\theta$.

Using the Pythagorean Theorem, we can find the missing side, which we have labeled c. $11^2 + (-5)^2 = c^2$. If we solve this for c, we get $c = \sqrt{146}$. Therefore, $\sec\theta = \frac{\sqrt{146}}{11}$.

Notice how we solved these last three examples. We drew a triangle to represent the information that we had been given, and labeled the angle θ to stand for the inverse function. Then we used the Pythagorean Theorem to find the missing side and found the appropriate trig function of θ. The only tricky part is to remember what is positive and what is negative.

Here is one more nuance.

Example 7:

Find $\text{Cos}^{-1}\left(\cos\frac{7\pi}{6}\right)$.

You might think that the cosine and the inverse cosine cancel and just leave you with $\frac{7\pi}{6}$, but you would be wrong.

First, we know from special angles that $\cos\frac{7\pi}{6} = -\frac{\sqrt{3}}{2}$, so we need to find $\text{Cos}^{-1}\left(-\frac{\sqrt{3}}{2}\right)$.

Because the inverse cosine is of a negative number, the answer will be in quadrant II. We know from special angles that $\cos\frac{\pi}{6} = \frac{\sqrt{3}}{2}$, so we are looking for the quadrant II angle that has a reference angle of $\frac{\pi}{6}$. The answer is $\frac{5\pi}{6}$. Tricky, huh?!

Let's do one more.

Example 8:

Find $\text{Sin}^{-1}(\sin 135°)$.

Once again, do not just cancel the sine and the inverse sine!

We know from special angles that $\sin 135° = \frac{\sqrt{2}}{2}$, so we need to find $\text{Sin}^{-1}\left(\frac{\sqrt{2}}{2}\right)$.

Because the inverse sine is of a positive number, the answer will be in quadrant I. We know from special angles that $\sin 45° = \frac{\sqrt{2}}{2}$, so the answer is $45°$.

PROBLEMS

1) Find $\text{Sin}^{-1}(-1)$.

2) Find $\text{Tan}^{-1}\left(-\frac{\sqrt{3}}{3}\right)$.

3) Find $\text{ArcCos}\left(\frac{\sqrt{3}}{2}\right)$.

4) Evaluate $\sin(\text{ArcTan} 1)$.

5) Evaluate $\sin\left(\text{Cos}^{-1} \dfrac{15}{17}\right)$.

6) Evaluate $\tan\left(\text{Cos}^{-1}\left(-\dfrac{3}{5}\right)\right)$.

7) Evaluate $\csc\left(\text{ArcCos}\left(\dfrac{\sqrt{5}}{3}\right)\right)$.

8) Evaluate $\sin\left(\text{Tan}^{-1}\left(\sqrt{3}\right)\right)$.

9) Evaluate $\text{Sin}^{-1}\left(\sin\left(225°\right)\right)$.

10) Evaluate $\text{Cos}^{-1}\left(\cos\left(\dfrac{5\pi}{4}\right)\right)$.

APPLICATIONS OF TRIGONOMETRY

Now we come to the applications that use three special trigonometric relationships, and that don't require right triangles. In all three, we make use of triangles that we label as follows. The sides are labeled a, b, and c. The angles opposite those sides are labeled A, B, and C, with the letters corresponding to the sides and their opposite angles.

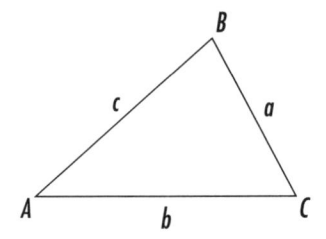

The actual lengths and labeling of the sides is arbitrary, unless the problem is written otherwise.

Law of Sines

The Law of Sines states that:

> Given the triangle, with sides a, b, and c, and with angles opposite those sides that are, respectively, A, B, and C, then $\frac{\sin A}{a} = \frac{\sin B}{b} = \frac{\sin C}{c}$.

Notice, this doesn't say that the sines and the sides are equal, but that the ratios of the sides to the sines of their opposite angles are equal. We use the Law of Sines when we are given a triangle and two sides and a non-included angle (SSA), or two angles and a side (ASA or SAA). Let's do some examples.

Example 1:

If $A = 30°$, $a = 7$, and $c = 10$, find $\sin C$.

Using the Law of Sines, we get: $\frac{\sin 30°}{7} = \frac{\sin C}{10}$.

We know that $\sin 30° = \frac{1}{2}$, so we get: $\frac{\frac{1}{2}}{7} = \frac{\sin C}{10}$.

Now, we cross-multiply and we get: $5 = 7 \sin C$.

Therefore, $\sin C = \frac{5}{7}$.

Notice that the problem didn't ask us for C, but for $\sin C$.

Example 2:

If $A = 30°$, $B = 70°$, and $a = 8$, find b.

Using the Law of Sines, we get: $\frac{\sin 30°}{8} = \frac{\sin 70°}{b}$.

If we cross-multiply, we get: $b \sin 30° = 8 \sin 70°$.

Now, we divide through by $\sin 30°$, and we get: $b = \frac{8 \sin 70°}{\sin 30°}$.

Using the calculator, we get $b \approx 15$.

Example 3:

If $A = 40°$, $B = 60°$, and $a = 5$, find c.

Notice that here we have one pair of opposites — A and a, but we don't have another. But, we can find angle C, because the sum of the angles in a triangle is always $180°$. Thus, $C = 180° - 40° - 60° = 80°$.

Now, we can use the Law of Sines: $\dfrac{\sin 40°}{5} = \dfrac{\sin 80°}{c}$.

If we cross-multiply, we get: $c \sin 40° = 5 \sin 80°$.

Next, we divide through by $\sin 40°$, and we get: $c = \dfrac{5 \sin 80°}{\sin 40°}$.

Using the calculator, we get $c \approx 7.7$.

Sometimes, we will get an answer that is impossible.

Example 4:

If $A = 110°$, $a = 8$, and $b = 9$, find B.

Using the Law of Sines, we get: $\dfrac{\sin 110°}{8} = \dfrac{\sin B}{9}$.

If we multiply through by 9, we get: $\dfrac{9 \sin 110°}{8} = \sin B$.

But, when we evaluate the left-hand expression, we get $\sin B \approx 1.06$.

Because the sine of an angle can never be greater than 1, this is impossible and there is no angle B.

There is a complicated aspect of the Law of Sines called *The Ambiguous Case*. This occurs when the arrangement of sides and angles can lead to more than one triangle (or none, as we saw above). Let's do an example.

Example 5:

If $b = 8$, $a = 5$, and $A = 25°$, find B.

If we draw a picture, we could get the following:

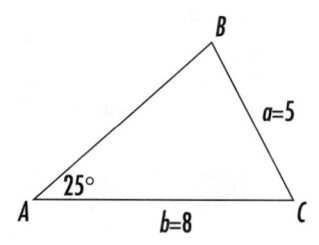

But, we could also get:

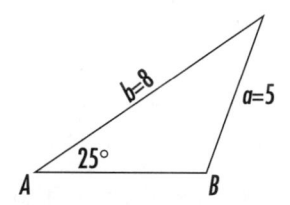

This is why this is called the Ambiguous Case. There is more than one triangle that can be drawn from this information. Let's use the Law of Sines and see why this is so.

We get: $\dfrac{\sin 25°}{5} = \dfrac{\sin B}{8}$.

If we multiply through by 8, we get: $\dfrac{8\sin 25°}{5} = \sin B$

This gives us: $\sin B \approx 0.6762$. Using the calculator, we get: $B = 42.5°$, which we will round to $B = 43°$.

This means that the third angle is $C = 180° - 25° - 43° = 112°$.

BUT, remember that the sine of an angle is also positive in quadrant II. Thus, if $\sin B \approx 0.6762$, B could also be $180° - 43° = 137°$. Then the third angle would be $C = 180° - 25° - 137° = 18°$.

Thus, as you can see, we get two triangles. The first has angles of 25°, 43°, and 112°, and the second has angles of 25°, 137°, and 18°. There is no correct answer, which is why this is called the *Ambiguous Case*.

There is a way to check that a triangle might involve the ambiguous case. First of all, it only applies to cases where we are given SSA (because if we are given two of the angles, then the third angle is determined), and the given angle is acute. Then, if we are given, for example, sides a and b, and angle A, then there will be two possible triangles if:

$$b \sin A < a < b.$$

Or, if we are given sides a and b, and angle B, then there will be two possible triangles if $a \sin B < b < a$. Etc.

In the example above, we were given $b = 8$, $a = 5$, and $A = 25°$. Applying the test, we get: $8 \sin 25° \approx 3.38$. And, $3.38 < 5 < 8$. Therefore, there will be two possible triangles.

If the test doesn't work, then there will be either one triangle or no triangle. If we give you a rule, it will be confusing, so we suggest that you work out the answer using the Law of Sines.

Example 6:

If $a = 16$, $b = 13$, and $B = 50°$, find A.

Applying our test, we get: $16 \sin 50° \approx 12.3$, and $12.3 < 13 < 16$, so we are going to get two triangles.

Using the Law of Sines, we get: $\dfrac{\sin 50°}{13} = \dfrac{\sin A}{16}$.

If we multiply through by 16, we get: $\dfrac{16 \sin 50°}{13} = \sin A$

This gives us: $\sin A \approx 0.9428$. Using the calculator, we get: $A \approx 70.5°$, which we will round to $A \approx 71°$.

This means that the third angle is $C = 180° - 50° - 71° = 59°$.

But, A could also be $180° - 71° = 109°$. Then the third angle would be $C = 180° - 50° - 109° = 21°$.

Therefore, the first triangle has angles of 50°, 71°, and 59°, and the second has angles of 50°, 109°, and 21°.

Example 7:

If $a = 10$, $c = 8$, and $C = 38°$, find A.

Applying our test, we get: $10 \sin 38° \approx 6.2$, and $6.2 < 8 < 10$, so we are going to get two triangles.

Using the Law of Sines, we get: $\dfrac{\sin 38°}{8} = \dfrac{\sin A}{10}$.

If we multiply through by 10, we get: $\dfrac{10 \sin 38°}{8} = \sin A$

This gives us: $\sin A \approx 0.7696$. Using the calculator, we get: $A \approx 50.3°$, which we will round to $A \approx 50°$.

This means that the third angle is $B = 180° - 38° - 50° = 92°$.

But, A could also be $180° - 50° = 130°$. Then the third angle would be $B = 180° - 38° - 130° = 12°$.

Therefore, the first triangle has angles of 38°, 50°, and 92°, and the second has angles of 38°, 130°, and 12°.

LAW OF COSINES

The next formula that we will learn is called the Law of Cosines. It, too, is used for any type of triangle. The Law of Cosines states that:

> Given the triangle, with sides a, b, and c, and with angles opposite those sides that are, respectively, A, B, and C, then $c^2 = a^2 + b^2 - 2ab \cos C$.

The choice of which side is labeled c is arbitrary, of course, so the law can also be written as:

$b^2 = a^2 + c^2 - 2ac \cos B$ or $a^2 = b^2 + c^2 - 2bc \cos A$.

(As long as the cosine is of the angle opposite the side that is on the left side of the equation, you are setting up the formula correctly.)

We use the Law of Cosines when we are given a triangle with two sides and an included angle (SAS), or three sides (SSS). *There is no ambiguous case.* Let's do some examples.

Example 8:

If $a = 8$, $b = 10$ and $C = 45°$, find c to the nearest tenth.
Let's draw a triangle and label the appropriate sides.

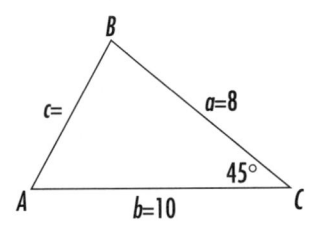

If we plug the information into the formula, we get: $c^2 = 8^2 + 10^2 - 2(8)(10)\cos 45°$.

Now we can solve for c:

$$c^2 = 64 + 100 - 160\left(\frac{\sqrt{2}}{2}\right)$$

$$c^2 = 164 - 80\sqrt{2}$$

$$c^2 \approx 50.86$$

$$c \approx 7.1$$

Example 9:

If $a = 5$, $b = 9$, and $c = 11$, find B to the nearest tenth.
Let's draw a picture.

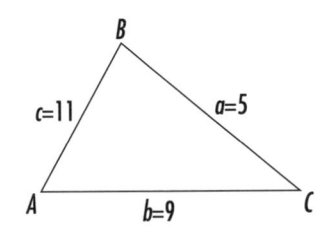

Here, the angle we are looking for is opposite side b, so we write the formula to solve for b: $b^2 = a^2 + c^2 - 2ac \cos B$.

Plugging in, we get: $9^2 = 5^2 + 11^2 - 2(5)(11)\cos B$

Now, we can solve for B:

$81 = 25 + 121 - 110 \cos B$

$81 = 146 - 110 \cos B$

$110 \cos B = 65$

$\cos B = \dfrac{65}{110}$

$B \approx 53.8°$

Now let's use both laws to find all of the unknown parts of a triangle. This is called *solving a triangle*.

Example 10:

Solve the triangle with $b = 7$, $c = 11$, and $A = 25°$. Round all answers to the nearest tenth.

Let's draw a picture.

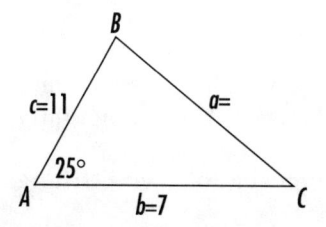

Notice that we are given two sides and an included angle. This means that we will first use the Law of Cosines to find side a.

$a^2 = 7^2 + 11^2 - 2(7)(11) \cos 25°$

$a^2 = 49 + 121 - 154 \cos 25°$

$a^2 = 170 - 154 \cos 25°$

$a^2 \approx 30.43$

$a \approx 5.5$

Now, we can use either the Law of Sines, or the Law of Cosines to solve for one of the other two angles. Just for variety's sake, let's use the Law of Sines and solve for angle B.

$$\frac{\sin B}{7} = \frac{\sin 25°}{5.5}$$

Multiplying through by 7, we get: $\sin B = \frac{7 \sin 25°}{5.5}$

$\sin B \approx 0.5379$

$B \approx 32.5°$

Now, we can find the last angle C by using the fact that the sum of the angles in a triangle must add up to $180°$.

$C = 180° - 25° - 32.5° = 122.5°$.

Thus, the triangle has sides $a = 5.5$, $b = 7$, and $c = 11$; and angles $A = 25°$, $B = 32.5°$, and $C = 122.5°$.

TRIGONOMETRIC AREA

The last formula that we will learn is a formula to find the area of a triangle using trigonometry. We are actually going to derive this one.

Suppose we are given the following triangle:

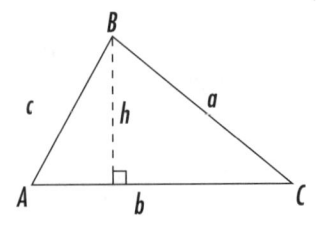

(h is the altitude of the triangle)

We know that the area of the triangle is $A = \frac{1}{2}bh$.

We also know that $\sin A = \dfrac{h}{c}$, which we can rewrite as $c \sin A = h$. Now, if we substitute this into the expression for area, we get:

$$\text{Area} = \frac{1}{2} bc \sin A$$

This is the trigonometric formula for area. As with the other two formulas, the choice of letters is arbitrary, and the area can also be found by $\text{Area} = \dfrac{1}{2} ab \sin C$ or $\text{Area} = \dfrac{1}{2} ac \sin B$

Let's make sure that we understand it. The formula says that, if we are given two sides and an included angle (SAS), then the area is: $\dfrac{1}{2}$ multiplied by the product of the two sides by the sine of the included angle.

Let's do some examples.

Example 11:

Find the area of the triangle with $b = 10$, $c = 20$, and $A = 30°$.

We are given SAS, so using the formula, we get:

$\text{Area} = \dfrac{1}{2}(10)(20)\sin 30° = 100\left(\dfrac{1}{2}\right) = 50$.

Example 12:

Solve the triangle with $a = 7$, $b = 10$, and $c = 6$, and find its area. Round all answers to the nearest tenth.

Let's draw a picture.

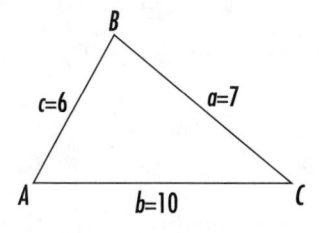

We are given SSS, so we will first use the Law of Cosines to find an angle. Let's find angle C.

$$6^2 = 7^2 + 10^2 - 2(7)(10)\cos C$$

$$36 = 49 + 100 - 140\cos C$$

$$36 = 149 - 140\cos C$$

$$140\cos C = 149 - 36 = 113$$

$$\cos C = \frac{113}{140}$$

$$C \approx 36.2°$$

Now, let's use the Law of Sines to find angle B.

$$\frac{\sin 36.2°}{6} = \frac{\sin B}{10}$$

$$\frac{10\sin 36.2°}{6} = \sin B$$

$$\sin B \approx 0.9843$$

$$B \approx 79.8°$$

Now we can find angle A.

$$A = 180° - 36.2° - 79.8° = 64°$$

Finally, let's find the area. Let's use sides b and c, and angle A.

$$Area = \frac{1}{2}(6)(10)\sin 64° = 30\sin 64° \approx 27.0.$$

Therefore, the triangle has sides $a = 7$, $b = 10$, and $c = 6$; angles $A = 64°$, $B = 79.8°$, and $C = 36.2°$; and Area = 27.0.

PROBLEMS

1) Given $\triangle ABC$, if $a = 5$, $\sin A = \frac{1}{3}$, and $\sin B = \frac{2}{5}$, find b.

2) Given $\triangle ABC$, if $a=11$, $b=7$, and $c=9$, find B.

3) Given $\triangle ABC$, if $a=8$, $b=13$, and $C=70°$, find c.

4) Given $\triangle ABC$, if $A=30°$, $a=5$, and $b=6$, solve the triangle.

5) Given $\triangle ABC$, if $A=34°$, $b=12$, and $c=10$, solve the triangle.

6) Given $\triangle ABC$, if $a=20$, $b=15$, and $c=30$, solve the triangle.

7) Given $\triangle ABC$, if $a=15$, $b=8$, and $C=45°$, find the area of the triangle.

8) Given $\triangle ABC$, if $a=9$, $b=11$, and $c=7$, find the area of the triangle.

9) An observer stands at point A and measures her angle of elevation to the top of a 70 meter pole as $40°$. She walks directly towards the pole to point B, where her angle of elevation measures $60°$. Find the distance from A to B to the nearest meter.

10) A ship sails for 75 kilometers. It then turns $30°$ clockwise and sails for 60 kilometers. How far, to the nearest kilometer, is the ship from its starting point?

CHAPTER 4

Complex Numbers

WHAT IS *i*?

How do we find the square root of a negative number? If we square a positive number, the answer is positive. If we square a negative number, the answer is positive. If we square zero, we get zero. So what real number, squared, will give us a negative number? The answer is: there *is no* real number that we can square and get a negative number. We need to use a new type of number called a *complex number*. These are sometimes called *imaginary numbers*, but the preferred term is *complex*.

Complex numbers were invented to solve the problem of defining the square root of a negative number. The fundamental unit of complex numbers is *i*. It is defined as follows:

$$i^2 = -1 \text{ or } i = \sqrt{-1}$$

We use this in the following way. Suppose that we want to find $\sqrt{-16}$. We could write $\sqrt{-16}$ as $\sqrt{-16} = \sqrt{16}\sqrt{-1}$. Now, because

$\sqrt{16} = 4$ and because $i = \sqrt{-1}$, we can rewrite this as: $\sqrt{-16} = \sqrt{16}\sqrt{-1} = 4i$. This is a complex number. If we take $4i$ and square it, we will get $(4i)^2 = (4^2)(i^2) = (16)(-1) = -16$.

In essence, when we want to take the square root of a negative number, we factor out the $\sqrt{-1}$ and then take the square root. That is, we pretend that the number is positive and find the square root. Then we multiply it by i and we are done.

Example 1:
Find $\sqrt{-36}$.

We know that $\sqrt{36} = 6$, so $\sqrt{-36} = \sqrt{36}\sqrt{-1} = 6i$.

$6i$ is an example of what we call a *pure imaginary number*. These are numbers that can be written in the form bi, where b is a real number other than zero, and i is $\sqrt{-1}$.

Example 2:
Find $\sqrt{-50}$.

$\sqrt{-50} = \sqrt{25}\sqrt{2}\sqrt{-1} = 5\sqrt{2}i$.

It is customary to write complex numbers with radicals by putting the i in front of the radical sign to avoid confusion, so the answer is usually written as $5i\sqrt{2}$.

Example 3:
Find $(12i)^2$.

$(12i)^2 = (12^2)(i^2) = (144)(-1) = -144$.

Now that we know what i is, let's learn a few nuances.

How do we find powers of i?

As with real numbers, we define $i^0 = 1$.

If we raise any number to the power **one**, we get the number, so $i^1 = i$.

If we raise i to the power **two**, we get $i^2 = -1$, by definition.

If we raise i to the power **three**, we get $i^3 = i^2 \cdot i = -i$.

If we raise i to the power **four**, we get $i^4 = i^3 \cdot i = -i \cdot i = 1$.

Let's write these again because they are VERY important.

$$i^0 = 1$$
$$i^1 = i$$
$$i^2 = -1$$
$$i^3 = -i$$
$$i^4 = 1$$

Why are these so important? Notice that i^4 is the same as i^0.

Now let's find i^5. We can rewrite this as $i^5 = i^4 \cdot i^1 = (1)(i) = i$. Notice that this is the same as i^1.

Now let's find i^6. We can rewrite this as $i^6 = i^4 \cdot i^2 = (1)(-1) = -1$. Notice that this is the same as i^2.

Now let's find i^7. We can rewrite this as $i^7 = i^4 \cdot i^3 = (1)(-i) = -i$. Notice that this is the same as i^3.

As you can see, the numbers are repeating. In fact, they run in a cycle of four numbers: $i, -1, -i, 1$. Thus, any power of i raised to a power higher than 3 is going to be one of these four numbers. For example, $i^{17} = (i^4)^4 (i) = (1)(i) = i$.

> There is a simple rule for finding higher powers of i. Take the power and divide it by four, and raise i to the power of the remainder.

Example 4:

Find i^{35}.

If we divide 35 by 4, the remainder is 3. Therefore, $i^{35} = i^3 = -i$.

Example 5:

Find i^{122}.

If we divide 122 by 4, the remainder is 2. Therefore, $i^{122} = i^2 = -1$.

Isn't this simple? In fact, if the power that i is raised to is a three digit number, or greater, we only have to divide the last *two* digits of the power by four and raise i to the remainder.

Example 6:

Find i^{13457}.

We only look at the last two digits, so if we divide 57 by 4, the remainder is 1. Therefore, $i^{13457} = i^1 = i$.

COMPLEX NUMBERS

Complex numbers are numbers that have both a real and an imaginary part. They are written in the form $a+bi$, where a and b are real numbers and i is $\sqrt{-1}$. The number a is called the real part and bi is the imaginary part of the complex number $a+bi$. For example, a complex number could be: $3+2i$ or $3-2i$ or $-3+2i$ or $-3-2i$. Furthermore, a complex number could have zero as either the real part or the imaginary part. For example, $0+2i$, which is the same as $2i$. Or $2+0i$, which is the same as 2. Thus we can see that a real number can be thought of as a complex number whose imaginary part is $0i$. If $a=0$, then the complex number is said to be a *pure imaginary number*.

If we want to add complex numbers, we add the real and the imaginary parts separately. That is, $(a+bi)+(c+di)=(a+c)+(b+d)i$.

Example 7:

Find $(3+2i)+(5+10i)$.

We add the real and imaginary parts separately, so we get: $(3+5)+(2+10)i = 8+12i$.

Example 8:

Find $(7-3i)+(4+9i)$.

We add the real and imaginary parts separately, so we get: $(7+4)+(-3+9)i = 11+6i$.

The rule for subtraction is the same as addition.

Example 9:

Find $(2+5i)-(7+4i)$.

We subtract the real and imaginary parts separately, so we get: $(2-7)+(5-4)i = -5+i$.

When we multiply complex numbers, we FOIL. That is, we multiply the First parts, the Outer parts, the Inner parts, and the Last parts.

Example 10:

Find $(2+7i)(3-4i)$.

We FOIL, which gives us:

$(2 \cdot 3)+(7i \cdot 3)+(2 \cdot -4i)+(7i \cdot -4i) = 6+21i-8i-28i^2$.

We can simplify this to: $6+13i-28i^2$.

Remember that $i^2 = -1$, so this simplifies to:

$6+13i+28 = 34+13i$.

Example 11:

Find $(5-3i)(5+3i)$.

We FOIL, which gives us:

$(5 \cdot 5) + (-3i \cdot 5) + (5 \cdot 3i) + (-3i \cdot 3i) = 25 - 15i + 15i - 9i^2$

We can simplify this to: $25 - 9i^2$.

Again, because $i^2 = -1$, this simplifies to: $25 + 9 = 34$.

Notice on this last one that, when we multiplied $a + bi$ by $a - bi$, the imaginary terms dropped out. Then, because $i^2 = -1$, we ended up with $a^2 + b^2$.

> Remember this: $(a + bi)(a - bi) = a^2 + b^2$

Division of imaginary numbers is a little trickier. Now we need to use something called the *complex conjugate*. We find this by changing the sign between the real and imaginary parts from positive to negative, or from negative to positive.

The complex conjugate of $a + bi$ is $a - bi$.

For example, the complex conjugate of $3 + 7i$ is $3 - 7i$. The complex conjugate of $7 - 2i$ is $7 + 2i$. And so on.

> When a complex number is divided by another complex number, we multiply the top and bottom of the fraction by the complex conjugate of the denominator.

Example 12:

Find $\dfrac{3 + 5i}{2 - i}$.

First, we multiply the top and bottom of the fraction by the complex conjugate of the denominator, which is $2 + i$. We get:

$\dfrac{3 + 5i}{2 - i} \cdot \dfrac{2 + i}{2 + i}$.

Notice that the bottom is of the form $(a + bi)(a - bi)$, where $a = 2$ and $b = -1$. Therefore, the bottom becomes $2^2 + (-1)^2 = 5$.

We FOIL the top:

$(3+5i)(2+i) = 6+10i+3i+5i^2 = 6+13i-5 = 1+13i$.

The fraction now becomes: $\dfrac{1+13i}{5}$, which is usually written as $\dfrac{1}{5}+\dfrac{13}{5}i$.

Example 13:

Find $\dfrac{4+2i}{5-3i}$.

First, we multiply the top and bottom by $5+3i$. We get: $\dfrac{4+2i}{5-3i} \cdot \dfrac{5+3i}{5+3i}$.

The bottom can be simplified to $5^2 + 3^2 = 34$.

We FOIL the top:

$(4+2i)(5+3i) = 20+12i+10i+6i^2 = 20+22i-6 = 14+22i$.

The fraction now becomes: $\dfrac{14+22i}{34} = \dfrac{7+11i}{17}$ or $\dfrac{7}{17}+\dfrac{11}{17}i$.

Example 14:

Find $\dfrac{3-4i}{3+4i}$.

We multiply top and bottom by $3-4i$. We get: $\dfrac{3-4i}{3+4i} \cdot \dfrac{3-4i}{3-4i}$.

The bottom can be simplified to: $3^2 + 4^2 = 25$.

We FOIL the top: $(3-4i)\cdot(3-4i) = 9-12i-12i+16i^2 = -7-24i$.

The fraction now becomes: $\dfrac{-7-24i}{25}$ or $-\dfrac{7}{25}-\dfrac{24}{25}i$.

THE COMPLEX PLANE

We are only going to cover the very basics of complex graphs.

A complex number $a+bi$ can be thought of as a pair of coordinates, where a corresponds to the x-coordinate and where bi corresponds to the y-coordinate. For example, $6+8i$ can be thought of as $(6,8i)$ in the complex plane. When we graph a complex number, we label the y-axis the yi-axis, and then plot the coordinates as we always do.

Example 15:

Graph the following points in the complex plane.

Point A: $2+3i$.   Point B: $4-7i$.   Point C: $5i$.
Point D: $-1-i$.

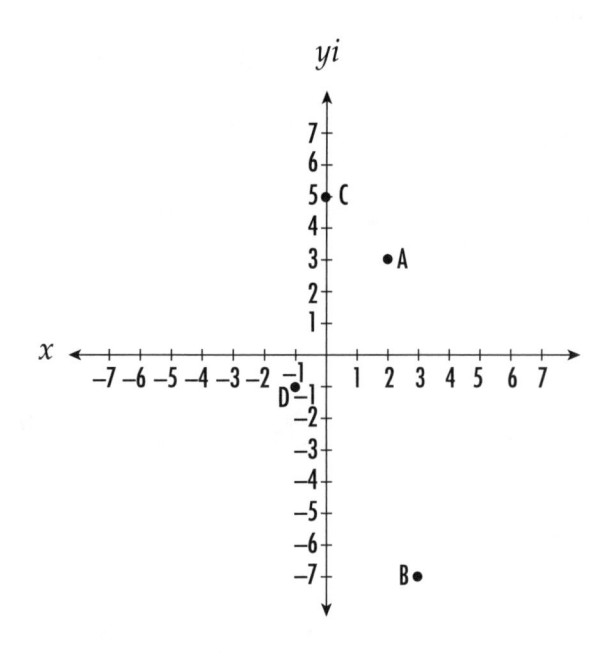

Notice how we now think of complex numbers as $x+yi$ instead of $a+bi$. The distinction is merely to help you think of the complex number as a pair of coordinates.

The *modulus* of a complex number $x+yi$ is the distance from the origin to the point (x, y) in the complex plane. It is written as: $|x + yi|$.

Example 16:

Find $|6 + 8i|$.

If we graph the point $(6, 8)$ in the complex plane and draw the distance from the origin (which we labeled D), it looks like this:

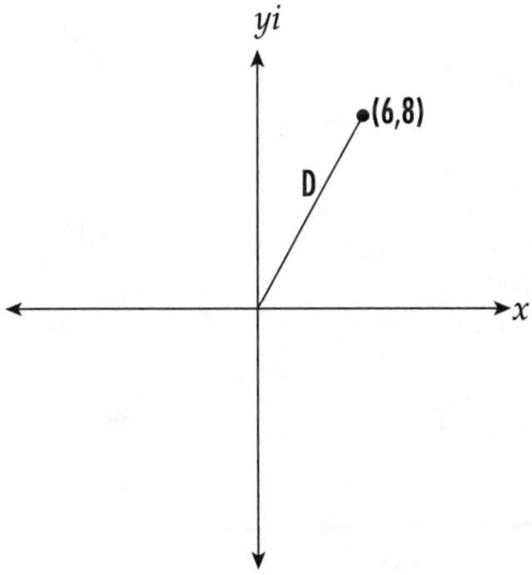

We can easily find the distance with the Pythagorean Theorem. It is: $6^2 + 8^2 = 100 = D^2$.

$$D = 10. \text{ Therefore, } |6 + 8i| = 10.$$

As you can see, we can always use the Pythagorean Theorem to find the modulus of a complex number. This leads us to a rule:

$$|x + yi| = \sqrt{x^2 + y^2}$$

Notice that we are squaring y, not yi.

As you can see, the modulus is the same as the square root of the product of a number and its complex conjugate.

Example 17:

Find $|8-15i|$.

Using the rule above,

$$|8-15i| = \sqrt{8^2 + (-15)^2} = \sqrt{289} = 17$$

COMPLEX TRIGONOMETRY

If we represent a complex number in the complex plane, and draw a right triangle connecting the point with the origin, we get a picture like this:

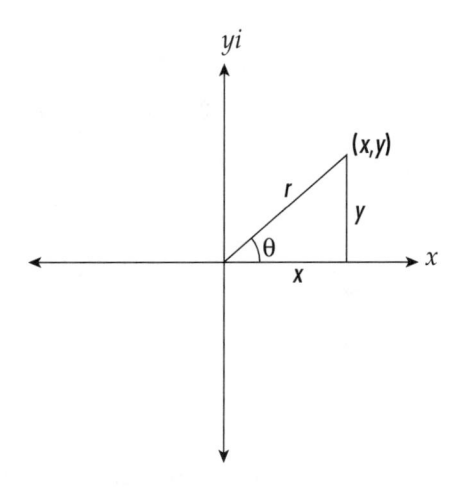

Notice that we have labeled the modulus of the point, r, and the angle that the modulus makes with the origin, θ. Using trigonometry, we know that $\cos\theta = \frac{x}{r}$ and $\sin\theta = \frac{y}{r}$. These can be rewritten as: $r\cos\theta = x$ and $r\sin\theta = y$. Thus, a complex number $x+yi$, can also be thought of as $r\cos\theta + ir\sin\theta$.

If we factor out the r, we get: $r\cos\theta + ir\sin\theta = r(\cos\theta + i\sin\theta)$. This is often abbreviated as $r\text{cis}\theta$.

Notice, in the figure above, that $\tan\theta = \frac{y}{x}$ and $r = \sqrt{x^2 + y^2}$.

This enables us to switch systems when thinking of a complex number. We can either think of it in terms of rectangular coordinates, $x+yi$ or (x,y), or in terms of polar (trigonometric) coordinates, $rcis\theta$ or (r,θ).

This gives us some rules:

> Given the number $x+yi$, then $\tan\theta = \frac{y}{x}$ and $r = \sqrt{x^2+y^2}$.
>
> Given the number $rcis\theta$, then $x = r\cos\theta$ and $y = r\sin\theta$.

Let's practice switching from one system to the other.

Example 18:

Convert $1+2i$ to complex polar coordinates.

Using the rules above, we know that $\tan\theta = \frac{y}{x}$, so $\tan\theta = \frac{2}{1}$. Using a calculator, we find that $\theta \approx 63°$. We also know from the rules above that $r = \sqrt{x^2+y^2}$, so $r = \sqrt{1^2+2^2} = \sqrt{5}$.

Therefore, we can write $1+2i$ as $\sqrt{5}cis64°$. The point has the coordinates $(1,2)$ in the rectangular system, or $(\sqrt{5}, 64°)$ in the polar system.

Example 19:

Convert $6cis30°$ to complex rectangular coordinates. Using the rules above, we know that $x = r\cos\theta$, so

$$x = 6\cos 30° = 6 \cdot \frac{\sqrt{3}}{2} = 3\sqrt{3}.$$

We also know that $y = r\sin\theta$, so $y = 6\sin 30° = 6 \cdot \frac{1}{2} = 3$.

Therefore, we can write $6cis30°$ as $3\sqrt{3}+3i$. The point has the coordinates $(3\sqrt{3}, 3)$ in the rectangular system, or $(6, 30°)$ in the polar system.

PROBLEMS

1) $(7+3i)+(4-5i) =$

2) $(6-8i)-(8-6i) =$

3) $(2+5i)(9-4i) =$

4) $\dfrac{6}{1-i} =$

5) $i^{143} =$

6) $\dfrac{(3-5i)}{(1+2i)} =$

7) $|8-15i| =$

8) Convert to trigonometric form: $9-12i$

9) Convert to rectangular form: $8cis30°$

10) Convert to trigonometric form: $7i$

11) Convert to rectangular form: $5cis270°$

12) $(1+i)^4 =$

CHAPTER 5
Quadratic Equations

You should be familiar with quadratic equations from your earlier Math courses. They are equations of the form $ax^2 + bx + c = 0$. In High School Math III, we learn only some of the finer points of quadratic equations.

COMPLETING THE SQUARE

There is a technique called "completing the square" that is very important to be able to do. You will need this for problems that ask you to complete the square (obviously), for conic sections, and for some messier trig problems. You will also find this very handy if you ever take BC Calculus, so if you are planning to do so, put this into your permanent bag of tricks. The technique is very easy, so let's learn it through an example.

Example 1:

Complete the square for the expression $x^2 + 8x + 2$.

Step 1: First, insert some parentheses into the expression $(x^2 + 8x) + 2$.

Step 2: Next, take the coefficient of the x term and cut it in half. Then throw away the x, and the power on the x^2 term, and rewrite the expression as: $(x + 4)^2 + 2$.

Step 3: Then, subtract the square of the constant in the parentheses from the term, like so: $\left[(x+4)^2-16\right]+2$.

Step 4: Simplify. $(x+4)^2-14$

You're done. That wasn't so bad, was it? Notice that if you took the final expression and expanded it out, you would get: $x^2+8x+16-14=x^2+8x+2$, which is what we started with. So completing the square just involves rewriting an expression. Let's do some more examples.

Example 2:

Complete the square for the expression $x^2+6x+11$.

Step 1: Insert the parentheses. $\left(x^2+6x\right)+11$

Step 2: Cut the coefficient of the x term in half, throw away the x and the power on the x^2 term, and rewrite the expression. $(x+3)^2+11$

Step 3: Subtract the square of the constant in the parentheses from the term: $\left[(x+3)^2-9\right]+11$

Step 4: Simplify: $(x+3)^2+2$

Example 3:

Complete the square for the expression $x^2-20x+5$.

Step 1: Insert the parentheses: $\left(x^2-20x\right)+5$

Step 2: Cut in half, throw away, and rewrite: $(x-10)^2+5$

Step 3: Subtract the square of the constant: $\left[(x-10)^2-100\right]+5$

Step 4: Simplify: $(x-10)^2-95$

Notice that we still **subtract** the square of the constant term, even though the constant term is negative.

Let's do a more annoying one.

Example 4:

Complete the square for the expression $x^2 + 7x - 4$.

Step 1: Insert the parentheses: $(x^2 + 7x) - 4$

Step 2: Cut in half, throw away, and rewrite: $\left(x + \frac{7}{2}\right)^2 - 4$.

Step 3: Subtract the square of the constant: $\left[\left(x + \frac{7}{2}\right)^2 - \frac{49}{4}\right] - 4$.

Step 4: Simplify: $\left(x + \frac{7}{2}\right)^2 - \frac{65}{4}$

There is one last aspect of completing the square that you need to learn. Notice that all of the problems that we did have a leading term of x^2. What do we do if the term has a coefficient other than 1? Simple. First, factor the coefficient out of the first two terms, then put it back when you are done. For example:

Example 5:

Complete the square for the expression $2x^2 + 20x + 6$.

Step 1: Insert the parentheses: $(2x^2 + 20x) + 6$

Step 1A: Factor the 2 out of the parentheses: $2(x^2 + 10x) + 6$

Step 2: Cut in half, throw away, and rewrite: $2(x + 5)^2 + 6$

Step 3: Square the constant and subtract: $2[(x + 5)^2 - 25] + 6$

Step 3A: Multiply through by the number that we factored out: $[2(x + 5)^2 - 50] + 6$

Step 4: Simplify: $2(x+5)^2 - 44$

That was harder, wasn't it?

Let's do a couple more examples of this type.

Example 6:

Complete the square for the expression $4x^2 + 16x - 18$.

Step 1: Insert the parentheses: $(4x^2 + 16x) - 18$

Step 1A: Factor the 4 out of the parentheses: $4(x^2 + 4x) - 18$

Step 2: Cut in half, throw away, and rewrite: $4[(x+2)^2] - 18$

Step 3: Square the constant and subtract: $4[(x+2)^2 - 4] - 18$

Step 3A: Multiply through by the number that we factored out: $[4(x+2)^2 - 16] - 18$

Step 4: Simplify. $4(x+2)^2 - 34$

Here's a really yucky one!

Example 7:

Complete the square for the expression $3x^2 - 11x + 5$.

Step 1: Insert the parentheses: $(3x^2 - 11x) + 5$

Step 1A: Factor the 3 out of the parentheses: $3\left(x^2 - \dfrac{11}{3}x\right) + 5$

Step 2: Cut in half, throw away, and rewrite: $3\left[\left(x - \dfrac{11}{6}\right)^2\right] + 5$

Step 3: Square the constant and subtract: $3\left[\left(x - \dfrac{11}{6}\right)^2 - \dfrac{121}{36}\right] + 5$

Step 3A: Multiply through by the number that we factored out: $3\left(x-\frac{11}{6}\right)^2 - \frac{121}{12} + 5$

Step 4: Simplify: $3\left(x-\frac{11}{6}\right)^2 - \frac{61}{12}$

If you could do that last one, you can complete the square on any quadratic.

Now let's use this technique to solve a quadratic equation.

Example 8:

Solve for x: $x^2 - 4x - 60 = 0$.

First, move the constant term to the other side. Then complete the square on the left side.

$(x^2 - 4x) = 60$

$(x-2)^2 - (-2)^2 = 60$

$(x-2)^2 - 4 = 60$

Add 4 to both sides: $(x-2)^2 = 64$

Take the square root of both sides: $(x-2) = \pm 8$

Add 2 to both sides: $x = 2 \pm 8$.

Simplify: $x = 10$ or $x = -6$.

Let's check this by factoring the quadratic. $(x-10)(x+6) = 0$. Correct!

Example 9:

Solve for x: $3x^2 - 12x + 16 = 0$.

First, move the 16 to the other side. Then complete the square on the left side.

$$(3x^2 - 12x) = -16$$

$$3(x^2 - 4x) = -16$$

$$3\left[(x-2)^2 - (-2)^2\right] = -16$$

$$3\left[(x-2)^2 - 4\right] = -16$$

$$3(x-2)^2 - 12 = -16$$

Now, add 12 to both sides: $3(x-2)^2 = -4$

Divide through by 3: $(x-2)^2 = -\dfrac{4}{3}$

Take the square root of both sides: $x - 2 = \pm \dfrac{2}{\sqrt{3}} i$.

If you don't know how to find the square root of a negative number, review the unit on complex numbers.

Add 2 to both sides: $x = 2 \pm \dfrac{2}{\sqrt{3}} i$.

Example 10:

Solve for x: $ax^2 + bx + c = 0$.

First, move the c to the other side. Then complete the square on the left side.

$$ax^2 + bx = -c$$

$$a\left(x^2 + \frac{b}{a}x\right) = -c$$

$$a\left[\left(x + \frac{b}{2a}\right)^2 - \left(\frac{b}{2a}\right)^2\right] = -c$$

$$a\left[\left(x + \frac{b}{2a}\right)^2 - \frac{b^2}{4a^2}\right] = -c$$

$$a\left(x + \frac{b}{2a}\right)^2 - \frac{b^2}{4a} = -c$$

Now, move the constant term outside of the parentheses to the right side:

$$a\left(x + \frac{b}{2a}\right)^2 = \frac{b^2}{4a} - c$$

Simplify the right side using a common denominator:

$$a\left(x + \frac{b}{2a}\right)^2 = \frac{b^2}{4a} - \frac{4ac}{4a} = \frac{b^2 - 4ac}{4a}$$

Divide through by a: $\quad \left(x + \frac{b}{2a}\right)^2 = \frac{b^2 - 4ac}{4a^2}$

Take the square root of both sides: $\quad x + \frac{b}{2a} = \frac{\pm\sqrt{b^2 - 4ac}}{2a}$.

Subtract $\frac{b}{2a}$ from both sides: $\quad x = -\frac{b}{2a} \pm \frac{\sqrt{b^2 - 4ac}}{2a}$ or

$$x = \frac{-b \pm \sqrt{b^2 - 4ac}}{2a}.$$

Now doesn't that look familiar?! That's the Quadratic Formula and we just derived it!

THE QUADRATIC FORMULA

The quadratic formula is what we usually use to solve a quadratic equation when we can't factor it easily. The formula is:

$$x = \frac{-b \pm \sqrt{b^2 - 4ac}}{2a}$$

If we plug the coefficients of a quadratic equation into the formula, we get the solutions to the equation. The solutions to the equation are also called the *roots*.

Example 11:

Use the quadratic formula to find the roots of: $4x^2 - 11x + 3 = 0$.

Here, $a = 4$, $b = -11$, and $c = 3$. Plugging into the formula, we get: $x = \dfrac{-(-11) \pm \sqrt{(-11)^2 - 4(4)(3)}}{2(4)}$

$x = \dfrac{11 \pm \sqrt{121 - 48}}{8} = \dfrac{11 \pm \sqrt{73}}{8}$.

We tend to leave the roots in this form unless it is easy to reduce them.

Example 12:

Use the quadratic formula to find the roots of: $x^2 + 6x + 13 = 0$.

Here, $a = 1$, $b = 6$, and $c = 13$. Plugging into the formula, we get: $x = \dfrac{-6 \pm \sqrt{6^2 - 4(1)(13)}}{2(1)}$

$x = \dfrac{-6 \pm \sqrt{36 - 52}}{2} = \dfrac{-6 \pm \sqrt{-16}}{2} = \dfrac{-6 \pm 4i}{2} = -3 \pm 2i$.

THE DISCRIMINANT

The nature of the quadratic formula enables us to make some interesting observations about the roots of a quadratic equation. The first one involves something called the "discriminant." The *discriminant* of a quadratic equation is the expression under the radical sign in the quadratic formula. That is, the discriminant is $b^2 - 4ac$.

If the discriminant turns out to be a **negative** number, then the formula will involve taking the square root of a negative number, and thus will be a complex number. Because this complex number is added to and subtracted from $-b$, we will get two complex roots. (They are actually called a *conjugate pair* of complex roots because they only differ by the sign in the middle. See the section on Complex Numbers.)

The graph of a parabola with two complex roots does **not** touch the x-axis. It could open either up or down. For example:

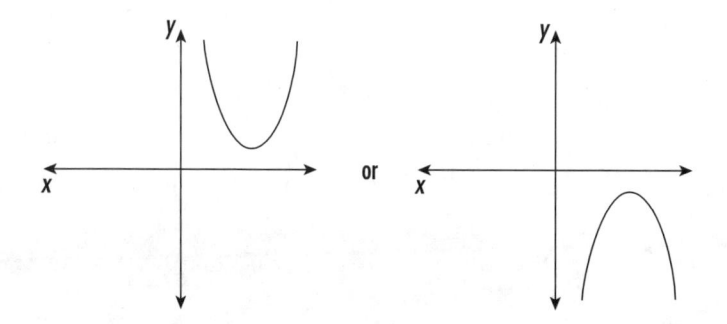

If the discriminant turns out to be **zero**, then there will be nothing to add to or subtract from $-b$, so we will only get one root — namely $-\dfrac{b}{2a}$. (Some teachers like to refer to this as a *double root*.)

The graph of a parabola with a double root touches the x-axis at one point. It could open either up or down. For example:

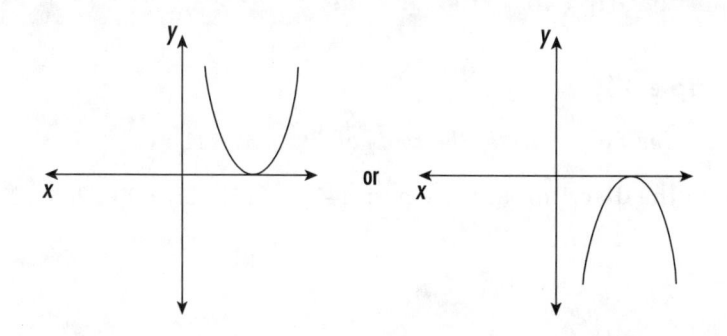

If the discriminant turns out to be a *perfect square* (other than zero), then an integer will be added to and subtracted from $-b$, and we will get two rational roots.

If the discriminant turns out to be a *positive number* that is not a perfect square, then an irrational number will be added to and subtracted from $-b$, and we will get two irrational roots.

The graph of a parabola with a two real roots touches the x-axis at two points. It could open either up or down. For example:

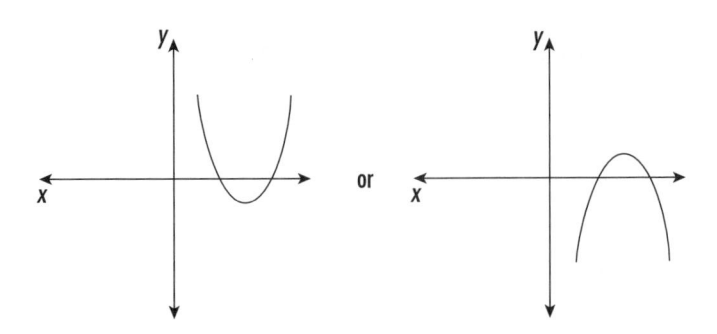

Let's put these into a rule:

We can determine the nature of the roots of a quadratic equation of the form $ax^2 + bx + c = 0$ by using the discriminant $b^2 - 4ac$.

If $b^2 - 4ac < 0$, the equation has **two complex roots**.

If $b^2 - 4ac = 0$, the equation has **one rational root**.

If $b^2 - 4ac > 0$, and $b^2 - 4ac$ is a perfect square, then the equation has **two rational roots**.

If $b^2 - 4ac > 0$, and $b^2 - 4ac$ is not a perfect square, then the equation has **two irrational roots**.

Example 13:

Determine the nature of the roots of $5x^2 - 3x - 11 = 0$.

Using the discriminant, we get: $(-3)^2 - 4(5)(-11) = 9 + 220 = 229$.

229 is not a perfect square, so the equation has two irrational roots.

Example 14:
Determine the nature of the roots of $5x^2 - 3x + 11 = 0$.

Using the discriminant, we get: $(-3)^2 - 4(5)(11) = 9 - 220 = -211$.

This is negative, so the equation has two complex roots.

Example 15:
Determine the nature of the roots of $x^2 - 6x + 9 = 0$.

Using the discriminant, we get: $(6)^2 - 4(1)(9) = 36 - 36 = 0$.

This is zero, so the equation has one root.

Sum and Product of Roots

If we take the quadratic equation and write the roots individually, we get:

$$x = \frac{-b + \sqrt{b^2 - 4ac}}{2a} \text{ and } x = \frac{-b - \sqrt{b^2 - 4ac}}{2a}.$$

If we were to add these two roots, we would get:

$$\frac{-b + \sqrt{b^2 - 4ac}}{2a} + \frac{-b - \sqrt{b^2 - 4ac}}{2a} = \frac{-2b}{2a} = -\frac{b}{a}.$$

Similarly, if we were to multiply these two roots, we would get:

$$\frac{-b + \sqrt{b^2 - 4ac}}{2a} \cdot \frac{-b - \sqrt{b^2 - 4ac}}{2a} = \frac{b^2 - (b^2 - 4ac)}{4a^2} = -\frac{4ac}{4a^2} = \frac{c}{a}.$$

This gives us a rule:

> Given a quadratic equation of the form $ax^2 + bx + c = 0$, the **sum of the roots** is $-\frac{b}{a}$ and the **product of the roots** is $\frac{c}{a}$.

Example 16:
Find the sum and product of the roots of $2x^2 - 12x + 18 = 0$.

Using the rule above, the sum of the roots is $-\frac{-12}{2} = 6$ and the product of the roots is $\frac{18}{2} = 9$.

Example 17:

Find the sum and product of the roots of $5x^2 - 3x - 11 = 0$.

The sum of the roots is $-\frac{-3}{5} = \frac{3}{5}$ and the product of the roots is $-\frac{11}{5}$.

Problems

1) Solve for x by completing the square: $2x^2 - 3x - 2 = 0$.

2) Solve for x by completing the square: $x^2 - 6x + 13 = 0$.

3) Solve for x using the quadratic formula: $2x^2 - 7x - 11 = 0$.

4) Solve for x by any means: $12x^2 - 19x - 21 = 0$.

5) Where does the graph of $y = x^2 + 12x - 28$ intersect the x-axis?

6) How are the roots of the equation $3x^2 + 2x - 3 = 0$ best described?

7) For which value of k will the roots of the equation $2x^2 - 4x + k = 0$ be equal?

8) What is the sum, s, and the product, p, of the roots of the equation $x^2 + 2x - 35 = 0$?

9) Find a quadratic equation with roots −7 and 4.

10) Find a quadratic equation with a root of 5−i.

CHAPTER 6
Transformations

In High School Math III, we are introduced to transformational geometry. Although the field is actually very complex, the areas that we study are fairly simple. A transformation refers to taking a set of points and changing them. The changed set of points is called the *image* of the original set of points.

TRANSLATIONS

A *translation* refers to moving a point or set of points the same distance in the same direction. For example, we might take a graph and translate all of the points 2 units in the x-direction and 3 units in the y-direction. When we translate a figure, its size and shape do not change.

> If point $P(x,y)$ is translated a units horizontally and b units vertically, its image is $P'(x+a, y+b)$. You will usually see this notation to indicate a translation: $(x,y) \xrightarrow{T_{a,b}} (x+a, y+b)$.

Example 1:

Given points $A(2,3)$, $B(1,-2)$, and $C(-2,0)$, find the image of $\triangle ABC$ under $T_{4,-1}$.

Let's understand what this says. We are given three points that form a triangle. We are then asked to translate the triangle 4 units to the right and 1 unit down.

Using the rule that we just learned, our translation is:
$$(x,y) \xrightarrow{T_{4,-1}} (x+4, y-1)$$

Therefore, $A(2,3) \to A'(6,2)$

$B(1,-2) \to B'(5,-3)$

$C(-2,0) \to C'(2,-1)$

which looks like this:

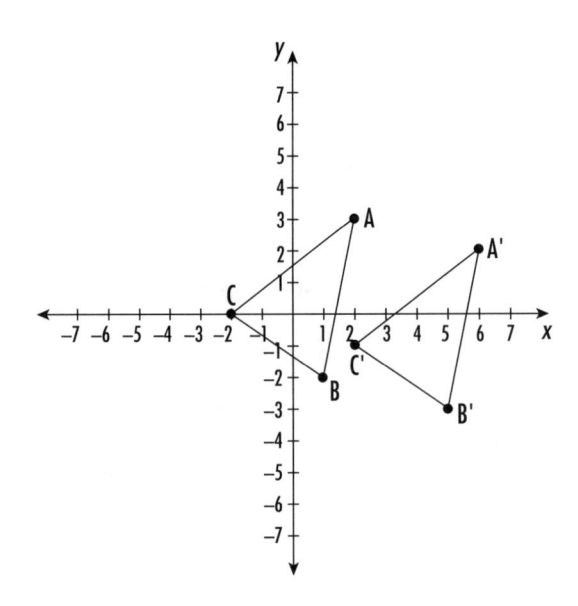

REFLECTIONS

A *reflection* refers to finding the mirror image of a point, where a given line acts as a mirror. The line connecting the original point to the image point is perpendicular to and bisected by the mirror line. Once again, when a figure is reflected, its size and shape do not change.

> If point $P(x,y)$ is reflected in the y-axis, its image is $P'(-x,y)$.
>
> $$(x,y) \xrightarrow{R_{y-axis}} (-x,y)$$

Notice that the y-coordinate of the image is unchanged, and the sign of the x-coordinate is changed.

Example 2:

Find the reflection in the y-axis of points $A(2,3)$ and $B(4,1)$.

Using the rule above, we get: $A(2,3) \xrightarrow{R_{x-axis}} A'(-2,3)$ and $B(4,1) \xrightarrow{R_{x-axis}} B'(-4,1)$.

It looks like this

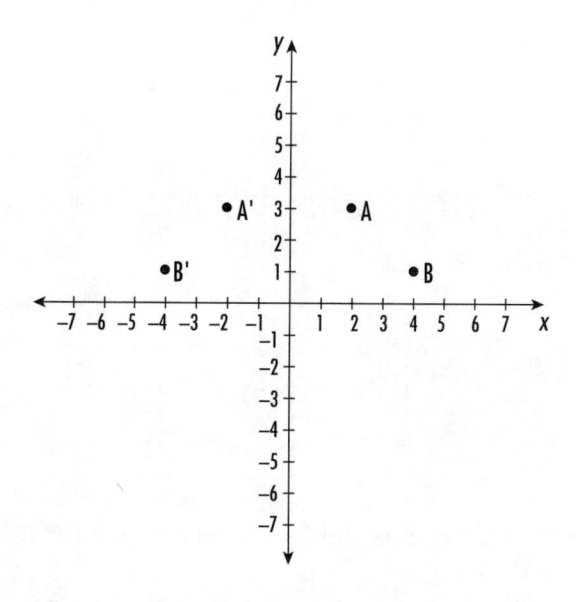

Notice how the *y*-axis is the line of symmetry for the points and their image.

Now let's do the *x*-axis.

If point $P(x,y)$ is reflected in the *x*-axis, its image is $P'(x,-y)$.

$$(x,y) \xrightarrow{R_{x-axis}} (x,-y)$$

Notice that the *x*-coordinate is unchanged, and the sign of the *y*-coordinate is changed.

Example 3:

Given the points in example 2 above, find their reflection in the x-axis.

Here, we get: $A(2,3) \to A'(2,-3)$ and $B(4,1) \to B'(4,-1)$.

It looks like this:

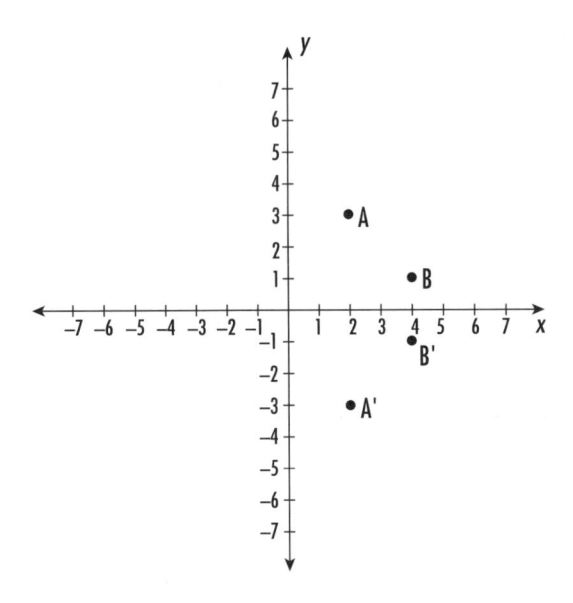

Notice how the *x*-axis is the line of symmetry for the points and their image.

Now let's reflect in the line $y = x$.

> If point $P(x, y)$ is reflected in the line $y = x$, its image is $P'(y, x)$.
>
> $$(x, y) \xrightarrow{R_{y=x}} (y, x)$$

Notice that the x-coordinate and the y-coordinate are interchanged.

Example 4:

Find the reflection in the line $y = x$ of points $A(2, -3)$ and $B(4, 1)$.

Here, we get: $A(2, -3) \xrightarrow{R_{y=x}} A'(-3, 2)$ and $B(4, 1) \xrightarrow{R_{y=x}} B'(1, 4)$.

It looks like this:

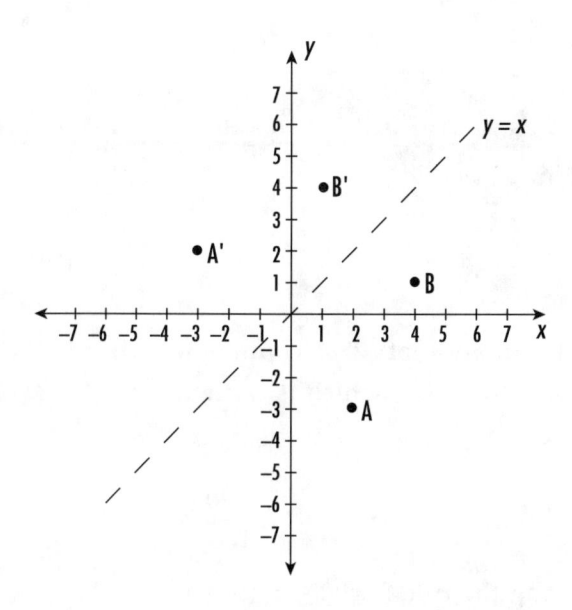

Notice how the line $y = x$ is the line of symmetry for the points and their image.

ROTATIONS

A *rotation* is a transformation that transforms a set of points by rotating them around a fixed point. Here, we will only discuss rotations about the origin. Unless a problem states otherwise, a rotation through a positive angle is counterclockwise, and a rotation through a negative angle is clockwise. Here, too, the size and shape of a figure is not changed.

If a point $P(x,y)$ is rotated 90° counterclockwise about the origin, its image is $P'(-y,x)$.

$$P(x,y) \xrightarrow{Rot_{90°}} P'(-y,x)$$

If a point $P(x,y)$ is rotated 180° counterclockwise (or clockwise) about the origin, its image is $P'(-x,-y)$.

$$P(x,y) \xrightarrow{Rot_{180°}} P'(-x,-y)$$

If a point $P(x,y)$ is rotated 270° counterclockwise about the origin, its image is $P'(y,-x)$.

$$P(x,y) \xrightarrow{Rot_{270°}} P'(y,-x)$$

Note that a rotation of 270° counterclockwise is the same as a rotation of 90° clockwise, which is written $Rot_{-90°}$.

Example 5:

Find the images of $A(2,1)$ and $B(4,3)$ under rotations of: (a) 90°, (b) 180°, and (c) 270°.

(a) Following the rule for 90° rotations:

$$A(2,1) \xrightarrow{Rot_{90°}} A'(-1,2) \text{ and } B(4,3) \xrightarrow{Rot_{90°}} B'(-3,4).$$

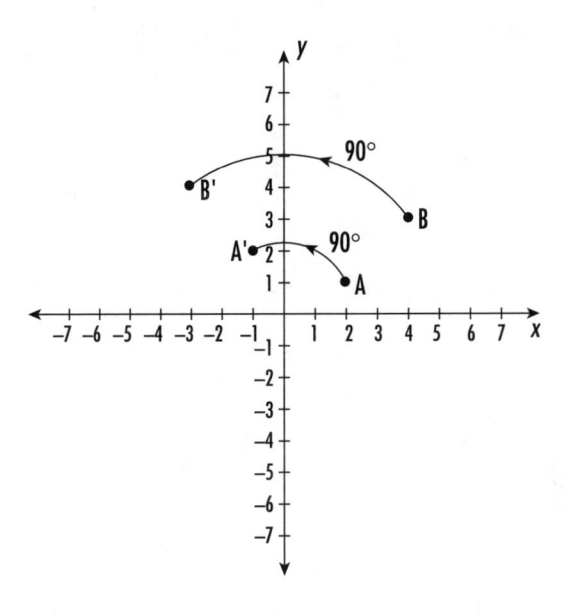

(b) Following the rule for 180° rotations:

$A(2,1) \xrightarrow{Rot_{180°}} A'(-2,-1)$ and $B(4,3) \xrightarrow{Rot_{180°}} B'(-4,-3)$.

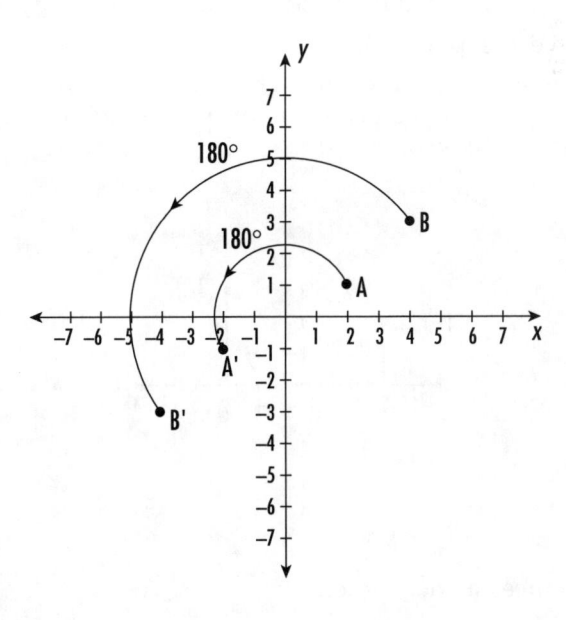

(c) Following the rule for $270°$ rotations:

$$A(2,1) \xrightarrow{Rot_{270°}} A'(1,-2) \text{ and } B(4,3) \xrightarrow{Rot_{270°}} B'(3,-4).$$

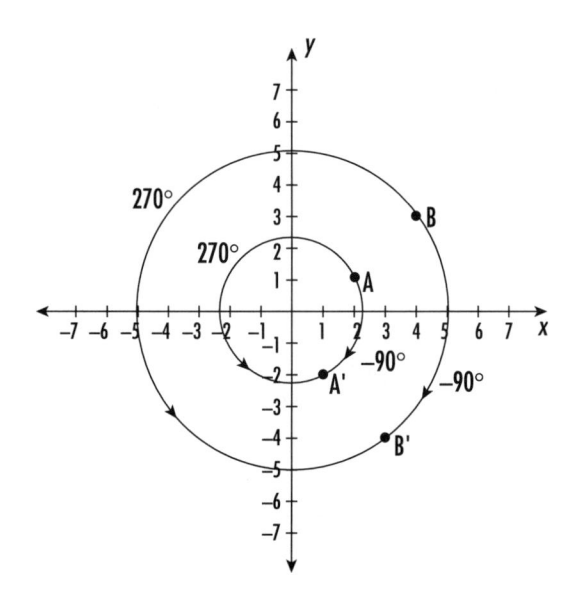

You may find it difficult to remember which rotation is which. If so, you can always learn the following derivation. Suppose that we initially have the point $A(2,3)$. This is found by starting at the origin and going 2 units to the right and 3 units up. A rotation of $90°$ means that we will start at the origin and go 3 units to the left and 2 units up, like so:

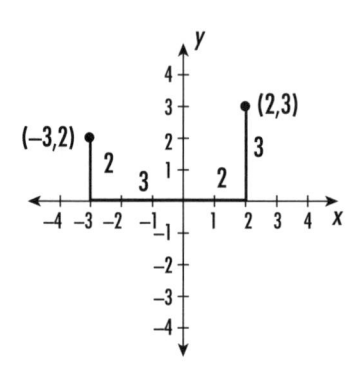

This produces a rotation of $90°$.

Similarly, a rotation of $180°$ means that we will start at the origin and go 2 units to the left and 3 units down, like so:

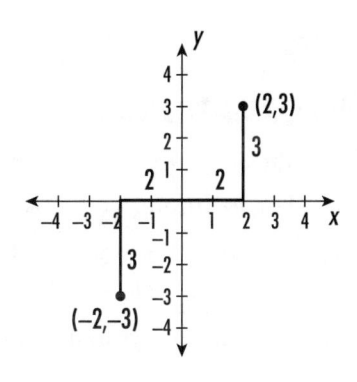

You should be able to figure out how to do a rotation of $270°$.

DILATIONS

The last transformation that we will learn is called a *dilation*. This refers to stretching or shrinking a set of points. The amount by which the points are stretched or shrunk is called a *scale factor*. **Notice that the size of a figure is different after a dilation.** The shape is the same, however, so the figures are *similar*, but not *congruent*.

> If point $P(x, y)$ is dilated with a scale factor of k, its image is $P'(kx, ky)$.
>
> $P(x, y) \xrightarrow{D_k} P'(kx, ky)$

All that we do is to multiply the x and y-coordinates by the scale factor.

Example 6:

Find the image of the triangle ABC, with $A(2, 3)$, $B(0, 5)$, and $C(-3, -7)$, under D_3.

All that we do is multiply the coordinates of each point by 3:

$A(2, 3) \xrightarrow{D_3} A'(6, 9)$

$B(0,5) \xrightarrow{D_3} B'(0,15)$

$C(-3,-7) \xrightarrow{D_3} C'(-9,-21)$

COMPOSITE TRANSFORMATIONS

In a composite transformations, two or more transformations are made to a set of points. For example, $(T_{3,1} \circ D_2)(1,4)$ means that we are going to take the point $(1,4)$ and dilate it **and** translate it. Which do we do first? *We go in order from right to left.* Thus here we would first dilate, $(1,4) \xrightarrow{D_2} (2,8)$, and then translate, $(2,8) \xrightarrow{T_{3,1}} (5,9)$.

Example 7:

Find the image under $(T_{-3,1} \circ R_{y-axis})$ of the triangle with the points $A(2,1)$, $B(3,4)$, and $C(0,5)$.

First, we perform the reflection. Following the rule that a reflection in the y-axis means $(x,y) \xrightarrow{R_{y-axis}} (-x,y)$, we get:

$A(2,1) \xrightarrow{R_{y-axis}} A'(-2,1)$

$B(3,4) \xrightarrow{R_{y-axis}} B'(-3,4)$

$C(0,5) \xrightarrow{R_{y-axis}} C'(0,5)$

Next, we perform the translation. Following the rule that a translation of *a* units horizontally and *b* units vertically means $(x,y) \xrightarrow{T_{a,b}} (x+a, y+b)$, we get:

$A'(-2,1) \xrightarrow{T_{-3,1}} A''(-5,2)$

$B'(-3,4) \xrightarrow{T_{-3,1}} B''(-6,5)$

$C'(0,5) \xrightarrow{T_{-3,1}} C''(-3,6)$

The transformation looks like this:

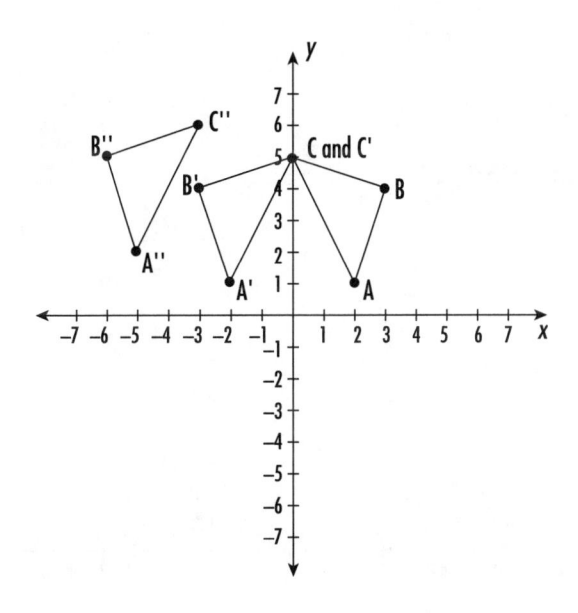

Example 8:

Find the image of the triangle under $(D_2 \circ Rot_{90°})$ of triangle with the points $A(2,1)$, $B(3,4)$, and $C(0,5)$.

First, we perform the rotation. Following the rule that a rotation of 90° counterclockwise about the origin means $P(x,y) \xrightarrow{Rot_{90°}} P'(-y, x)$, we get:

$A(2,1) \xrightarrow{Rot_{90°}} A'(-1, 2)$

$B(3,4) \xrightarrow{Rot_{90°}} B'(-4, 3)$

$C(0,5) \xrightarrow{Rot_{90°}} C'(-5, 0)$

Next, we perform the dilation. Following the rule that a dilation of scale factor k, means $P(x,y) \xrightarrow{D_2} P'(kx, ky)$, we get:

$A'(-1,2) \xrightarrow{D_2} A''(-2,4)$

$B'(-4,3) \xrightarrow{D_2} B''(-8,6)$

$C'(-5,0) \xrightarrow{D_2} C''(-10,0)$

The transformation looks like this:

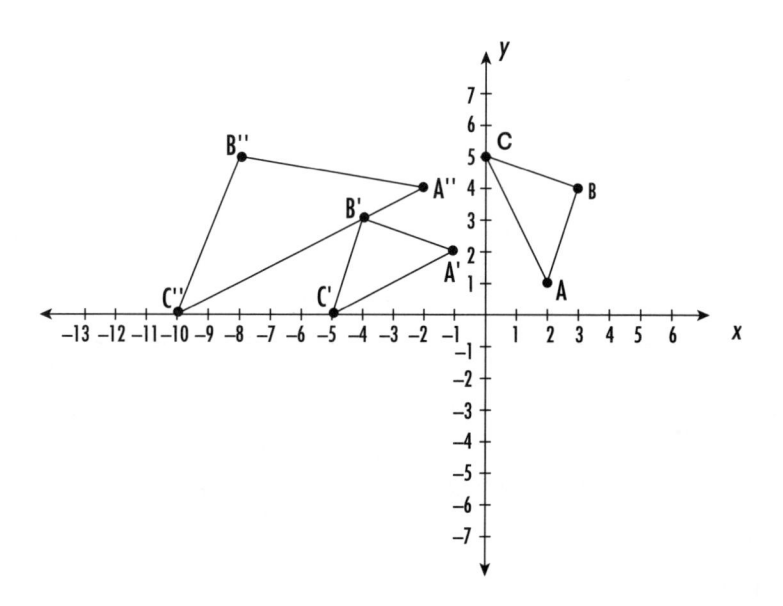

PROBLEMS

Triangle ABC has coordinates $A(2,5)$, $B(-1,1)$, and $C(0,-2)$:

1. Find the coordinates of the image $A'B'C'$ after the transformation $ABC \xrightarrow{T_{(-2,2)}} A'B'C'$.

2. Find the coordinates of the image $A''B''C''$ after the transformation $ABC \xrightarrow{r_{x-axis}} A''B''C''$.

3. Find the coordinates of the image $A'''B'''C'''$ after the transformation $ABC \xrightarrow{D_2} A'''B'''C'''$.

Triangle ABC has coordinates $A(3,-1)$, $B(3,4)$, *and* $C(0,0)$:

4. Find the coordinates of the image $A'B'C'$ after the transformation $ABC \xrightarrow{rot_{90°}} A'B'C'$.

5. Find the coordinates of the image $A''B''C''$ after the transformation $ABC \xrightarrow{T_{(1,-3)}} A''B''C''$.

6. Find the coordinates of the image $A'''B'''C'''$ after the transformation $ABC \xrightarrow{r_{y-axis}} A'''B'''C'''$.

Triangle ABC has coordinates $A(4,3)$, $B(-4,3)$, *and* $C(1,0)$:

7. Find the coordinates of the image $A'B'C'$ after the transformation $ABC \xrightarrow{rot_{180°}} A'B'C'$.

8. Find the coordinates of the image $A''B''C''$ after the transformation $A'B'C' \xrightarrow{r_{x-axis}} A''B''C''$.

9. Find the coordinates of the image $A'''B'''C'''$ after the transformation $A''B''C'' \xrightarrow{D_{\frac{1}{2}}} A'''B'''C'''$.

Triangle ABC has coordinates $A(4,2)$, $B(-1,-1)$, *and* $C(-3,3)$:

10. Find the coordinates of the image $A'B'C'$ after the transformation $ABC \xrightarrow{rot_{180°} \circ\, r_{x-axis}} A'B'C'$.

11. Find the coordinates of the image $A''B''C''$ after the transformation $ABC \xrightarrow{T_{(2,2)} \circ\, D_2} A''B''C''$.

12. Find the coordinates of the image $A'''B'''C'''$ after the transformation $ABC \xrightarrow{rot_{180°} \circ\, r_{y-axis}} A'''B'''C'''$.

CHAPTER 7
Circle Rules

When you first studied circles, you learned about circumference and area. Then you learned how to find the arc length and area of a sector of a circle. A third aspect of circles has to do with the properties of circles and their relationship to various lines. First, let's review some basics.

1. The number of degrees in a circle is 360°.
2. The sum of the degrees of the central angles in a circle is 360°.
3. The sum of the degrees of the arcs that make up the circle is 360°.
4. A line segment that connects two points on a circle is called a *chord*. The largest chord of a circle is its diameter.
5. A line that passes through two points on a circle is called a *secant*.
6. A line that touches the edge of a circle at only one point is called a *tangent*. A tangent is a special case of a secant.

7. A tangent is perpendicular to the radius that it meets at the point of intersection with the circle.

Are you familiar with all of these terms? If not, go back to your Sequential II book and review them. First, the angle rules.

Rule #1:

> A central angle has the same measure as the arc it subtends.

A central angle is formed by two radii and looks like this:

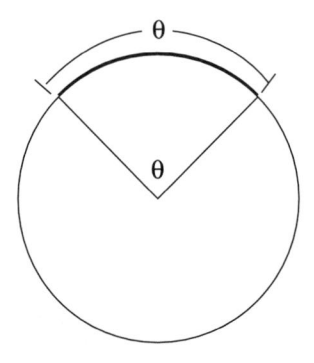

The darkened arc has the same degree measure as the angle. By the way, *subtends* means the same thing as *intercepts*.

Example 1:
Find the measures of A, B, C, and D.

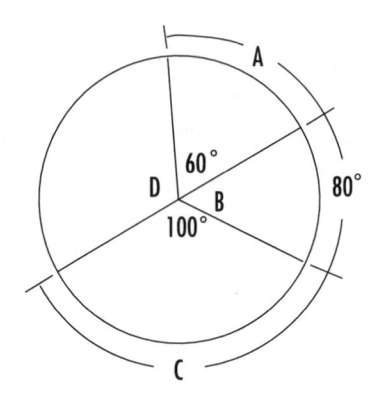

Using the rule above, because $\angle A = 60°$, we know that $\widehat{A} = 60°$.

Because $\widehat{B} = 80°$, we know that $\angle B = 80°$.

Because $\angle C = 100°$, we know that $\widehat{C} = 100°$.

Finally, because the sum of the central angles of a circle is $360°$, we know that $\angle D = 360° - 60° - 80° - 100° = 120°$.

Rule #2:

> The measure of an inscribed angle is half of the arc it subtends.

An inscribed angle is one that subtends an arc, but is formed by two chords emanating from a single point on a circle, rather than being made by two radii. Like so:

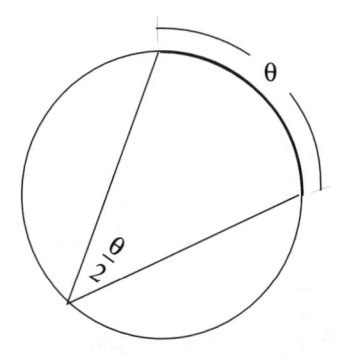

Notice here that, the arc has measure θ, but the angle has measure $\frac{\theta}{2}$.

An arc can only have one central angle, but it can have an infinite number of inscribed angles, all of which have the same measure. For example, all of the inscribed angles in the circle below are 50°.

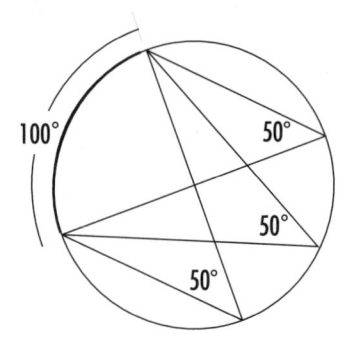

Example 2:

Find the measures of A *and* B.

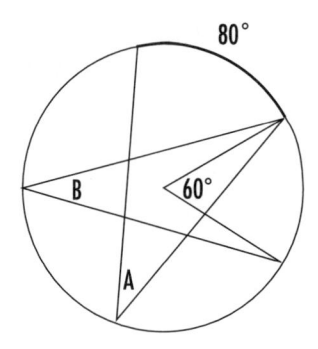

Because ∠A subtends an arc of measure 80°, ∠A = 40°.

In order to find the measure of ∠B, we need to find the measure of its arc. The arc has a central angle of measure 60°, so the arc also has measure 60°. Therefore, ∠B = 30°.

Rule #3:

> If two chords intersect within a circle, then the angle between the two chords is the average of their intercepted arcs.

Notice that we use the *measures* of the arcs, not the *lengths* of the arcs.

In the circle below, two chords intersect and form a pair of intercepted arcs $\widehat{A}$ and $\widehat{B}$. The measure of angle θ is $\frac{m\widehat{A} + m\widehat{B}}{2}$.

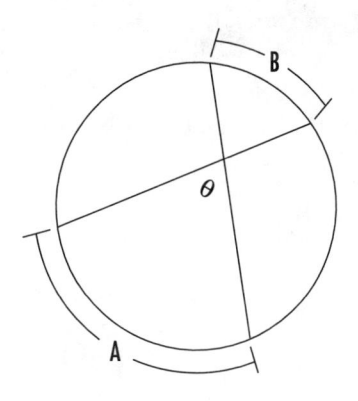

Example 3:

Find the measures of $\angle A$ and $\angle B$.

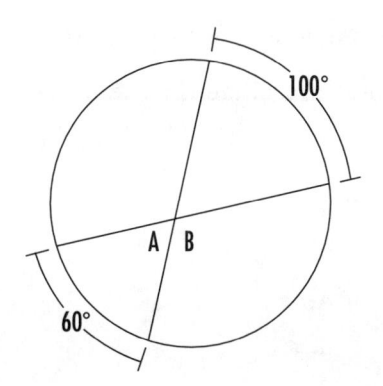

The two chords subtend arcs of measure 60° and 100°. Therefore, $\angle A = \frac{60° + 100°}{2} = 80°$.

Then, because angle A and angle B are supplementary, they add to 180°. Therefore, $\angle B = 180° - 80° = 100°$.

Rule #4:

> The measure of an angle formed by a pair of secants, or a secant and a tangent, is equal to half of the difference between measures of the larger and the smaller arcs that are intercepted by the secants or the secant and the tangent.

In other words, in the figure below, $\angle A = \dfrac{x-y}{2}$.

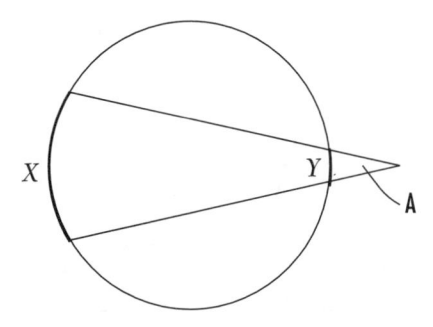

If one of the lines is a tangent, we use the same rule.

If both of the lines are tangents, the bigger arc is called the *major arc* and the smaller arc is called the *minor arc*. We still use the same rule.

Let's do some examples.

Example 4:

Find the measure of A.

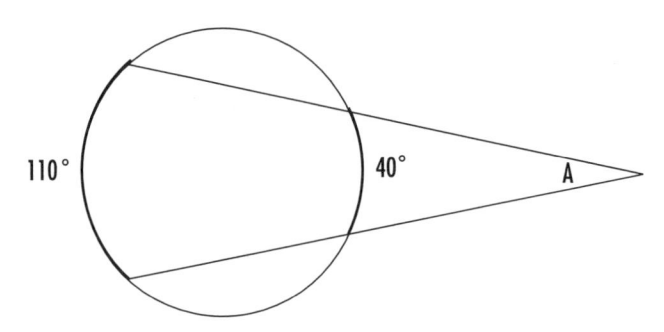

From Rule #4 above, we know that $\angle A = \dfrac{110° - 40°}{2} = 35°$.

Example 5:

Find the measure of $\angle A$.

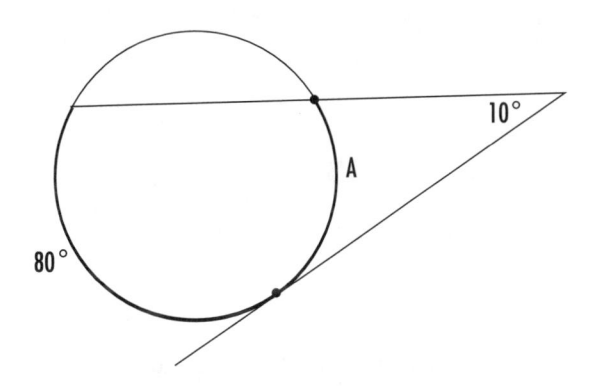

From Rule #4 above, we know that $\dfrac{80° - A}{2} = 10°$. If we solve for A, we get $\angle A = 60°$.

Rule #5:

> The measure of an angle formed by a tangent and a chord is equal to half of the measure of its intercepted arc.

Thus, in the figure below, angle A is equal to $\dfrac{1}{2} \cdot 100° = 50°$.

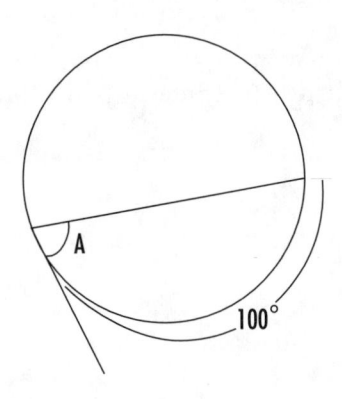

Now let's combine a few things.

Example 6:

Find the measures of: (a) $\widehat{DC}$, (b) $\angle E$, and (c) $\angle DBC$.

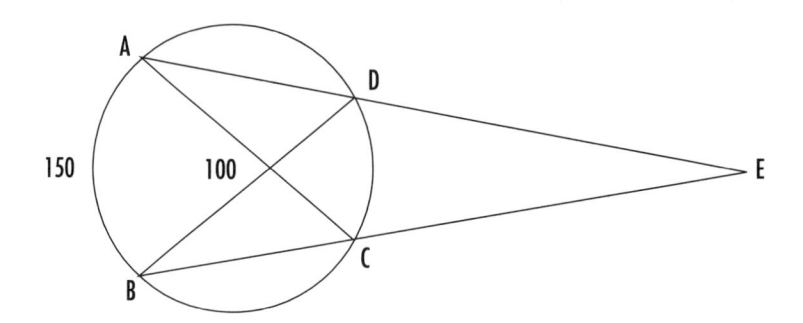

(a) We can find the measure of $\widehat{DC}$ using Rule #3. We get:
$$100° = \frac{150° + \widehat{DC}}{2}.$$
Now we can solve for $\widehat{DC}$: $200° = 150° + \widehat{DC}$, so $\widehat{DC} = 50°$.

(b) We can find the measure of $\angle E$ using Rule #4. We get:
$$\angle E = \frac{150° - 50°}{2} = 50°.$$

(c) We can find the measure of $\angle DBC$ using Rule #5. We get: $\angle DBC = \frac{50°}{2} = 25°.$

Now we are going to learn the segment rules.

Rule #6:

A diameter of a circle that intersects a chord at right angles **bisects** the chord.

In the figure above, $AB = BC$.

This is a very simple rule. Obviously, the rule is also true for a radius that intersects a chord at right angles.

Rule #7:

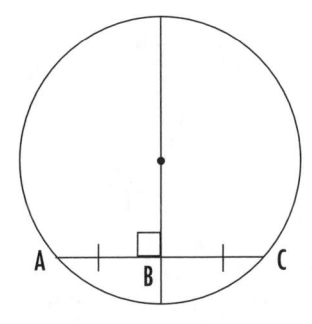

> The two tangents drawn to a circle from the same point are congruent.

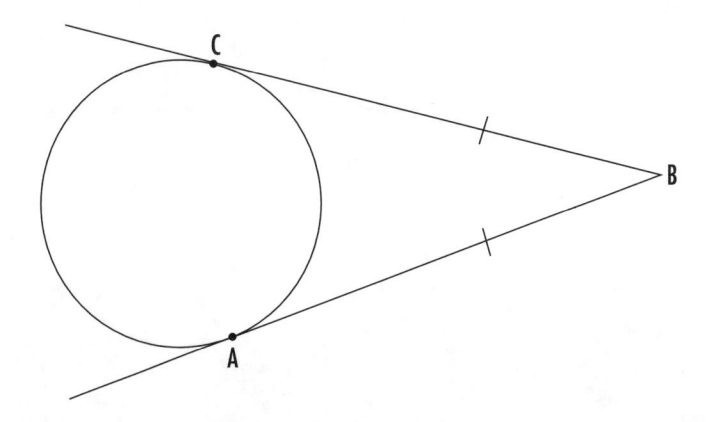

In the figure above, $AB = BC$. This, too, is a very simple rule.

Rule #8:

> If two chords intersect within a circle, then the product of the lengths of the segments of one chord is equal to the product of the lengths of the other.

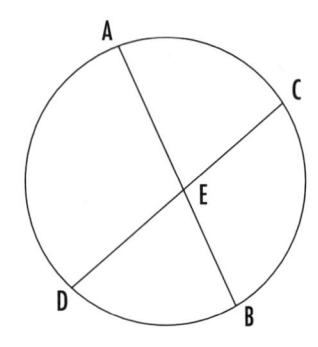

In the figure above, $AE \cdot EB = CE \cdot ED$.

This follows from the fact that $\triangle CAE$ is similar to $\triangle BDE$. Can you prove this?

Example 7:

In the figure below, given $AE = 12$, $EB = 8$, $CE = 6$, and $FA = 20$, find the perimeter of quadrilateral $FAED$.

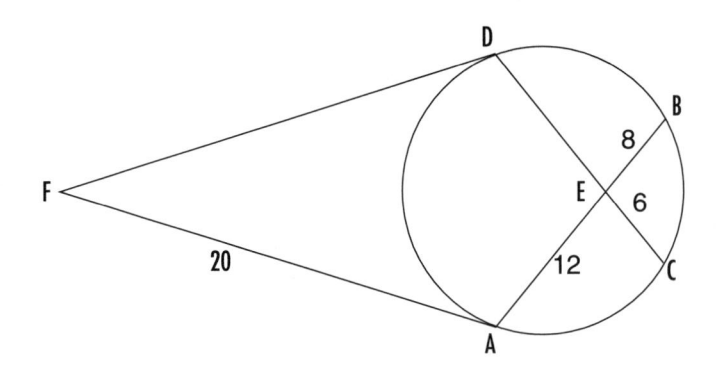

From Rule #8, we know that $AE \cdot EB = CE \cdot ED$, so $12 \cdot 8 = 6 \cdot ED$. If we solve this for ED, we get $ED = 16$.

From Rule #7, we know that $FA = FD$, so $FD = 20$.

Therefore, the perimeter of quadrilateral $FAED$ is

$12 + 16 + 20 + 20 = 68$.

Rule #9:

> Given a point exterior to a circle, the square of the tangent segment to the circle is equal to the product of the lengths of the secant and its external segment.

In other words, in the figure below, $AB^2 = AD \cdot AC$.

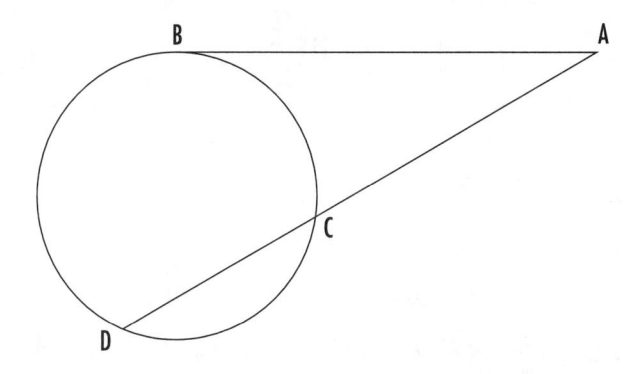

Example 8:

Find the value of x in the figure below.

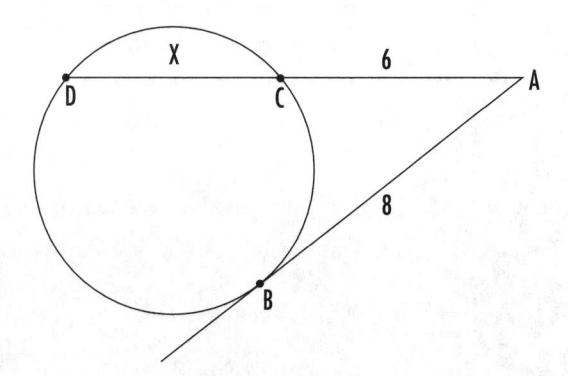

From Rule #9, we know that $AB^2 = AD \cdot AC$, so $8^2 = (6+x)6$.

We can easily solve this for x. $64 = 36 + 6x$ $28 = 6x$

$x = \dfrac{28}{6} = \dfrac{14}{3}$.

Now for a cumulative example.

Example 9:

In the figure below, rectangle ABCD is inscribed in the circle. PB is tangent to the circle at B. The length of side AD is 2, and the length of side DC is 4.

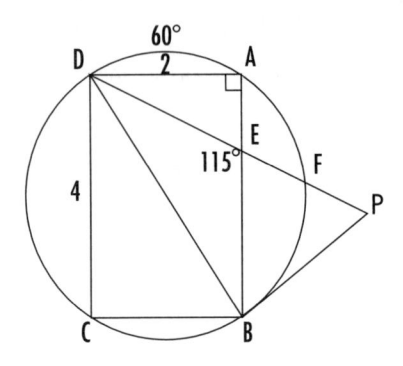

DB is a diameter of the circle.

The measure of angle DEB is 115 and the measure of arc AD is 60.

Find: (a) $m\angle ABD$; (b) $m\widehat{AF}$; (c) the length of PB to the nearest tenth; and (d) the length of PF to the nearest tenth.

(a) From Rule #2, we know that $m\angle ABD = \dfrac{m\widehat{AD}}{2}$, so
$m\angle ABD = \dfrac{60}{2} = 30$.

(b) Because $\angle DAB$ is a right angle, we know that $m\widehat{DCB} = 180°$. Next, using Rule #3, we know that $\dfrac{m\widehat{DCB} + m\widehat{AF}}{2} = 115°$. This gives us: $\dfrac{180° + \widehat{AF}}{2} = 115°$. If we solve for $\widehat{AF}$, we get $\widehat{AF} = 50°$.

(c) First, let's find the length of DB using the Pythagorean Theorem.

$$2^2 + 4^2 = DB^2$$

$$20 = DB^2$$

$$DB = \sqrt{20}.$$

Next, let's find the measure of $\angle BDE$. We know that $\angle DBE = 30°$, so $\angle BDE = 180° - 115° - 30° = 35°$.

We also know that PB is perpendicular to DB because a tangent is always perpendicular to a radius at its point of tangency.

Now, we can find PB using trigonometry. We know that $\tan 35° = \dfrac{PB}{\sqrt{20}}$, so $PB = \sqrt{20} \tan 35° \approx 3.1$

(d) We can find the length of PD using the Pythagorean Theorem.

$$\sqrt{20}^2 + 3.1^2 = PD^2$$

$$29.61 = PD^2$$

$$PD \approx 5.4.$$

Now, using Rule #9, we know that $PB^2 = PD \cdot PF$. Let's designate length PF as x. Then, $3.1^2 = 5.4x$. Let's solve this for x.

$$9.61 = 5.4x$$

$$x \approx 1.8$$

PROBLEMS

1. In the accompanying diagram of circle O, the measure of $\overarc{AB}$ equals 80°. What is the number of degrees in the measure of inscribed angle ACB?

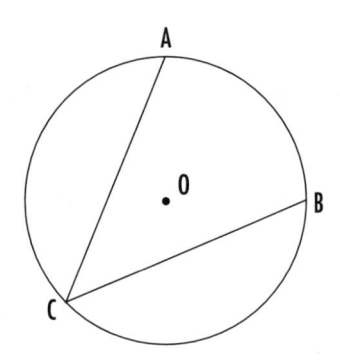

2. In the accompanying diagram, $\overline{AD}$ is tangent to the circle at D and $\overline{ABC}$ is a secant. Find $m\angle A$ if $m\overarc{DC} = 120$ and $m\overarc{CB} = 170$.

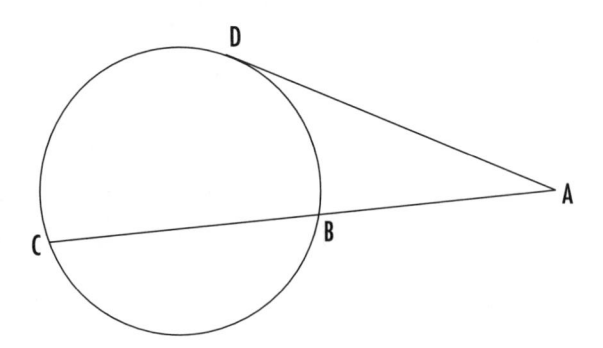

3. In the accompanying diagram of circle O, chords $\overline{AB}$ and $\overline{CD}$ intersect at E, $m\angle AEC = 65$, $AE = 6$, $EB = 8$, and $ED = 12$. Find CE.

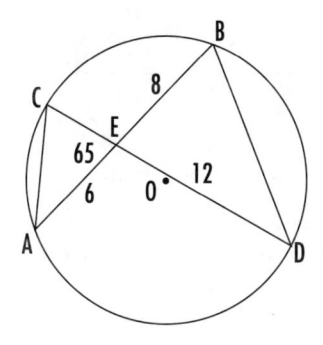

4. Using the diagram from Problem 3, find BD to the *nearest tenth*.

5. In the accompanying diagram of circle O, $\overrightarrow{PA}$ is tangent to the circle at A, and $\overline{PBC}$ is a secant. If $\widehat{AB}:\widehat{BC}:\widehat{CA} = 2:3:4$, find $m\angle P$.

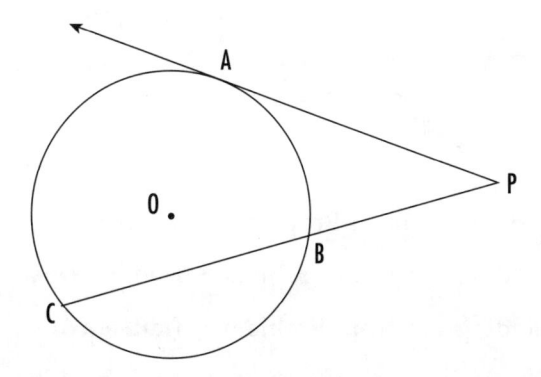

6. In the accompanying diagram, $\triangle ABC$ is inscribed in circle O, $BC = 10$, $AC = 18$, $\overline{PD}$ is tangent to the circle at D, $\overline{PCA}$ is a secant, and $m\widehat{AB} = 130$. Find AB to the *nearest tenth*.

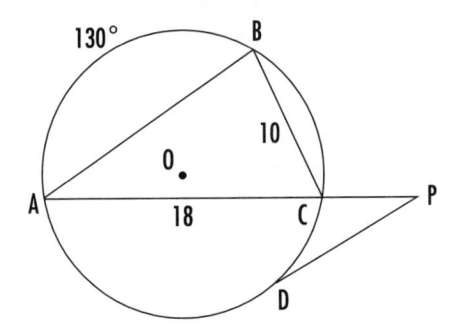

7. Using the diagram from Problem 6, find PD if $CP = 6$.

8. In the accompanying diagram of the circle, $\overline{PBA}$ and $\overline{PCD}$ are secants, chords $\overline{AC}$ and $\overline{BD}$ intersect at E, $\overline{BA} \cong \overline{CD}$, chord $\overline{BC}$ is drawn, $m\angle ABD = 60$ and $m\widehat{BC} = 40$. Find $m\angle ACD$.

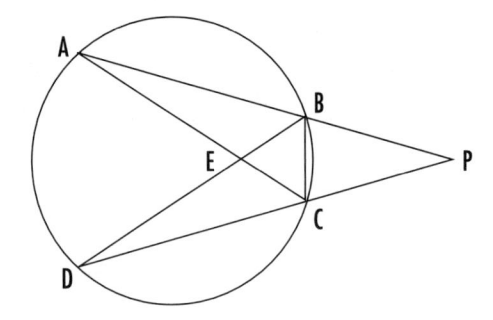

9. Using the diagram from Problem 8, find $m\angle P$.
10. Using the diagram from Problem 8, find $m\angle DBC$.
11. Using the diagram from Problem 8, find $m\angle AED$.
12. Using the diagram from Problem 8, find $m\angle PCB$.

CHAPTER 8
Probability

BASIC PROBABILITY

The probability that an event occurs is found by dividing the number of favorable outcomes in an event by the set of all equally possible outcomes. In probability notation: $p(E) = \frac{n(E)}{n(S)}$.

For example, there are two sides to a fair coin — heads and tails — thus the set of possible outcomes is 2. The number of outcomes for one toss that is heads is 1. Therefore, the probability of tossing a coin and getting heads is $p(H) = \frac{1}{2}$. Similarly, the probability of tossing a coin and *not* getting heads (in other words, getting *tails*) is $p(\text{not } H) = \frac{1}{2}$.

This leads us to some important rules:

> The total of a set of probabilities is 1.
>
> The probability of an impossible event is 0.
>
> The probability of a certain event is 1.
>
> The probability of an event, E, is $0 \leq p(E) \leq 1$.
>
> Because the total probability of a set is 1, the probability that an event, E, does not occur is $p(notE) = 1 - p(E)$.

Example 1:
What is the probability of rolling a fair die and getting a 4?
There are six numbers on a die and one of them is a 4, so $p(4) = \frac{1}{6}$.

Example 2:
What is the probability of rolling one die and not getting a 4?
$p(not4) = 1 - p(4) = 1 - \frac{1}{6} = \frac{5}{6}$.

Notice that there are 5 numbers that are not a 4, so we expect the answer to be $\frac{5}{6}$.

Example 3:
A jar contains 5 red and 7 blue marbles. What is the probability of pulling out 1 blue marble?
There are a total of 12 marbles, and 7 of them are blue, therefore $p(blue) = \frac{7}{12}$.

> If you want to find the probability of independent events occurring in a row, you multiply the probabilities of each event's occurrence.

In other words, if the probability of an event occurring is x, and the probability of a different event occurring is y, then the probability that x occurs followed by y is xy.

Example 4:

What is the probability of tossing a coin and getting heads twice in a row?

The probability of getting heads on an individual toss is $p(H) = \frac{1}{2}$.

The probability of getting two heads in a row is $p(HH) = \frac{1}{2} \cdot \frac{1}{2} = \frac{1}{4}$.

Example 5:

What is the probability of tossing a coin and getting heads three times in a row?

The probability of getting three heads in a row is $p(HHH) = \frac{1}{2} \cdot \frac{1}{2} \cdot \frac{1}{2} = \frac{1}{8}$.

Example 6:

A jar contains 5 red and 7 blue marbles. What is the probability of pulling out 2 blue marbles in a row, without replacement? (Without replacement means that, after you pull out the first marble, you don't put it back.)

The probability of getting a blue marble on the first pull is $\frac{7}{12}$.

After you have pulled out a blue marble, there are only 6 blue ones left, and the total number of marbles has dropped to 11, so the probability of getting a blue marble on the second pull drops to $\frac{6}{11}$. Therefore, the probability of getting two blues in a row is $\frac{7}{12} \cdot \frac{6}{11} = \frac{7}{22}$.

PERMUTATIONS

A *permutation* is an arrangement of a set of objects. The number of objects in the set is n and the number of objects in the arrangement is r.

> The number of permutations of n things taken all at a time is
> $n(n-1)(n-2)(n-3)\ldots 1$

The reason for this formula is quite simple. There are n possible objects that can go in spot number one. Now that an object has been used, there are $n-1$ objects that can go in spot number two. Now there are $n-2$ that can go in spot number three. And so on.

Example 1:

How many ways can six people be seated in six seats?

$(6)(5)(4)(3)(2)(1) = 720$

Six people can sit in the first seat, five in the second seat, four in the third seat, etc.

There is a symbol used for describing "the number of permutations of n things taken all at a time." It is called the factorial and we use the exclamation point to stand for it. Thus, $n(n-1)(n-2)(n-3)\ldots 1$ is written as $n!$.

Example 2:

$5! = 5 \cdot 4 \cdot 3 \cdot 2 \cdot 1 = 120$.

There are a couple of special factorials to know. $0! = 1$ *and* $1! = 1$

Usually, you will be asked to find the number of permutations of n things taken r at a time. This is found by evaluating $\dfrac{n!}{(n-r)!}$. The symbol for this is $_nP_r$. Notice that

$$\dfrac{n!}{(n-r)!} = \dfrac{n(n-1)(n-2)\ldots(n-r+1)(n-r)(n-r-1)\ldots(1)}{(n-r)(n-r-1)\ldots(1)} = n(n-1)(n-2)\ldots(n-r+1)$$

Example 3:

How many four-letter "words" with no letter used more than once, can be made from the letters A,B,C,D,E, and F?

We just have to find $_6P_4$ or $\frac{6!}{(6-4)!}$. Using the rule for factorials, this is $\frac{6 \cdot 5 \cdot 4 \cdot 3 \cdot 2 \cdot 1}{2 \cdot 1} = 6 \cdot 5 \cdot 4 \cdot 3 = 360$.

Example 4:

How many three-letter "words" with no letter used more than once, can be made from the letters A,B,C,D,E, and F?

Now we have to find $_6P_3$ or $\frac{6!}{(6-3)!}$.

This is $\frac{6 \cdot 5 \cdot 4 \cdot 3 \cdot 2 \cdot 1}{3 \cdot 2 \cdot 1} = 6 \cdot 5 \cdot 4 = 120$.

Example 5:

A baseball team has 15 players. How many different nine-player lineups can be made from these players?

We want to find $_{15}P_9$ or $\frac{15!}{(15-9)!}$.

This is $\frac{15 \cdot 14 \cdot 13 \cdot 12 \cdot 11 \cdot 10 \cdot 9 \cdot 8 \cdot 7 \cdot 6 \cdot 5 \cdot 4 \cdot 3 \cdot 2 \cdot 1}{6 \cdot 5 \cdot 4 \cdot 3 \cdot 2 \cdot 1} = 1,816,214,400$.

COMBINATIONS

A combination is very similar to a permutation with one big difference — in a combination, the *order* of the objects *doesn't* matter; in a permutation the *order does* matter. What does this mean? Suppose that you have a hand of 7 playing cards. Does it matter which one is first, which one is second, and so on? No. It doesn't matter how you hold them, so the order doesn't matter. Now suppose that you have a phone number of 7 digits. Does it matter which one you dial first? Of course, so the order does matter. The former is a combination, the latter is a permutation. *In a given group of objects, the number* of combinations is never bigger than the number of permutations.

The number of combinations of n things taken r at a time is $\dfrac{n!}{r!(n-r)!}$ and is symbolized as ${}_nC_r$.

Notice how it looks like the permutation formula, but divided by an additional $r!$.

This is because the number of ways that any particular group of r objects can be arranged is $r!$.

In a combination, as opposed to a permutation, we want to avoid "double counting." Thus, we divide out all of the different arrangements of the same set of things. For example, in a permutation, the group *ABC* is different from *ACB*, which is different from *BAC*, and so on. In a combination they are all the same because their order doesn't matter. How many ways can these letters be arranged? $3!$ different ways.

Example 6:

How many different groups of five people can be made from eight people?

Does the order of the people in the group matter? Not unless they have positions or titles or reserved seats or something similar. Therefore, we want to find a combination. We need to find ${}_8C_5$ or $\dfrac{8!}{5!(8-5)!}$.

$$\dfrac{8!}{5!(8-5)!} = \dfrac{8\cdot 7\cdot 6\cdot 5\cdot 4\cdot 3\cdot 2\cdot 1}{5\cdot 4\cdot 3\cdot 2\cdot 1(3\cdot 2\cdot 1)} = 56.$$

Example 7:

How many different five-card poker hands can be made from a standard 52-card deck?

The order of the cards doesn't matter, so this is a combination.

We need to find ${}_{52}C_5$ or $\dfrac{52!}{5!(52-5)!}$. You are going to need your calculator for this one. The answer is $2{,}598{,}960$.

There are a couple of combinations that you will find it handy to memorize.

The combination ${}_nC_n = 1$, and the combination ${}_nC_0 = 1$.

The combination $_nC_{n-1} = n$ and the combination $_nC_1 = n$.

Example 8:

How many committees of five people can be chosen from a group of six people?

The answer is $_6C_5 = 6$.

Example 9:

How many committees of three people — a president, a vice-president, and a treasurer — can be made from seven candidates?

Here, the order of the people matters. In other words, a committee where Amy is president, Evan is vice-president, and Lesly is treasurer is different from a committee where Evan is president, Lesly is vice-president, and Amy is treasurer.

The answer is $_7P_3 = 210$.

Suppose that we were just asked to find committees of three people from seven candidates. Then the answer would have been $_7C_3 = 35$.

BINOMIAL PROBABILITY

Now we are going to combine probability with combinations. This is something called *binomial probability*.

> The rule is: If the probability of a particular outcome is **p**, then the probability of that outcome occurring **r** times out of a possible **n** times is $_nC_r(p)^r(1-p)^{n-r}$.

Example 10:

If a fair coin is tossed five times, what is the probability of getting exactly three heads?

Here we use binomial probability. This is because there are several ways of getting three heads out of five tosses. For example, HHHTT, HHTHT, HTTHH, HHTTH, etc. So binomial probability finds the probability of one of these arrangements occurring, and then multiplies it by the number of possible arrangements, $_5C_3$.

The probability of getting heads on a toss is $\frac{1}{2}$, so, using the formula above, we need to find $_5C_3\left(\frac{1}{2}\right)^3\left(1-\frac{1}{2}\right)^{5-3}$. This can be simplified to $_5C_3\left(\frac{1}{2}\right)^3\left(\frac{1}{2}\right)^2 = {_5C_3}\left(\frac{1}{2}\right)^5$.

We know that $_5C_3 = \frac{5!}{3!\,2!} = 10$, so the answer is

$$10\left(\frac{1}{2}\right)^5 = \frac{10}{32} = \frac{5}{16}.$$

Example 11:
The probability that it rains in New York on a given day in the summer is $\frac{1}{3}$. Find the probability that it rains exactly three days in a week in the summer.
Using the binomial probability formula, we need to find:

$$_7C_3\left(\frac{1}{3}\right)^3\left(1-\frac{1}{3}\right)^{7-3}.$$

This can be simplified to $_7C_3\left(\frac{1}{3}\right)^3\left(\frac{2}{3}\right)^4$.

We know that $_7C_3 = \frac{7!}{3!\,4!} = 35$, so the answer is

$$35\left(\frac{1}{3}\right)^3\left(\frac{2}{3}\right)^4 = \frac{560}{2187}.$$

Example 12:
The probability that it snows in Minneapolis on a given day in the

winter is $\frac{1}{4}$. Find the probability that it snows at most *two days in a week*.

Now we need to find several probabilities — the probability that it snows two days, the probability that it snows one day, and the probability that it snows zero days — and add them up.

The probability that it snows two days is:

$$_7C_2\left(\frac{1}{4}\right)^2\left(1-\frac{1}{4}\right)^{7-2} = {_7C_2}\left(\frac{1}{4}\right)^2\left(\frac{3}{4}\right)^5.$$

The probability that it snows one day is:

$$_7C_1\left(\frac{1}{4}\right)^1\left(1-\frac{1}{4}\right)^{7-1} = {_7C_1}\left(\frac{1}{4}\right)^1\left(\frac{3}{4}\right)^6.$$

The probability that it snows zero days is:

$$_7C_0\left(\frac{1}{4}\right)^0\left(1-\frac{1}{4}\right)^{7-0} = {_7C_0}\left(\frac{1}{4}\right)^0\left(\frac{3}{4}\right)^7.$$

We know that $_7C_2 = \frac{7!}{2!(5!)} = 21$, $_7C_1 = 7$, and $_7C_0 = 1$ **Remember those special combinations that we told you about?**

The probability that it snows two days is:

$$21\left(\frac{1}{4}\right)^2\left(\frac{3}{4}\right)^5 = \frac{5103}{16384}.$$

The probability that it snows one day is: $7\left(\frac{1}{4}\right)^1\left(\frac{3}{4}\right)^6 = \frac{5103}{16384}$ (A coincidence!).

The probability that it snows zero days is: $1\left(\frac{1}{4}\right)^0\left(\frac{3}{4}\right)^7 = \frac{2187}{16384}.$

Therefore, the probability that it snows at most two days is $\frac{5103}{16384} + \frac{5103}{16384} + \frac{2187}{16384} = \frac{12393}{16384}.$

PROBLEMS

1) If two dice are tossed, what is the probability of getting a ten or higher?

2) If two dice are tossed, what is the probability of getting a seven or an eleven?

3) If two coins are tossed, what is the probability of getting at least one head?

4) A jar contains 7 red and 10 black balls. What is the probability of pulling out 2 red balls in a row without replacement?

5) A jar contains 5 red, 8 white, and 7 blue balls. What is the probability of pulling out 3 white balls in a row without replacement?

6) If a fair coin is tossed five times, what is the probability of getting *exactly* three tails?

7) In a family of five children, what is the probability that *at most* two of the children are girls?

8) The probability of hitting a bull's eye is $\frac{1}{4}$. If three darts are tossed, what is the probability of getting *at least* two bull's eyes?

9) The probability of getting an x in a game is $\frac{1}{4}$. If four plays are made, what is the probability of getting an x exactly 2 times?

10) The probability of getting a y in a game is $\frac{1}{3}$. If four plays are made, what is the probability of getting a y *at least* three times?

CHAPTER 9
Statistics

MEAN

In the field of Statistics, you will learn a few ways to interpret data. The first is called the "mean." The *mean* is the same thing as the average and you find it by adding up the total of the scores (or whatever you are measuring) and dividing by the number of scores. By the way, the symbol that is usually used for mean is $\bar{x}$, and is read "x bar."

Example 1:

Find the mean test grade for a class whose grades are: $\{85, 88, 91, 93, 90, 75, 81, 100, 74, 85\}$.

All that we do is add up the scores and divide by the number.

The sum of the scores is: 862

The number of scores is: 10

The mean is: $\frac{862}{10} = 86.2$.

Example 2:

Find the mean weight of a group of people whose weights are:
$\{189, 124, 130, 175, 210, 114, 133, 140, 155, 160, 199, 167\}$.

The sum of the weights is: 1896

The number of weights is: 12

The mean is: $\frac{1896}{12} = 158$.

There is another kind of average that you should be able to find called a *weighted average*. This is also the mean of a set of data. We find a weighted average when we have a set of data where we are given a set of scores and a number of people who got each score. We find the weighted average by multiplying each score by the number of people who got that score, finding the sum of those products, and dividing by the total number of scores.

Example 3:

The ages of a group of people are listed below. Find the mean age.

Age	18	19	20	21	22	23	24	25	26	27	28
Number of People	5	7	8	11	16	19	14	10	6	3	2

First, we multiply each age by the number of people and sum the products:

$(18 \cdot 5) + (19 \cdot 7) + (20 \cdot 8) + (21 \cdot 11) +$
$(22 \cdot 16) + (23 \cdot 19) + (24 \cdot 14) +$
$(25 \cdot 10) + (26 \cdot 6) + (27 \cdot 3) + (28 \cdot 2) = 2282$

Next, find the total number of people:

$5 + 7 + 8 + 11 + 16 + 19 + 14 + 10 + 6 + 3 + 2 = 101$

The mean age is: $\frac{2282}{101} \approx 22.59$.

MEDIAN

The next statistic that you need to know is called the "median." The *median* of a set of data is the middle score. It means the score where the same *number* of people scored at or below the median as the number of people who scored at or above the median. What we do is to put the scores in order and then count the number of scores. If the *number* is odd, the median is the middle score. If the number is even, the median is halfway between the two scores closest to the middle.

Example 4:

Find the median of the test scores from the first example $\{85, 88, 91, 93, 90, 75, 81, 100, 74, 85\}$.

First, we put the scores in order:

$\{74, 75, 81, 85, 85, 88, 90, 91, 93, 100\}$.

Next, count the scores: 10.

This is even, so the median score will be halfway between the 5th and the 6th score.

$\frac{85 + 88}{2} = 86.5$.

Example 5:

If the weights of a group of people are

$\{122, 170, 142, 130, 157, 210, 141, 158, 115, 175, 106, 221, 156\}$, *find the median weight.*

First, put the weights in order:

$\{106, 115, 122, 130, 141, 142, 156, 157, 158, 170, 175, 210, 221\}$.

The number of weights is: 13 .

The number is odd, so the median is the middle score: 156 .

Example 6:

Given the sample of ages in Example 3, find the median age.

Age	18	19	20	21	22	23	24	25	26	27	28
Number of People	5	7	8	11	16	19	14	10	6	3	2

There are 101 ages (see example 3), so the median age will be the 51st age. The median age is 23.

MODE

The third statistic is called the *mode*. The *mode* is the most frequently occurring score in a data set. It is possible to have more than one mode, or to have no mode.

Example 7:

Find the mode of the sample in Example 6.

The most frequently occurring score is 23.

Example 8:

Find the mode of the following scores: $\{4, 8, 6, 8, 4, 8\}$.

The most frequently occurring score is 8.

Example 9:

Find the mode of the following scores: $\{4, 5, 8, 6, 5, 8, 4, 5, 8\}$.

Notice that both 5 and 8 occur most frequently, so the modes are 5 and 8.

Example 10:

Find the mode of the following scores: $\{4, 6, 4, 6, 4, 6\}$.

No score occurs most frequently, so there is no mode.

Notice in the last example that the scores 4 and 6 each occur more than once, but, in order for there to be a mode, there must be a score that occurs **less** often than some other score.

When a set is said to have a *normal distribution*, the mean, median, and mode of a set of data are all equal. There are other aspects to the distribution as well, but they aren't relevant here.

STANDARD DEVIATION

The final statistic that we will learn is called the "standard deviation." The *standard deviation* of a set of data is a measure of the dispersion of the data. In other words, how much the data deviates from the average score. By the way, the symbol that is usually used for standard deviation is σ and is read "sigma." We will only deal with standard deviations of a normal distribution. Other types of distributions are not covered, except in Statistics courses.

Example 12:

If a normally distributed set of data has a mean of 100 and a standard deviation of 5, and another set of the same size has a mean of 100 and a standard deviation of 10, then the first set has more scores close to 100 than the second set does.

There is a rule for this that goes as follows:

In a normal distribution, with a mean of $\bar{x}$ and a standard deviation of σ:

> approximately 68% of the outcomes will fall between $\bar{x} - \sigma$ and $\bar{x} + \sigma$
>
> approximately 95% of the outcomes will fall between $\bar{x} - 2\sigma$ and $\bar{x} + 2\sigma$
>
> approximately 99.5% of the outcomes will fall between $\bar{x} - 3\sigma$ and $\bar{x} + 3\sigma$.

Example 13:

If a set of data is normally distributed and has a mean of 80 and a standard deviation of 3, then:

- approximately 68% of the outcomes will fall between 77 and 83

- approximately 95% of the outcomes will fall between 74 and 86

- approximately 99.5% of the outcomes will fall between 71 and 89.

Example 14:

A set of data is normally distributed and 25% of the scores lie below 100 and 2.5% lie above 108. What is the mean and standard deviation of the set?

Using the rule above, we know that $\bar{x} + 2\sigma = 108$ and $\bar{x} - 2\sigma = 100$.

If we add these two equations together, we get: $2\bar{x} = 208$.

Next, we divide through by 2: $\bar{x} = 104$.

Now, we can find that $\sigma = 2$.

Another rule for normal distributions is: **the closer a score is to the mean, the more likely it is to occur.**

Example 15:

If a set of data is normally distributed and the mean is 100, then a score of 101 is more likely to occur than a score of 102. A score of 103 is more likely to occur than a score of 95. Etc.

The method for finding a standard deviation is simple, but time-consuming.

It consists of six steps:

- First, find the mean.
- Second, subtract the mean from each actual score.
- Third, square each of these differences.
- Fourth, find the sum of these squares.
- Fifth, divide the sum by the number of scores. This is called the *variance*.
- Sixth, take the square root of the variance. This is the standard deviation.

This is easiest to do with an example.

Example 16:

Find the standard deviation of the set $\{6,8,9,7,9,3\}$.

First, find the mean.

The sum of the scores is 42. There are 6 scores. The mean is $\frac{42}{6} = 7$.

Second, subtract 7 from each actual score:

$6 - 7 = -1$ $\quad$ $8 - 7 = 1$ $\quad$ $9 - 7 = 2$

$7 - 7 = 0$ $\quad$ $9 - 7 = 2$ $\quad$ $3 - 7 = -4$

Third, square each difference.

$(-1)^2 = 1$ $\quad$ $(1)^2 = 1$ $\quad$ $(2)^2 = 4$

$(0)^2 = 0$ $\quad$ $(2)^2 = 4$ $\quad$ $(-4)^2 = 16$

Fourth, add up the squares of the differences.

$1 + 1 + 4 + 0 + 4 + 16 = 26$

Fifth, divide this sum by the total number of scores.

$\frac{26}{6} = 4.3\overline{3}$.

Last, take the square root of this number. This is the standard deviation. $\sigma = \sqrt{4.3\overline{3}} \approx 2.08$

Wasn't that fun? This isn't particularly hard, but it is time consuming, and you can't afford to make any mistakes.

Example 17:

Find the standard deviation of the data set in Example 1 $\{85, 88, 91, 93, 90, 75, 81, 100, 74, 85\}$.

First, we found the mean in example 1. It is 86.2 .

Second, subtract 86.2 from each actual score:

$85 - 86.2 = -1.2$

$88 - 86.2 = 1.8$

$91 - 86.2 = 4.8$

$93 - 86.2 = 6.8$

$90 - 86.2 = 3.8$

$75 - 86.2 = -11.2$

$81 - 86.2 = -5.2$

$100 - 86.2 = 13.8$

$74 - 86.2 = -12.2$

$85 - 86.2 = -1.2$

Third, square each difference.

$(-1.2)^2 = 1.44$

$(1.8)^2 = 3.24$

$(4.8)^2 = 23.04$

$(6.8)^2 = 46.24$

$(3.8)^2 = 14.44$

$(-11.2)^2 = 125.44$

$(-5.2)^2 = 27.04$

$(13.8)^2 = 190.44$

$(-12.2)^2 = 148.84$

$(-1.2)^2 = 1.44$

Fourth, add up the squares of the differences.

$1.44 + 3.24 + 23.04 + 46.24 + 14.44 + 125.44$
$+ 27.04 + 190.44 + 148.84 + 1.44 = 581.60$

Fifth, divide this sum by the total number of scores.

$$\frac{581.60}{10} = 58.16.$$

Last, take the square root of this number. This is the standard deviation.

$$\sigma = \sqrt{58.16} \approx 7.626$$

If you have a set of data where we are given a set of scores and the number of people who got each score, we find the standard deviation in a way that is similar to how we found the weighted average. That is, we multiply the square of each difference by the number of people who got that difference, then find the sum, and divide by the total number of scores.

Example 18:

Find the standard deviation of the data set in Example 3

Age	18	19	20	21	22	23	24	25	26	27	28
Number of People	5	7	8	11	16	19	14	10	6	3	2

First, find the mean (which we did in example 3): The mean was 22.59, which we will round to 22.6 (to make life easier).

Second, subtract 22.6 from each actual score:

$18 - 22.6 = -4.6$

$19 - 22.6 = -3.6$

$20 - 22.6 = -2.6$

$21 - 22.6 = -1.6$

$22 - 22.6 = 0.6$

$23 - 22.6 = 0.4$

$24 - 22.6 = 1.4$

$25 - 22.6 = 2.4$

$26 - 22.6 = 3.4$

$27 - 22.6 = 4.4$

$28 - 22.6 = 5.4$

Third, square each difference.

$(-4.6)^2 = 21.16$

$(-3.6)^2 = 12.96$

$(-2.6)^2 = 6.76$

$(-1.6)^2 = 2.56$

$(0.6)^2 = 0.36$

$(0.4)^2 = 0.16$

$(1.4)^2 = 1.96$

$(2.4)^2 = 5.76$

$(3.4)^2 = 11.56$

$(4.4)^2 = 19.36$

$(5.4)^2 = 29.16$

Fourth, multiply each squared difference by the number of people who got that score and add them up:

$(21.16 \cdot 5) + (12.96 \cdot 7) + (6.76 \cdot 8) + (2.56 \cdot 11) + (0.36 \cdot 16) + (0.16 \cdot 19)$
$+ (1.96 \cdot 14) + (5.76 \cdot 10) + (11.56 \cdot 6) + (19.36 \cdot 3) + (29.16 \cdot 2) = 558.36$

Fifth, divide this sum by the total number of scores.

$\dfrac{558.36}{101} \approx 5.53$.

Last, take the square root of this number. This is the standard deviation.

$$\sigma = \sqrt{5.53} \approx 2.4$$

PROBLEMS

The distribution of quiz scores for a class of 12 students is $\{8,6,7,9,10,8,5,1,9,10,7,7,\}$.

1) Find the mean quiz score for the class.
2) Find the median quiz score for the class.
3) Find the mode for the class.
4) **Find the standard deviation for the class (to the nearest tenth).**

During a 10-week softball season, Jo got the following number of hits per week: $\{3,8,6,1,5,7,6,5,6,3\}$.

5) Find the mean number of hits Jo got per week.
6) Find the median number of hits Jo got per week.
7) Find the mode of the number of hits.
8) **Find the standard deviation of the number of hits.**

The table shows the average snowfall in centimeters recorded one winter at a ski resort over a period of days.

Snowfall (cm.)	18	19	20	21	22	23	24	25	26	27
Frequency (days)	6	4	4	3	5	3	14	10	6	3

9) Find the mean snowfall per day.
10) Find the standard deviation of the snowfall (to the nearest *tenth* of a cm.).
11) The test scores of 50 students resulted in a mean of 82 and a standard deviation of 7.5. If the distribution were normal, between what two numbers would 95% of the scores be expected to fall?
12) On a standardized test, the mean is 37 and the standard deviation is 2.5. Approximately what percent of the scores fall in the range $32-42$?

CHAPTER 10
Logarithms

WHAT IS A LOGARITHM?

Quite simply, a logarithm is an exponent. What do we mean by this? Look at the following and we will show you where logs come from. By the way, most people say "log" for logarithm. It's shorter.

We know that $10^1 = 10$.

We also know that $10^2 = 100$.

So, there must be a power of 10 that gives us 50. And that power is somewhere between 1 and 2. Of course it's not 1.5—that would be too easy! We don't know exactly what this power is so we give it a name. It's called "the log of 50".

In other words, $\log 50$ is the power that we raise 10 to, in order to get 50.

What if we wanted to find the power that we raise 10 to in order to get 70? We would use $\log 70$. This is also between 1 and 2, but should be bigger than $\log 50$. (Does this make sense to you? It should.)

But there's a problem. Consider the following:

We know that $8^1 = 8$.

We also know that $8^2 = 64$.

So, there must be a power of 8 that gives us 50. And that power is also somewhere between 1 and 2. Shouldn't this also be called "the log of 50". It shouldn't be the same as the power that we raised 10 to in order to get 50 because 10 is bigger than 8. So how can we tell them apart? Simple. The power that we raise 10 to in order to get 50 we write as $\log_{10} 50$, and the power that we raise 8 to in order to get 50 we write as $\log_8 50$. The subscript stands for the base that we raise the exponent to. We read these as "log base 10 of 50" and "log base 8 of 50" respectively.

Let's recap. $\log_{10} 50$ is the power that we raise 10 to in order to get 50. $\log_8 50$ is the power that we raise 8 to in order to get 50.

It is traditional to leave off the 10 from logs that are base 10, and to include them for all other logs. The base 10 logs are called *common logs* and are the ones that we frequently learn first. Later in this chapter we will learn about *natural logs* which have a different base.

Now that we have an idea of what a log is, let's do some basic examples and learn some rules.

Example 1:

What is $\log 1,000$*?*

$\log 1,000$ is the power that we raise 10 to in order to get 1,000.

$10^3 = 1,000$. In other words, $\log 1,000 = 3$.

Example 2:

What is $\log 1,000,000,000$*?*

Because $10^9 = 1,000,000,000$, we know that

$\log 1,000,000,000 = 9$.

Example 3:

What is $\log 0.0001$*?*

Because $10^{-4} = 0.0001$, we know that $\log 0.0001 = -4$.

Example 4:

What is $\log_4 64$?

Because $4^3 = 64$, we know that $\log_4 64 = 3$.

Example 5:

What is $\log_3 \frac{1}{9}$?

Because $3^{-2} = \frac{1}{9}$, we know that $\log_3 \frac{1}{9} = -2$.

Example 6:

What is $\log_2 \sqrt{2}$?

Because $2^{\frac{1}{2}} = \sqrt{2}$, we know that $\log_2 \sqrt{2} = \frac{1}{2}$.

Example 7:

What is $\log_5 1$?

Because $5^0 = 1$, we know that $\log_5 1 = 0$.

Got the idea? Notice that a log can be zero, a fraction, or a negative number.

Now let's learn some rules.

As we said before, a log is the power that we raise a base to in order to get a desired number. Therefore:

$$\log_B x = A \text{ means } B^A = x$$

What power do we raise a number to in order to get 1? The power zero. In fact, anything to the power zero is 1. Therefore:

$$\log_B 1 = 0$$

What power do we raise a number to in order to get itself? The power 1.
Therefore:

$$\log_B B = 1$$

For example, $\log_7 1 = 0$; $\log_7 7 = 1$; $\log_9 1 = 0$; $\log_9 9 = 1$; and so on.

What power do we raise B to in order to get B^x? The power x. Therefore:

$$\log_B B^x = x$$

and, $\log_B x$ is the power we raise B to, to get x. Therefore:

$$B^{\log_B x} = x$$

What power do we raise a number to in order to get zero? There is no power! Therefore, we can't evaluate $\log_B 0$. Similarly, there is no power we can raise a positive number to in order to get a negative number, so we can't evaluate the log of a negative number (we restrict ourselves to a positive base B). Therefore:

When we evaluate $\log_B x$, x must be a positive number.

Let's do a few more examples.

Example 8:

What is $\log_8 8^{3.7}$?

Following the rule that $\log_B B^x = x$, the answer is 3.7.

Example 9:

What is $2^{\log_2 x}$?

Following the rule that $B^{\log_B x} = x$, the answer is x.

LOG RULES

Now let's do some more complicated things with logs. There are three rules to learn.

Rule #1:

$$\log(AB) = \log A + \log B$$

Where does this come from? When you multiply two like bases, you add the exponents. The log is the exponent.

Rule #2:

$$\log\left(\frac{A}{B}\right) = \log A - \log B$$

Why? When you divide two like bases, you subtract the exponents.

Rule #3:

$$\log(A^B) = B \log A$$

Why? When you raise a power to a power, you multiply the exponents.

Let's do some examples.

Example 10:

Simplify $\log A^2 B^5$.

Using rule #1, we can rewrite this as: $\log A^2 + \log B^5$.

Now, using rule #3, we can rewrite this as: $2 \log A + 5 \log B$.

Why would we want to do this? Suppose we were told that $\log A = 3$ and $\log B = 2$. Then,

$\log A^2 B^5 = 2 \log A + 5 \log B = 6 + 10 = 16$.

Example 11:

Simplify $\log \dfrac{x^3 \sqrt{y}}{z^5}$.

Using rule #2, we can rewrite this as: $\log x^3 \sqrt{y} - \log z^5$.

Next, using rule #1, we can rewrite this as:

$\log x^3 + \log \sqrt{y} - \log z^5$.

Finally, using rule #3, we can rewrite this as:

$3 \log x + \dfrac{1}{2} \log y - 5 \log z$.

Notice how this enables us to take complex logarithmic expressions and turn them into simpler ones.

Now let's learn our final rule, called the *change of base rule*. The first thing to know is that, just as we can square both sides of an equation, or square root it, or the like, we can take the log of both sides of an equation.

Suppose that we want to find the value of x that solves $7^x = 55$. We know from our definition of a logarithm that $\log_7 55 = x$.

But, if we take the log base 10 of both sides of the equation, we get: $\log 7^x = \log 55$.

Now, using rule #3 above, we can rewrite this as: $x \log 7 = \log 55$, and solving for x we get: $x = \dfrac{\log 55}{\log 7}$.

Because x has to be the same as that found by using the definition of a logarithm, we know that $\log_7 55 = \dfrac{\log 55}{\log 7}$.

Now let's generalize this. Start with $B^x = A$. Using the definition of a logarithm we get: $\log_B A = x$. If we instead take the log of both sides using a *different* base (call it C), we get: $x \log_C B = \log_C A$ and $x = \dfrac{\log_C A}{\log_C B}$. Therefore:

> **Change of Base Rule:** $\log_B A = \dfrac{\log_C A}{\log_C B}$

Example 12:

Solve for x: $8^{3x+2} = 77$.

We can take the log of both sides, and we get $\log 8^{3x+2} = \log 77$.

Next, using the rule #3 above, we get: $(3x+2)\log 8 = \log 77$, which gives us: $3x + 2 = \dfrac{\log 77}{\log 8}$.

Now we can solve for x: $x = \dfrac{\dfrac{\log 77}{\log 8} - 2}{3}$.

Why do we want to do this? Because we can use a calculator to find common logs (Remember, those are base 10.) so we can come up with an answer. We get that x is approximately 0.030.

Example 13:

Find $\log_6 300$.

Using the change of base rule, $\log_6 300 = \dfrac{\log 300}{\log 6} \approx 3.183$.

Example 14:

Solve for x: $7^{2x} = 5^{3x+1}$.

Take the log of both sides: $\log 7^{2x} = \log 5^{3x+1}$.

Use rule #3: $2x \log 7 = (3x+1)\log 5$.

Now we solve for x.

First, distribute the log on the right side:

$2x \log 7 = 3x \log 5 + \log 5$.

Next, move the terms containing x to the same side:

$2x \log 7 - 3x \log 5 = \log 5$.

Factor out x: $x(2\log 7 - 3\log 5) = \log 5$.

Isolate x: $x = \dfrac{\log 5}{(2\log 7 - 3\log 5)}$.

Now we can find x with a calculator if we want to. We get:

$x \approx -1.72$.

By the way, let's check the result:

$7^{(2)(-1.72)} \approx 0.0012$ and $5^{3(-1.72)+1} \approx 0.0012$

What is *e*?

Now we are going to learn about logarithms with base e. Where does e come from? Study the following.

Suppose that we put 1000 dollars in the bank at 10% interest, compounded annually. How much money would we have at the end of the year?

We multiply the amount that we have in the bank by 0.1 and add it to the amount that we started with.

We get: $1000 + 1000(0.1) = 1100$ dollars.

Now suppose that we factor 1000 out of the solution to get: $1000(1+0.1)$. Thus we could say that, at the end of the year, we had $1000(1+0.1)$ dollars. Now, how much would we have at the end of the second year?

Again, we multiply the amount that we have in the bank by 0.1 and add it to the amount that we started with. We get: $1000(1+0.1) + 1000(1+0.1)(0.1)$ dollars.

If we factor out the starting amount we get: $1000(1+0.1)(1+0.1)$, which we can write as: $1000(1+0.1)^2$.

At the end of a third year, we would have $1000(1+0.1)^3$. And so on.

Therefore, at the end of T years, we would have $1000(1+0.1)^T$ dollars.

If we had put P dollars in the bank at the beginning, we would have $P(1+0.1)^T$.

If we let $r = \frac{R}{100}$; that is, the decimal equivalent of the percent R, then, if we had earned an interest rate of R percent, we would have $P(1+r)^T$.

Now we have a formula for compound interest.

> If we put P dollars in the bank, for T years, at R percent interest compounded annually, we get: $P(1+r)^T$ dollars.

If the interest compounds more than once a year, we divide the interest rate by the number of times it compounds in a year, and we multiply the number of years by the number of compounding periods in a year. Thus, if the interest compounds semi-annually, we have: $P\left(1+\frac{r}{2}\right)^{2T}$. If the interest compounds quarterly, we have: $P\left(1+\frac{r}{4}\right)^{4T}$. Now we can come up with a general formula for compound interest:

If we put P dollars in the bank, for T years, at R percent interest compounded N times a year, the final amount, A, is:

$$A = P\left(1 + \frac{r}{N}\right)^{NT} \text{ dollars} \quad \left(\text{where } r = \frac{R}{100}\right).$$

Example 15:

If we put $100 in the bank, for 5 years, at 12% interest, then how much will we have if the interest compounds: (a) annually; (b) semi-annually; (c) quarterly; or (d) monthly?

Using the formula, we get:

(a) $A = 100\left(1 + \frac{.12}{1}\right)^5 = 176.23$

(b) $A = 100\left(1 + \frac{.12}{2}\right)^{2(5)} = 179.08$

(c) $A = 100\left(1 + \frac{.12}{4}\right)^{4(5)} = 180.61$

(d) $A = 100\left(1 + \frac{.12}{12}\right)^{12(5)} = 181.67$

What does this have to do with e? If we let N get infinitely large, in other words, if we compound *continuously*, then instead of the usual growth factor $\left(1 + \frac{r}{N}\right)^N$ we substitute an irrational number with a value of ≈ 2.71828, which we call e^r. The formula is: If we compound **continuously**, then the final amount is:

$$A = Pe^{rt}$$

Note that because e is an irrational number, like π, we will never have the exact value. But with money, we usually only care about two decimal places, so the approximation is good enough.

Example 16:

If we put $100 in the bank, for 5 years, at 12% interest, then how much will we have if the interest compounds continually?

Using the formula, we get: $A = 100e^{0.12(5)} = 182.21$

Notice how the final amount increases as we compound more frequently.

Natural Logarithms

Natural logarithms are logarithms with a base of e. Why would we want to use e as a base? It turns out that these show up when we are looking at the growth or decay of something. In calculus, you will learn many uses for e and for natural logarithms, so you should get comfortable with natural logarithms.

First, let's define a natural logarithm. $\log_e A = x$ means that $e^x = A$.

By the way, we write $\log_e$ as ln (which stands for *log natural*) and pronounce it "log." Don't ask why!

Thus, $\ln A = x$ means that $e^x = A$.

All of the rules for natural logs are the same as for common logs.

- $\ln 1 = 0$
- $\ln e = 1$
- $\ln e^x = x$
- $\ln AB = \ln A + \ln B$
- $\ln \dfrac{A}{B} = \ln A - \ln B$
- $\ln A^B = B \ln A$

Because e is an irrational number, we will use a calculator to get decimal approximations of answers. Or, we will leave answers in terms of e, the way we do with π.

Let's do some examples.

Example 17:

Simplify $\ln \dfrac{A^2 B^3}{\sqrt{C}}$.

First, we rewrite this as: $\ln A^2 B^3 - \ln \sqrt{C}$.

Next, we get: $\ln A^2 + \ln B^3 - \ln \sqrt{C}$.

Finally, we get: $2\ln A + 3\ln B - \dfrac{1}{2}\ln C$.

Example 18:

Solve for x: $e^x = 17$

Take the log of both sides: $\ln e^x = \ln 17$

This simplifies to: $x = \ln 17 \approx 2.833$

Example 19:

Solve for x: $8^x = 5^{x-1}$.

We could do this with any type of logs, so let's solve it twice — once using common logs, and one using natural logs.

Common Logs	**Natural Logs**

Take the log of both sides:

$$\log 8^x = \log 5^{x-1} \qquad\qquad \ln 8^x = \ln 5^{x-1}$$

Bring down the power:

$$x \log 8 = (x-1)\log 5 \qquad\qquad x \ln 8 = (x-1)\ln 5$$

Distribute on the right side

$$x \log 8 = x \log 5 - \log 5 \qquad\qquad x \ln 8 = x \ln 5 - \ln 5$$

Group the terms containing x:

$$x \log 8 - x \log 5 = -\log 5 \qquad\qquad x \ln 8 - x \ln 5 = -\ln 5$$

Factor out x:

$$x(\log 8 - \log 5) = -\log 5 \qquad\qquad x(\ln 8 - \ln 5) = -\ln 5$$

Solve for x:

$$x = \frac{-\log 5}{\log 8 - \log 5} \qquad\qquad x = \frac{-\ln 5}{\ln 8 - \ln 5}$$

Now use a calculator:

$$x \approx -3.424 \qquad\qquad x \approx -3.424$$

Notice, we got the same answer using both common logs and natural logs. Interesting, isn't it?

PROBLEMS

1. Solve for x: $8^{2x-2} = 16^x$
2. Solve for x: $\log 0.00001 = x$
3. Solve for x: $\log_7 x = 2$
4. Simplify: $\log \dfrac{A^2}{B}$
5. Write as a single log: $5 \log A - 3 \log B$
6. If $\log A = 3$ and $\log B = 5$, find $\log \dfrac{A^4}{B^{10}}$.
7. Solve for x (to three decimal places): $3^x = 35$
8. Solve for x (to three decimal places): $5^{3x-2} = 8^{x+1}$
9. Simplify: $\ln \dfrac{C^2 \sqrt{A}}{B^3}$
10. Solve for x: $\ln x - \ln 3 = 5$
11. If you invest $1000 at 8%, compounded quarterly, how long will it take to double?
12. If you invest $1000 at 8%, compounded continuously, how much will you have after 7 years?

CHAPTER 11
Conic Sections

There is a family of curves in mathematics called *conic sections* that consists of parabolas, circles, ellipses, and hyperbolas. Although you have probably seen parabolas before, it is unlikely that you have studied the others in any depth. We will not be exploring all of the nuances of conic sections here (which is often a full semester course), but we will teach you the basics.

PARABOLAS

A *parabola* is the set of all points in the plane equidistant from a fixed point and a line. The point is called the *focus* and the line is called the *directrix*.

A parabola is a curve where y is in terms of x^2, or x is in terms of y^2. For example, $y = x^2$ or $y = 4x^2 - 8x + 24$ or $x = -3y^2 + 12y$.

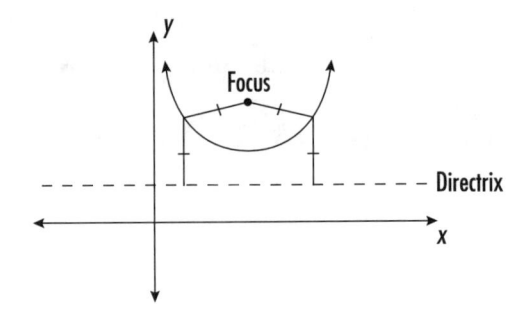

By using the above definition and the distance formula, we could show that equations of parabolas that open *up* or *down* are of the form $y = ax^2 + bx + c$.

If $a > 0$, the parabola will open up. If $a < 0$, the parabola will open down.

In order to graph a parabola, we will only be concerned with the vertex of the parabola, the x-intercepts, and the y-intercept.

The **y-intercept** is the point where the curve crosses the y-axis. If we want to find the y-intercept of any curve, we plug in 0 for x. Here, we get $y = c$. Therefore, the parabola will go through the point $(0, c)$.

The **vertex** of a parabola is the minimum point, if it opens up; or the maximum point, if it opens down. It occurs at the point where $x = -\frac{b}{2a}$. To find the corresponding y-coordinate, plug $-\frac{b}{2a}$ in for x into the equation and find y.

The **x-intercepts** are the points where the curve crosses the x-axis; that is, where $ax^2 + bx + c = 0$. These are also called the *roots* of the equation. Not all parabolas have roots because not all parabolas cross the x-axis. In the chapter on quadratic equations, we learned how to find solutions to $ax^2 + bx + c = 0$ either by factoring or by using the quadratic formula.

Let's do an example.

Example 1:

Find the intercepts and the vertex of $y = x^2 - 3x - 4$ *and graph the equation.*

Here we have $a = 1$, $b = -3$, and $c = -4$.

The y-intercept is at the point $(0,c)$ so the y-intercept is at $(0,-4)$.

The vertex is at $x = -\frac{b}{2a}$, so the vertex is at $x = -\frac{(-3)}{2(1)} = \frac{3}{2}$.

When we plug $\frac{3}{2}$ into the equation, we get:

$y = \left(\frac{3}{2}\right)^2 - 3\left(\frac{3}{2}\right) - 4 = -\frac{25}{4}$. Thus, the vertex is at $\left(\frac{3}{2}, -\frac{25}{4}\right)$.

The x-intercepts are where $x^2 - 3x - 4 = 0$. We can easily factor the equation into: $(x-4)(x+1) = 0$, so the x-intercepts are at $(4,0)$ and $(-1,0)$.

It looks like this:

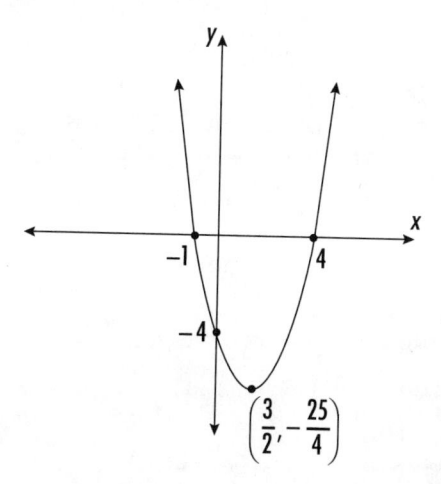

Sometimes you will be given a parabola where x is in terms of y rather than the other way around. Then the parabola opens *sideways* instead of up or down. The equation of a sideways parabola is $x = ay^2 + by + c$.

If $a > 0$, the parabola opens to the right. If $a < 0$, the parabola opens to the left.

As with the parabola that opens up or down, we are only concerned with a few points: the vertex, the x-intercepts, and the y-intercept. We will find these points in the same manner as the previous parabola, but with the roles of x and y reversed.

The **x-intercept** is the point where the curve crosses the x-axis. If we want to find the x-intercept of any curve, we plug in 0 for y. Here, we get $x = c$. Therefore, the parabola will go through the point $(c, 0)$.

The **vertex** of a parabola occurs at the point where $y = -\frac{b}{2a}$. To find the corresponding x-coordinate, plug $-\frac{b}{2a}$ in for y into the equation and find x.

The **y-intercepts** are the points where the curve crosses the y-axis; that is, where $ay^2 + by + c = 0$. These are also called the *roots* of the equation. Not all parabolas will cross the y-axis, but to find the points, either factor the equation or use the quadratic formula.

Example 2:

Find the intercepts and the vertex of $x = y^2 + 2y - 8$ and graph the equation.

Here we have $a = 1$, $b = 2$, and $c = -8$.

The x-intercept is at the point $(c, 0)$ so the x-intercept is at $(-8, 0)$.

The vertex is at $y = -\frac{b}{2a}$, so the vertex is $y = -\frac{(2)}{2(1)} = -1$. When we plug -1 into the equation, we get: $x = (-1)^2 + 2(-1) - 8 = -9$. Thus, the vertex is at $(-9, -1)$.

The y-intercepts are where $y^2 + 2y - 8 = 0$. We can factor the equation into: $(y + 4)(y - 2) = 0$, so the y-intercepts are at $(0, 2)$ and $(0, -4)$.

It looks like this:

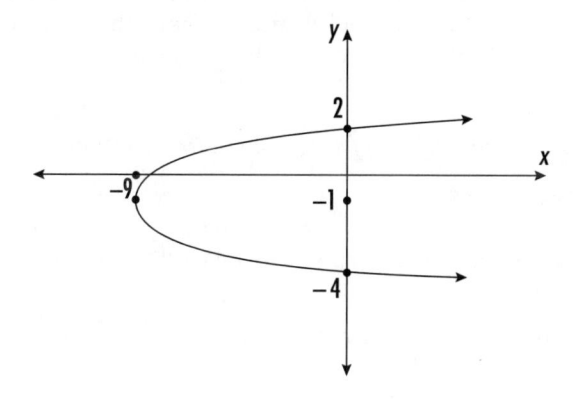

CIRCLES

A *circle* is a set of all points in the plane equidistant from a fixed point called a *center*. The line segment from the center to any point on the circle is the *radius*.

The equation of a circle with a center at (h,k) and a radius r is given by $(x-h)^2 + (y-k)^2 = r^2$.

Example 3:

Find the equation of a circle with a center at $(3,-1)$ and radius of 6.

Using the formula, the equation is $(x-3)^2 + (y-(-1))^2 = 6^2$, which can be simplified to $(x-3)^2 + (y+1)^2 = 36$. It looks like this:

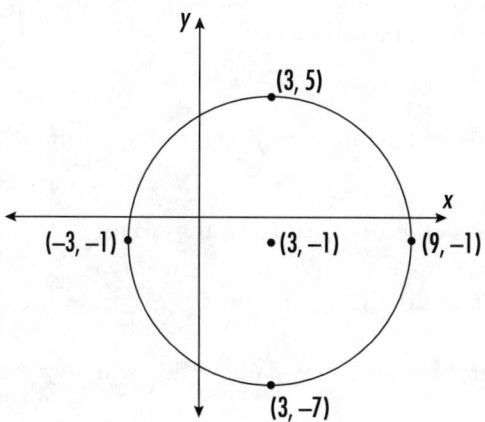

Sometimes we will need to complete the square on x or y to put the equation in a form that we can work with. If you are unfamiliar or uncomfortable with this technique, review the chapter on quadratic equations. Let's do an example.

Example 4:

Find the center and radius of the circle with equation
$x^2 + y^2 + 4x - 6y = 68$.

First, group the x and y terms. $x^2 + 4x + y^2 - 6y = 68$

Complete the square on the x term: $(x+2)^2 - 4 + y^2 - 6y = 68$.

Complete the square on the y term:

$(x+2)^2 - 4 + (y-3)^2 - 9 = 68$.

Move the constant terms to the right side:

$(x+2)^2 + (y-3)^2 = 68 + 4 + 9$.

Therefore, the equation of the circle is $(x+2)^2 + (y-3)^2 = 81$.

The circle has center $(-2, 3)$ and radius 9.

ELLIPSES

An *ellipse* is the set of all points in the plane the sum of whose distances from two fixed points is a constant. Each point is called a *focus*, and together are called *foci*.

> The equation of an ellipse centered at the origin is $\dfrac{x^2}{a^2} + \dfrac{y^2}{b^2} = 1$.
>
> The value a is the distance from the origin to the x-intercepts.
>
> The value b is the distance from the origin to the y-intercepts.
>
> The greater of a and b is called the *major axis*.
>
> The lesser of a and b is called the *minor axis*.

The foci are found by the square root of the positive difference between a^2 and b^2. That is, if the foci are designated by c, then $c = \pm\sqrt{a^2 - b^2}$ (or $c = \pm\sqrt{b^2 - a^2}$), and are located on the major axis.

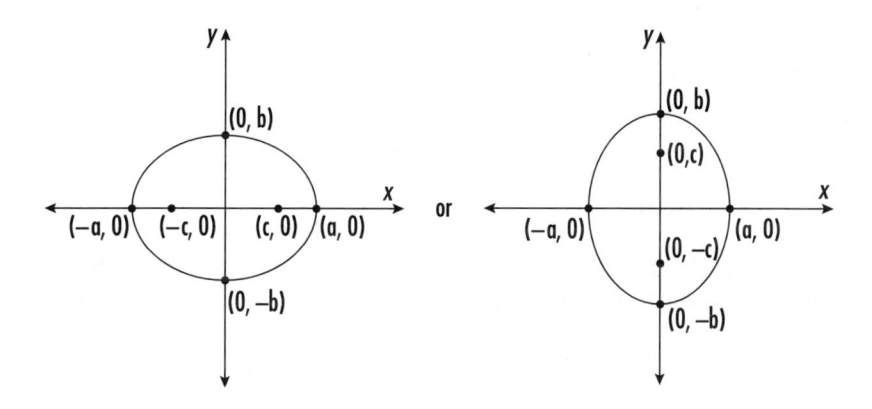

Example 5:

Find the foci and graph $\dfrac{x^2}{4} + \dfrac{y^2}{9} = 1$.

First, rewrite the equation as: $\dfrac{x^2}{2^2} + \dfrac{y^2}{3^2} = 1$.

Thus $a = 2$ and $b = 3$, so the major axis is 3 and the minor axis it 2.

We find the foci by $c = \pm\sqrt{9 - 4} = \pm\sqrt{5}$. Thus, the foci are $\left(0, \sqrt{5}\right)$ and $\left(0, -\sqrt{5}\right)$.

The graph looks like this:

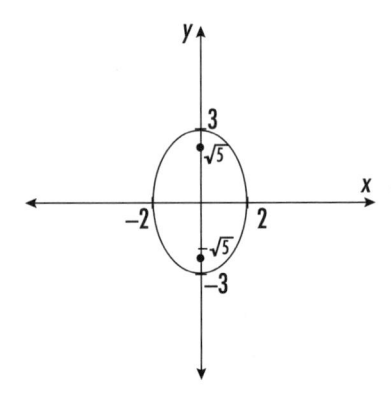

There are more complicated aspects to ellipses, particularly when they aren't centered at the origin, but we won't treat them here.

Hyperbolas

A *hyperbola* is the set of all points in the plane the difference of whose distances from two fixed points is a constant. Each point is called a *focus*, and together are called *foci*.

The equation of a hyperbola centered at the origin is either:

$$\frac{x^2}{a^2} - \frac{y^2}{b^2} = 1 \text{ (if it opens sideways);}$$

$$\text{or } \frac{y^2}{a^2} - \frac{x^2}{b^2} = 1 \text{ (if it opens up and down).}$$

A hyperbola will only intercept one of the two coordinate axes. For a "sideways" hyperbola:

- The value a is the distance from the origin to the x-intercepts.
- There are no y-intercepts.

For an "up and down" hyperbola:

- The value a is the distance from the origin to the y-intercepts.

- There are no x-intercepts.
- The foci are designated by c, and are found by $c = \pm\sqrt{a^2 + b^2}$. The foci are located on the same axis as the intercepts.

There are oblique asymptotes for a hyperbola. They can be found by drawing a rectangle with sides parallel to the axes that passes through the points a, −a, b, and −b. The rectangle is not part of the graph, of course, but makes it much easier to draw the graph.

Let's do an example.

Example 6:

Find the intercepts and foci and graph the hyperbola with equation $\frac{x^2}{4} - \frac{y^2}{9} = 1$.

We can rewrite the equation as $\frac{x^2}{2^2} - \frac{y^2}{3^2} = 1$.

The x-intercepts are $(2, 0)$ and $(-2, 0)$.

The foci are found by $c = \pm\sqrt{4+9} = \pm\sqrt{13}$.

We can now draw a rectangle connecting $(2, 0), (-2, 0), (0, 3),$ and $(0, -3)$.

The graph looks like this:

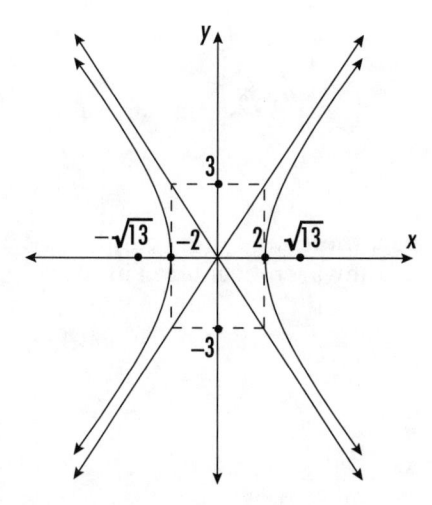

Example 7:

Find the intercepts and foci and graph the hyperbola with equation $\frac{y^2}{16} - \frac{x^2}{4} = 1$.

We can rewrite the equation as $\frac{y^2}{4^2} - \frac{x^2}{2^2} = 1$.

The y-intercepts are $(4, 0)$ and $(-4, 0)$.

The foci are found by $c = \pm\sqrt{4+16} = \pm\sqrt{20}$.

We can now draw a rectangle connecting $(2, 0), (-2, 0), (0, 4),$ and $(0, -4)$.

The graph looks like this:

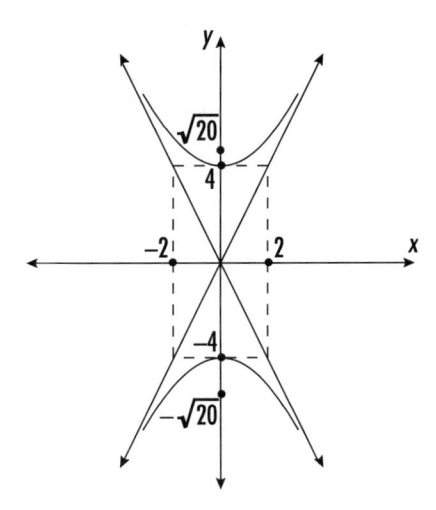

As with the ellipse, there are more complicated aspects to hyperbolas, particularly if they aren't centered at the origin, but we won't treat them here.

PROBLEMS

Find the relevant points and graph the following.

1. $y = x^2 + x - 12$
2. $x = y^2 - 4y + 3$
3. $x^2 + y^2 = 16$
4. $x^2 + y^2 - 2x + 4y - 4 = 0$
5. $\dfrac{x^2}{25} + \dfrac{y^2}{9} = 1$
6. $25x^2 + 4y^2 = 100$
7. $\dfrac{x^2}{16} - \dfrac{y^2}{9} = 1$
8. $y^2 - x^2 = 25$

CHAPTER 12
Solutions to Practice Problems

Rational and Radical Expressions
1. x
2. $3-x$
3. $x = 2$
4. $x = 3$
5. $x = 4 \pm 2\sqrt{2}$
6. $x = -1$
7. $x = 2, 5$
8. $x = 13$
9. $x = 9, 25$
10. $x = -7$

Degrees and Radians

1. 120°
2. 30°
3. 315°
4. $\dfrac{720°}{\pi}$ or ≈ 229.2°
5. $\dfrac{7\pi}{6}$
6. $\dfrac{\pi}{2}$
7. $\dfrac{6\pi}{5}$
8. $\dfrac{2\pi}{9}$
9. 2
10. a. $\dfrac{8\pi}{3}$ b. $\dfrac{32\pi}{3}$
11. a. $\dfrac{4\pi}{3}$ b. 4π
12. 90°

Definitions of Trig Functions

1. $\sin A = \dfrac{5}{13}$ $\cos A = \dfrac{12}{13}$ $\tan A = \dfrac{5}{12}$

   $\cot A = \dfrac{12}{5}$ $\sec A = \dfrac{13}{12}$ $\csc A = \dfrac{13}{5}$

2. $\sin B = \dfrac{12}{13}$ $\cos B = \dfrac{5}{13}$ $\tan B = \dfrac{12}{5}$

   $\cot B = \dfrac{5}{12}$ $\sec B = \dfrac{13}{5}$ $\csc B = \dfrac{13}{12}$

3. $\sin A = \dfrac{7}{25}$ $\cos A = \dfrac{24}{25}$ $\tan A = \dfrac{7}{24}$

$$\cot A = \frac{24}{7} \qquad \sec A = \frac{25}{24} \qquad \csc A = \frac{25}{7}$$

4. $\sin B = \dfrac{24}{25} \qquad \cos B = \dfrac{7}{25} \qquad \tan B = \dfrac{24}{7}$

$$\cot B = \frac{7}{24} \qquad \sec B = \frac{25}{7} \qquad \csc B = \frac{25}{24}$$

5. $\sin A = \dfrac{4}{\sqrt{65}} \qquad \cos A = \dfrac{7}{\sqrt{65}} \qquad \tan A = \dfrac{4}{7}$

$$\cot A = \frac{7}{4} \qquad \sec A = \frac{\sqrt{65}}{7} \qquad \csc A = \frac{\sqrt{65}}{4}$$

6. $\sin B = \dfrac{7}{\sqrt{65}} \qquad \cos B = \dfrac{4}{\sqrt{65}} \qquad \tan B = \dfrac{7}{4}$

$$\cot B = \frac{4}{7} \qquad \sec B = \frac{\sqrt{65}}{4} \qquad \csc B = \frac{\sqrt{65}}{7}$$

How to Remember the Special Angles

1. $-\dfrac{\sqrt{3}}{2}$
2. $-\dfrac{\sqrt{3}}{2}$
3. $-\sqrt{3}$
4. $\dfrac{2}{\sqrt{3}}$
5. 2
6. 1
7. $\dfrac{1}{2}$
8. $-\dfrac{\sqrt{2}}{2}$
9. -1
10. $-\dfrac{1}{2}$

Trig Formulas

1. $-\dfrac{\sqrt{104}}{15}$
2. $-\dfrac{24}{25}$
3. $\dfrac{\sqrt{55}}{8}$
4. $\dfrac{-11}{\sqrt{96}}$
5. $\dfrac{1-\sqrt{3}}{1+\sqrt{3}}$
6. $\dfrac{\sqrt{6}+\sqrt{2}}{4}$
7. $-\dfrac{\sqrt{3}}{2}$
8. $\dfrac{\sqrt{6}+\sqrt{2}}{4}$
9. 0
10. -1
11. 1
12. -1
13. a. $\dfrac{63}{65}$ b. $\dfrac{16}{65}$ c. $\dfrac{33}{56}$
14. a. $\dfrac{2-2\sqrt{10}}{9}$ b. $\dfrac{\sqrt{5}-4\sqrt{2}}{9}$ c. $\dfrac{-2\sqrt{10}-2}{\sqrt{5}-4\sqrt{2}}$

Double Angle Formulas

1. $\dfrac{23}{25}$
2. $\dfrac{4\sqrt{7}}{121}$
3. $-\sqrt{3}$

4. $-\dfrac{24}{25}$

5. $-\dfrac{3}{5}$

6. $\dfrac{\sqrt{3}}{2}$

7. $-\dfrac{1}{2}$

8. $-\dfrac{\sqrt{3}}{3}$

9. $-\dfrac{\sqrt{3}}{2}$

10. $-\dfrac{\sqrt{3}}{2}$

11. $-\dfrac{79}{81}$

Trig Equations

1. $30°, 90°, 150°, 270°$
2. $60°, 90°, 270°, 300°$
3. $0°, 180°$
4. $31°, 180°, 329°$
5. $60°, 90°, 120°, 270°$
6. $90°, 183°, 270°, 357°$
7. $30°, 60°, 210°, 240°$
8. $0°, 30°, 60°, 120°, 150°, 180°, 240°, 270°, 300°$
9. $15°, 22.5°, 67.5°, 75°, 105°, 112.5, 157.5°, 165°$
10. $0°, 45°, 60°, 105°, 120°, 165°, 180°$

SINE AND COSINE GRAPHS

1. Amplitude is: 3

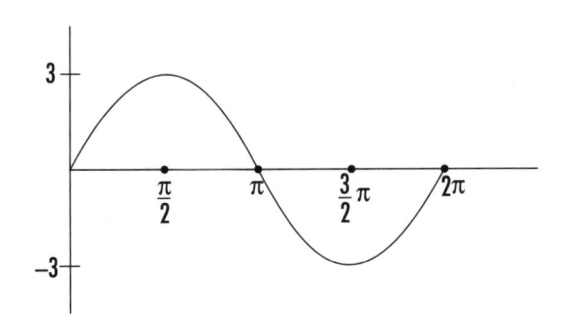

2. Amplitude is: 2; Vertical Shift is: up 3

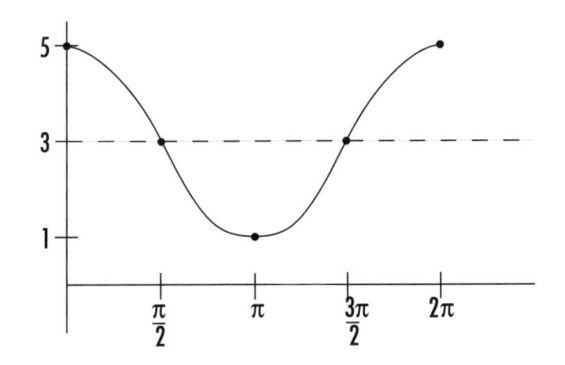

3. Amplitude is: $\frac{1}{2}$; Period is: π; Inverted

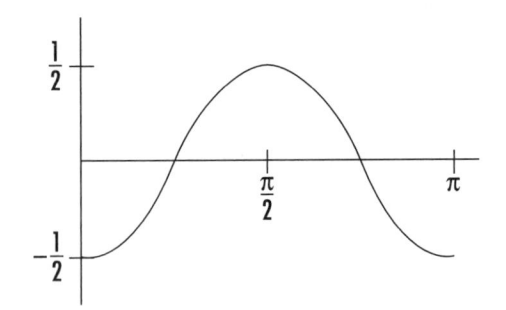

4) Amplitude is: 4; Period is: $\frac{\pi}{2}$

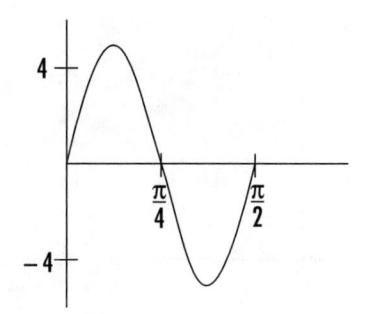

5) Horizontal Shift is: left $\frac{\pi}{2}$

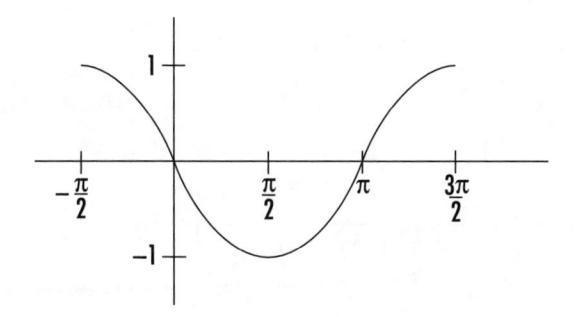

6) Period is: 8; Horizontal Shift is: left 1

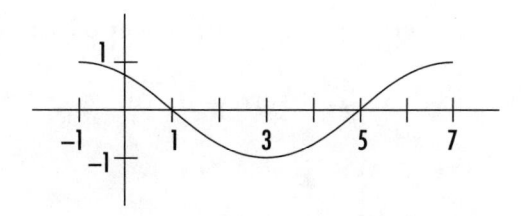

7) Amplitude is: 3; Period is: π; Horizontal Shift is: left $\frac{\pi}{4}$

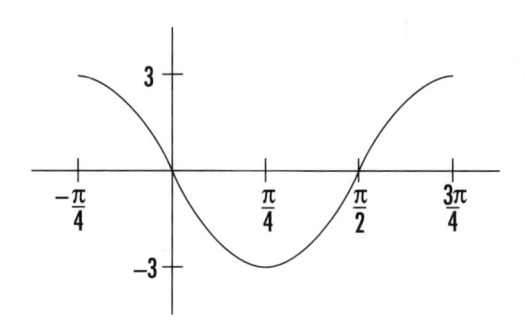

8) Period is: π; Horizontal Shift is: right $\frac{\pi}{6}$

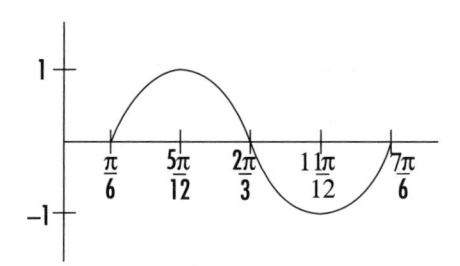

9) Amplitude is: 2; Vertical Shift is: up 1; Period is: $\frac{2\pi}{3}$; Horizontal Shift is: right $\frac{\pi}{8}$; Inverted

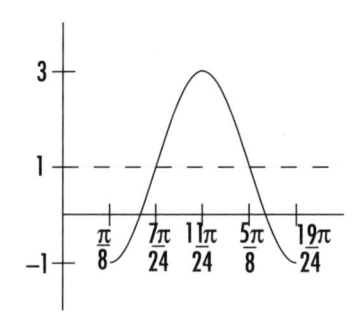

10) Amplitude is: 4; Period is: 12; Horizontal Shift is: left 2; Vertical Shift is: down 1

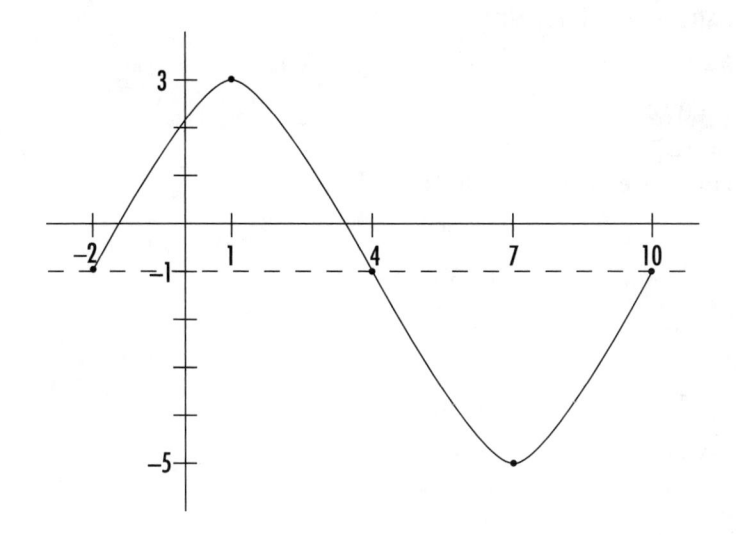

INVERSE TRIG FUNCTIONS

1. $270°$ or $\dfrac{3\pi}{2}$

2. $330°$ or $\dfrac{11\pi}{6}$

3. $30°$ or $\dfrac{\pi}{6}$

4. $\dfrac{\sqrt{2}}{2}$

5. $\dfrac{8}{17}$

6. $-\dfrac{4}{3}$

7. $\dfrac{3}{2}$

8. $\dfrac{\sqrt{3}}{2}$

9. $315°$ or $\dfrac{7\pi}{4}$

10. $\frac{3\pi}{4}$ or $135°$

APPLICATIONS OF TRIGONOMETRY

1. $b = 6$
2. $B = 39.4°$
3. $c = 12.7$
4. There are two possible triangles.

   $a = 5$ $A = 30°$
   $b = 6$ $B = 37°$
   $c = 9.2$ $C = 113°$
   and
   $a = 5$ $A = 30°$
   $b = 6$ $B = 143°$
   $c = 1.2$ $C = 7°$

5. $a = 6.7$ $A = 34°$
   $b = 12$ $B = 89.6°$
   $c = 10$ $C = 56.4°$

6. $a = 20$ $A = 36.3°$
   $b = 15$ $B = 26.4°$
   $c = 30$ $C = 117.3°$

7. Area is $30\sqrt{2}$
8. Area is 31.4
9. $y = 43$
10. Distance is 130 km.

COMPLEX NUMBERS

1. $11 - 2i$
2. $-2 - 2i$
3. $38 + 37i$
4. $3 + 3i$
5. $-i$

6. $-\dfrac{7}{5} - \dfrac{11}{5}i$
7. 17
8. $15cis307°$
9. $4\sqrt{3} + 4i$
10. $7cis90°$
11. $-5i$
12. -4

PROBABILITY

1. $\dfrac{1}{6}$
2. $\dfrac{2}{9}$
3. $\dfrac{3}{4}$
4. $\dfrac{21}{136}$
5. $\dfrac{14}{285}$
6. $\dfrac{5}{16}$
7. $\dfrac{1}{2}$
8. $\dfrac{5}{32}$
9. $\dfrac{27}{128}$
10. $\dfrac{1}{9}$

STATISTICS

1. 7.25
2. 7.5
3. 7
4. 2.4

5. 5
6. 5.5
7. 6
8. 2
9. 22.9 cm.
10. 2.7 cm.
11. 67 and 97
12. 95%

TRANSFORMATIONS

1. $A'(0,7)$ $B'(-3,3)$ $C'(-2,0)$
2. $A''(2,-5)$ $B''(-1,-1)$ $C''(0,2)$
3. $A'''(4,10)$ $B'''(-2,2)$ $C'''(0,-4)$
4. $A'(1,3)$ $B'(-4,3)$ $C'(0,0)$
5. $A''(4,-4)$ $B''(4,1)$ $C''(1,-3)$
6. $A'''(-3,-1)$ $B'''(-3,4)$ $C'''(0,0)$
7. $A'(-4,-3)$ $B'(4,-3)$ $C'(-1,0)$
8. $A''(-4,3)$ $B''(4,3)$ $C''(-1,0)$
9. $A'''\left(-2,\frac{3}{2}\right)$ $B'''\left(2,\frac{3}{2}\right)$ $C'''\left(-\frac{1}{2},0\right)$
10. $A'(-4,2)$ $B'(1,-1)$ $C'(3,3)$
11. $A''(10,6)$ $B''(0,0)$ $C''(-4,8)$
12. $A'''(4,-2)$ $B'''(-1,1)$ $C'''(-3,-3)$

Quadratic Equations

1. $x = 2$ and $x = -\frac{1}{2}$
2. $x = 3 + 2i$ and $x = 3 - 2i$
3. $x = \frac{7}{4} + \frac{\sqrt{137}}{4}$ and $x = \frac{7}{4} - \frac{\sqrt{137}}{4}$

4. $x = -\dfrac{3}{4}$ and $x = \dfrac{7}{3}$
5. $x = 2$ and $x = -14$
6. Two, real, irrational roots.
7. $k = 2$
8. $s = -2$ and $p = -35$
9. $x^2 + 3x - 28 = 0$
10. $x^2 - 10x + 26 = 0$

Circle Rules
1. 40
2. 25
3. 4
4. 11.3
5. 40
6. 16.5
7. 12
8. 60
9. 40
10. 50
11. 80
12. 70

Logarithms
1. $x = 3$
2. $x = -5$
3. $x = 49$
4. $2 \log A - \log B$
5. $\log \dfrac{A^5}{B^3}$
6. -38
7. $x \approx 3.236$
8. $x \approx 1.927$
9. $2 \ln C + \dfrac{1}{2} \ln A - 3 \ln B$

10. $x = 3e^5 \approx 445$
11. 8.75 years
12. $1750.67

Conic Sections

1. Vertex is: $\left(-\dfrac{1}{2}, -\dfrac{49}{9}\right)$; x-intercepts are: $(-4,0)$ and $(3,0)$;
   y-intercept is: $(0,-12)$

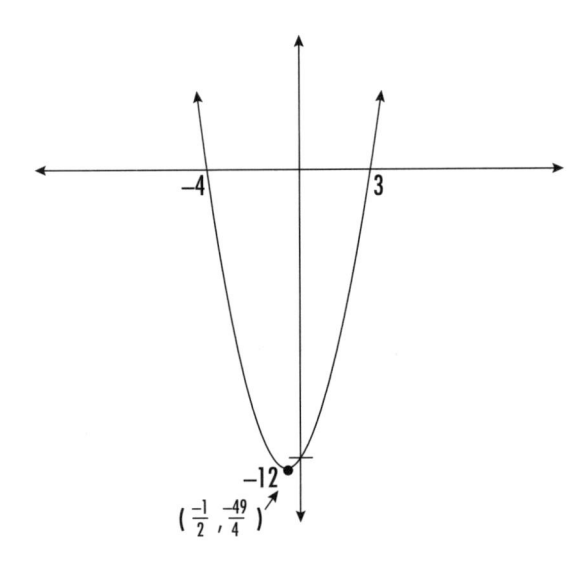

2. Vertex is: $(-1,2)$; y-intercepts are: $(0,1)$ and $(0,3)$;
   x-intercept is: $(3,0)$

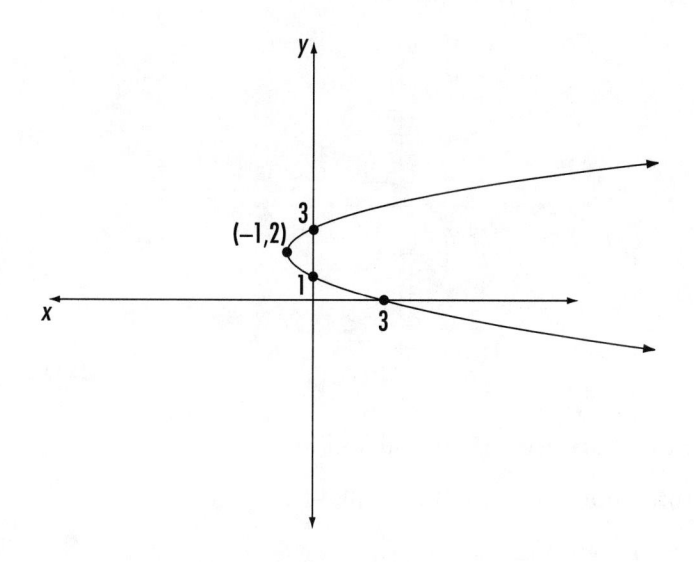

3. Center is: $(0,0)$; Radius is: 4.

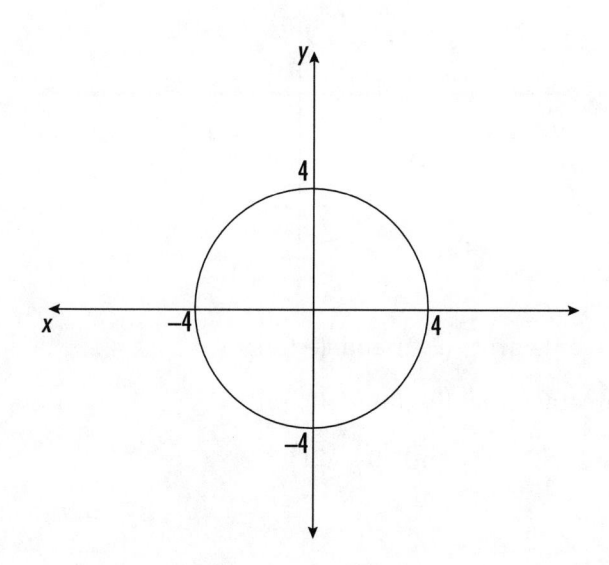

4. Center is: $(1,-2)$; Radius is: 3.

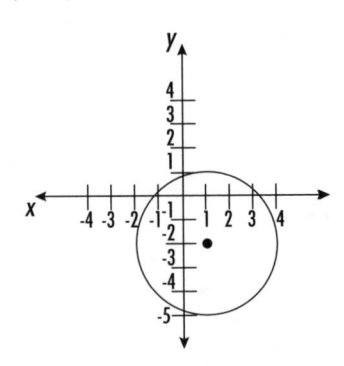

5. x-intercepts are: $(5,0)$ and $(-5,0)$;
   y-intercepts are: $(0,3)$ and $(0,-3)$;
   Foci are: $(4,0)$ and $(-4,0)$.

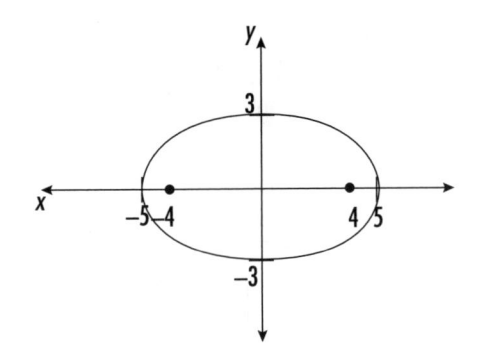

6. x-intercepts are: $(2,0)$ and $(-2,0)$;
   y-intercepts are: $(0,5)$ and $(0,-5)$;
   Foci are: $\left(0,\sqrt{21}\right)$ and $\left(0,-\sqrt{21}\right)$.

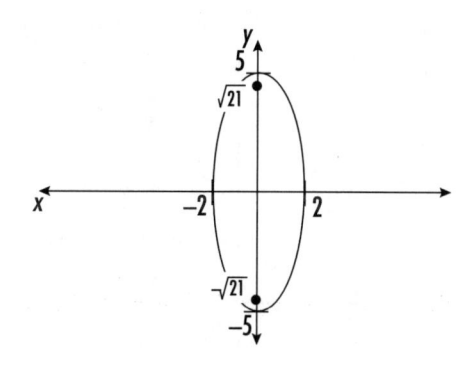

7. x-intercepts are: $(4,0)$ and $(-4,0)$;

    Foci are: $(5,0)$ and $(-5,0)$

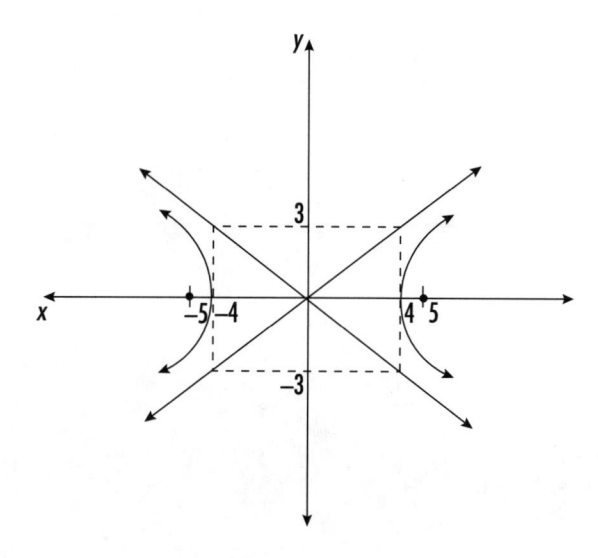

8. y-intercepts are: $(0,5)$ and $(0,-5)$;

    Foci are: $\left(0,\sqrt{50}\right)$ and $\left(0,-\sqrt{50}\right)$

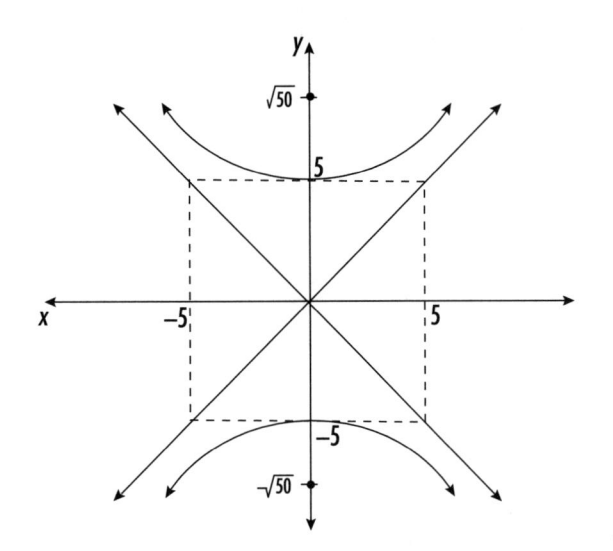

Practice Exams

Formulas

Pythagorean and Quotient Identities

$\sin^2 A + \cos^2 A = 1$ $\tan A = \dfrac{\sin A}{\cos A}$

$\tan^2 A + 1 = \sec^2 A$ $\cot A = \dfrac{\cos A}{\sin A}$

$\cot^2 A + 1 = \csc^2 A$

Functions of the Sum of Two Angles

$\sin(A + B) = \sin A \cos B + \cos A \sin B$

$\cos(A + B) = \cos A \cos B - \sin A \sin B$

$\tan(A + B) = \dfrac{\tan A + \tan B}{1 - \tan A \tan B}$

Functions of the Difference of Two Angles

$\sin(A - B) = \sin A \cos B - \cos A \sin B$

$\cos(A - B) = \cos A \cos B + \sin A \sin B$

$\tan(A - B) = \dfrac{\tan A - \tan B}{1 + \tan A \tan B}$

Law of Sines

$\dfrac{a}{\sin A} = \dfrac{b}{\sin B} = \dfrac{c}{\sin C}$

Law of Cosines

$a^2 = b^2 + c^2 - 2bc \cos A$

Functions of the Double Angle

$\sin 2A = 2 \sin A \cos A$

$\cos 2A = \cos^2 A - \sin^2 A$

$\cos 2A = 2 \cos^2 A - 1$

$\cos 2A = 1 - 2 \sin^2 A$

$\tan 2A = \dfrac{2 \tan A}{1 - \tan^2 A}$

Functions of the Half Angle

$\sin \dfrac{1}{2} A = \pm \sqrt{\dfrac{1 - \cos A}{2}}$

$\cos \dfrac{1}{2} A = \pm \sqrt{\dfrac{1 + \cos A}{2}}$

$\tan \dfrac{1}{2} A = \pm \sqrt{\dfrac{1 - \cos A}{1 + \cos A}}$

Area of Triangle

$A = \dfrac{1}{2} ab \sin C$

Standard of Division

$\text{S.D.} = \sqrt{\dfrac{1}{n} \sum_{i=1}^{n} (\overline{x} - x_i)^2}$

PRACTICE EXAM ONE

Part I

Answer 30 questions from this part. Each correct answer will receive 2 credits. No partial credit will be allowed. Write your ansers in the spaces procided on the separate answer sheet. Where applicable, answers may be left in terms of π or in radical form.

---

1. If $f(x) = \sqrt{3x} + \sqrt{12x}$, express f(-3) as a monomial in terms of i.

2. If $7^{x^2+x} = 49$, find the positive value of x.

3. Express 160° in radian measure.

4. If cos 72° = sin x, find the number of degrees in the measure of acute angle x.

5. If $f(x) = x^{\frac{1}{2}} + x^{-2}$, what is the value of f(4)?

6. Find the value of $\sum_{x=0}^{2} 2^x$.

7. Perform the indicated operations and express in simplest form:

   $$\frac{a+8}{7a^2} \cdot \frac{3a^2 - 24a}{a^2 - 64}$$

8. Express sin 75° cos 15°− cos 75° sin 15° as a single trigonometric function of a positive acute angle.

9. If $f(x) = x^2$ and $g(x) = x + 1$, what is (f ∘ g)(2)?

10. In which quadrant does the graph of the sum of 6 + 4i and 3 − 5i lie?

11. Two tangents are drawn to circle O from external point P. If the major arc formed has a measure of 280°, find m∠P.

12. If $\sin\theta = -\frac{8}{17}$ and $\tan\theta$ is positive, what is the value of $\cos\theta$?

13. Find, to the *nearest tenth*, the positive value of x in the equation $\sqrt{x^2+21} = 2x$.

14. If the coordinates of A are (2,−3), what are the coordinates of A′, the image of A after $R_{90°} \, r_{\text{y-axis}}(A)$?

15. In the accompanying diagram, $\overline{AD}$ is tangent to circle O at D and $\overline{ABC}$ is a secant. If AD = 6 and AC = 9, find AB.

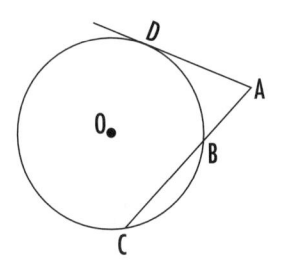

Directions (16-35): For *each* question chosen, write on the separate answer sheet the *numeral* preceding the word or expression that best completes the statement or answers the question.

16. In the accompanying table, y varies inversely as x.

x	3	6	12
y	8	4	z

    What is the value of z?

    (1) $\frac{1}{2}$ (3) 3

    (2) 2   (4) $\frac{1}{4}$

17. What is the solution set of the equation $|2x+1|=9$?
    (1) {-5}   (3) {4,-5}
    (2) {-4,5}   (4) {4}

18. The expression $\log\left(\dfrac{x^n}{\sqrt{y}}\right)$ is equivalent to

    (1) $n \log x - \frac{1}{2}\log y$
    (2) $n \log x - 2 \log y$
    (3) $\log(nx) - \log\left(\frac{1}{2}y\right)$
    (4) $\log(nx) - \log(2y)$

19. Which value is *not* in the range of the equation $y = \sin x$?

    (1) 1   (3) $\frac{1}{2}$

    (2) 2   (4) $-\frac{1}{2}$

20. Which trigonometric function is equivalent to the expression $\dfrac{\sin 2x}{2\sin x}$?

(1) tan x
(2) cot x
(3) sin x
(4) cos x

21. For which value of θ is the expression $\dfrac{2}{\tan\theta - 1}$ undefined?

(1) 0
(2) $\dfrac{3\pi}{4}$
(3) $\dfrac{\pi}{4}$
(4) $-\dfrac{\pi}{4}$

22. The value of $\sin\left(\dfrac{3\pi}{2}\right) - \cos\left(\dfrac{\pi}{3}\right)$ is

(1) $-1\dfrac{1}{2}$
(2) $1\dfrac{1}{2}$
(3) $\dfrac{1}{2}$
(4) $-\dfrac{1}{2}$

23. In which quadrants does the equation $xy = 10$ lie?
  (1) I and II
  (2) I and III
  (3) II and IV
  (4) III and IV

24. A set of scores with a normal distribution has a mean of 32 and a standard deviation of 3.7. Which score could be expected to occur the *least* often?
  (1) 26
  (2) 29
  (3) 36
  (4) 40

25. Which equation is represented in the graph below?

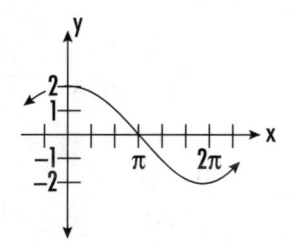

(1) $y = 2 \cos 2x$
(2) $y = \frac{1}{2} \cos 2x$
(3) $y = 2 \cos \frac{1}{2}x$
(4) $y = \frac{1}{2} \cos \frac{1}{2}x$

26. The product of $5 - 2i$ and i is
    (1) 7
    (2) $2 + 5i$
    (3) $5 - 2i$
    (4) $-2 + 5i$

27. Expressed in simplest form, $\dfrac{n - \frac{1}{n}}{1 + \frac{1}{n}}$ is equivalent to

    (1) $n - 1$
    (2) $n + 1$
    (3) $\dfrac{n-1}{n+1}$
    (4) n

28. Which is the equation of the inverse of $y = \frac{3}{2}x$?

    (1) $y = \frac{2}{3}x$
    (2) $y = -\frac{3}{2}x$
    (3) $y = 3x - 2$
    (4) $y = \dfrac{x+3}{2}$

29. In a triangle, the sides measure 3, 5, and 7. What is the measure, in degrees, of the largest angle?
    (1) 60
    (2) 90
    (3) 120
    (4) 150

30. In △ABC, m∠A = 45, m∠B = 30, and side a = 10. What is the length of side b?
    (1) $5\sqrt{2}$
    (2) $5\sqrt{3}$
    (3) $10\sqrt{2}$
    (4) $10\sqrt{3}$

31. Which relation is *not* a function?
    (1) $\{(x,y) | y = \cos x\}$
    (2) $\{(x,y) | x = y\}$
    (3) $\{(x,y) | y = 3^x\}$
    (4) $\{(x,y) | x = 3\}$

32. The roots of the quadratic equation $4x^2 = 2 + 7x$ are best described as
    (1) real, equal, and rational
    (2) real, unequal, and rational
    (3) real, unequal, and irrational
    (4) imaginary

33. What is the area of a parallelogram if two adjacent sides measure 4 and 5 and an included angle measures 60°?
    (1) $5\sqrt{2}$
    (2) $10\sqrt{2}$
    (3) $5\sqrt{3}$
    (4) $10\sqrt{3}$

34. Which quadratic equation has roots $2 + i$ and $2 - i$?
    (1) $x^2 + 4x + 5 = 0$
    (2) $x^2 - 4x - 5 = 0$
    (3) $x^2 + 4x - 5 = 0$
    (4) $x^2 - 4x + 5 = 0$

35. If three fair coins are tossed, what is the probability of getting *at least* two heads?
    (1) $\frac{1}{8}$
    (2) $\frac{3}{8}$
    (3) $\frac{1}{2}$
    (4) $\frac{2}{3}$

PART TWO

Directions: *Answer four questions from this part. Clearly indicate the necessary step, including appropriate formula substitutions, diagrams, graphs, charts, etc. Calculations that may be obtained by mental arithmetic or the calculator do not need to be shown.*

36a. Given the equation: $y = 2\sin\frac{1}{2}x$

  (1) On graph paper, sketch and label the graph of this equation in the interval $0 \leq x \leq 2\pi$.

  (2) On the same set of axes, sketch the image of the graph drawn in part $a(1)$ after the transformation $r_{\text{x-axis}}$. Label the graph T.

  (3) Write the equation of the graph drawn in part $a(2)$.

b. The graph below *incorrectly* represents the equation $y = 2\cos x$. Write a mathematical explanation of why this graph is incorrect.

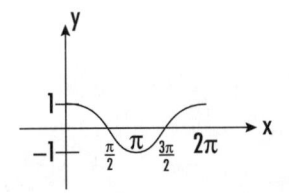

37a. On graph paper, sketch the graph of the equation $y = 2^x$ the interval $-3 \leq x \leq 3$.

b. On the same set of axes, reflect the graph drawn in part a in the y–axis and label it b.

c. Write an equation of the function graphed in part b.

d. On the same set of axes, reflect the graph drawn in part a in line $y = x$ and label the reflection d.

e. Write an equation of the function graphed in part d.

38a. In the accompanying diagram, regular pentagon $ABCDE$ is inscribed in circle O, chords $\overline{EC}$ and $\overline{DB}$ intersect at F, chord $\overline{DB}$ is extended to G, and tangent $\overline{GA}$ is drawn.

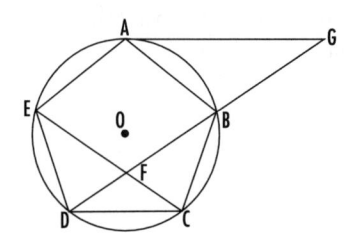

Find:

(1) $m\angle BDE$

(2) $m\angle BFC$

(3) $m\angle AGD$

b. In the accompanying diagram of circle O, chords $\overline{AB}$ and $\overline{CD}$ intersect at E, AE = x, EB = x + 1, CE = x − 1, and ED = 2x. Find AE.

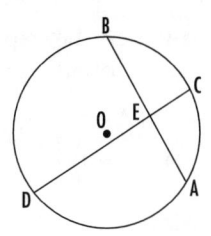

39a. Solve for x to the *nearest hundredth*:

$$6^x = 45$$

b. Find, to the *nearest degree*, all values of x in the interval $0° \leq x \leq 360°$ that satisfy the equation $3 \sin^2 x - 2 \sin x = 1$

40. Two forces act on an object. The first force has a magnitude of 85 pounds and makes an angle of 31°30′ with the resultant. The magnitude of the resultant is 130 pounds.

   a. Find the magnitude of the second force to the *nearest tenth of a pound*.

   b. Using the results from part *a*, find to the *nearest ten minutes* or *nearest tenth of a degree*, the angle that the second force makes with the resultant.

41a. If a letter is selected at random from the name **MARILYN** in five separate trials, what is the probability that the M is chosen *exactly* three times?

   b. If a letter is selcted at random from the name **DAPHNE** in seven separate trials, what is the probability that a vowel is chosen *at least* six times?]

c. If a letter is selected at random from the name **NORMA** in six separate trials, what is the probability that a consonant is chosen *at most* once?

42a. For all values of x for which the expressions are defined, prove that the following is an identity:
$$\frac{\sin(A+B)+\sin(A-B)}{\sin(A+B)-\sin(A-B)} = \frac{\tan A}{\tan B}$$

b. During a 10-game season, a high school football team scored the following number of points:
14, 17, 21, 10, 35, 27, 13, 7, 45, 21

Find the standard deviation of these scores to the *nearest tenth*.

ANSWER KEY

Part I

(1) $9i$
(2) 1
(3) $\dfrac{8\pi}{9}$
(4) 18
(5) $2\dfrac{1}{16}$
(6) 7
(7) $\dfrac{3}{7a}$
(8) $\sin 60°$
(9) 9
(10) IV
(11) 100
(12) $-\dfrac{15}{17}$

(13) 2.6
(14) (3,–2)
(15) 4
(16) 2
(17) 3
(18) 1
(19) 2
(20) 4
(21) 3
(22) 1
(23) 2
(24) 4

(25) 3
(26) 2
(27) 1
(28) 1
(29) 3
(30) 1
(31) 4
(32) 2
(33) 4
(34) 4
(35) 3

Part II

(36) a (3) $y = -2 \sin \frac{1}{2}x$
   b   Amplitude should be 2.
       or
       an equivalent statement

(37) c $y = 2^{-x}$
   e $x = 2^y$ or $y = \log_2 x$

(38) a (1) 72
       (2) 72
       (3) 36
   b 3

(39) a   2.12
   b   90°, 199°, 341°

(40) a   72.7
   b   37.7° or 37°40′

(41) a $\dfrac{360}{16807}$

   b $\dfrac{15}{2187}$

   c $\dfrac{640}{15625}$

(42) b   11.2

Formulas

Pythagoream and Quotient Identities

$\sin^2 A + \cos^2 A = 1 \qquad \tan A = \dfrac{\sin A}{\cos A}$

$\tan^2 A + 1 = \sec^2 A \qquad \cot A = \dfrac{\cos A}{\sin A}$

$\cot^2 A + 1 = \csc^2 A$

Functions of the Sum of Two Angles

$\sin(A + B) = \sin A \cos B + \cos A \sin B$

$\cos(A + B) = \cos A \cos B - \sin A \sin B$

$\tan(A + B) = \dfrac{\tan A + \tan B}{1 - \tan A \tan B}$

Functions of the Difference of Two Angles

$\sin(A - B) = \sin A \cos B - \cos A \sin B$

$\cos(A - B) = \cos A \cos B + \sin A \sin B$

$\tan(A - B) = \dfrac{\tan A - \tan B}{1 + \tan A \tan B}$

Law of Sines

$\dfrac{a}{\sin A} = \dfrac{b}{\sin B} = \dfrac{c}{\sin C}$

Law of Cosines

$a^2 = b^2 + c^2 - 2bc \cos A$

Functions of the Double Angle

$\sin 2A = 2 \sin A \cos A$

$\cos 2A = \cos^2 A - \sin^2 A$

$\cos 2A = 2 \cos^2 A - 1$

$\cos 2A = 1 - 2 \sin^2 A$

$\tan 2A = \dfrac{2 \tan A}{1 - \tan^2 A}$

Functions of the Half Angle

$\sin \dfrac{1}{2} A = \pm \sqrt{\dfrac{1 - \cos A}{2}}$

$\cos \dfrac{1}{2} A = \pm \sqrt{\dfrac{1 + \cos A}{2}}$

$\tan \dfrac{1}{2} A = \pm \sqrt{\dfrac{1 - \cos A}{1 + \cos A}}$

Area of Triangle

$A = \dfrac{1}{2} ab \sin C$

Standard of Division

$\text{S.D.} = \sqrt{\dfrac{1}{n} \sum_{i=1}^{n} (\bar{x} - x_i)^2}$

PRACTICE EXAM TWO

Part I

Answer 30 questions from this part. Each correct answer will receive 2 credits. No partial credit will be allowed. Write your answers in the spaces provided. Where applicable, answers may be left in terms of π or in radical form.

---

1. Express 240° in the radian measure.

2. In $\triangle ABC$, $a = 12$, $\sin A = 0.45$, and $\sin B = 0.15$. Find b.

3. Find the value of $\sum_{k=1}^{3}(3k-5)$.

4. Solve for x: $4^{(3x+5)} = 16$.

5. Express the sum of $\sqrt{-64}$ and $3\sqrt{-4}$ as a monomial in terms of i.

6. Solve for all values of x: $|2x+5| = 7$.

7. What will be the amplitude of the image of the curve $y = 2 \sin 3x$ after a dilation of scale factor 2?

8. What is the solution of the equation $\sqrt{5x-9} - 3 = 1$?

9. In the interval $90° \leq \theta \leq 180°$, find the value of θ that satisfies the equation $2 \sin \theta - 1 = 0$.

10. Express in simplest form: $\dfrac{1}{\dfrac{1}{a}+\dfrac{1}{b}}$.

11. If $f(x) = x^0 + x^{\frac{2}{3}} + x^{-\frac{2}{3}}$, find $f(8)$.

12. When the sum of $4 + 5i$ and $-3 - 7i$ is represented graphically, in which quadrant does the sum lie?

13. In the accompanying diagram, $\overline{AP}$ is a tangent and $\overline{PBC}$ is a secant to circle O. If $PC = 12$ and $BC = 9$, find the length of $\overline{AP}$.

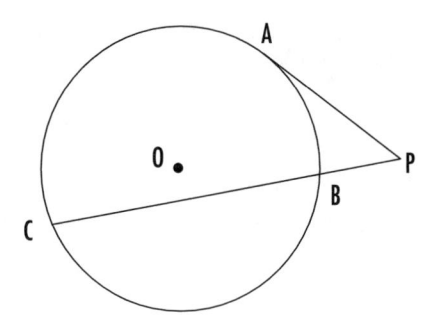

14. Circle O has a radius of 10. Find the length of an arc subtended by a central angle measuring 1.5 radians.

15. If $f(x) = 5x - 2$ and $g(x) = \sqrt[3]{x}$, evaluate $(f \circ g)(-8)$.

Directions (16-35): For *each* question chosen, write on the separate answer sheet the *numeral* preceding the word or expression that best completes the statement or answers the question.

16. For which value of x is the expression $\dfrac{1}{1-\cos x}$ undefined?
    (1) 90°
    (2) 180°
    (3) 270°
    (4) 360°

17. The expression $\log \sqrt{\dfrac{x}{y}}$ is equivalent to
    (1) $\dfrac{1}{2}(\log x - \log y)$
    (2) $\log \dfrac{1}{2}x - \log \dfrac{1}{2}y$
    (3) $\dfrac{1}{2}\log x - \log y$
    (4) $\log \dfrac{1}{2}x - \log y$

18. If $f(x) = \cos 3x + \sin x$, then $f\left(\dfrac{\pi}{2}\right)$ equals
    (1) 1
    (2) 2
    (3) –1
    (4) 0

19. Expessed in $a + bi$ form, $(1 + 3i)^2$ is equivalent to
    (1) 10 + 6i
    (2) –8 + 6i
    (3) 10 – 6i
    (4) –8 – 6i

20. The expression $\dfrac{\tan\theta}{\sec\theta}$ is equivalent to
    (1) cot θ
    (2) csc θ
    (3) cos θ
    (4) sin θ

21. Which equation is represented by the graph below?

(1) $y = -2 \sin \frac{1}{2}x$ 　　(3) $y = \frac{1}{2} \sin 2x$

(2) $y = -\frac{1}{2} \sin 2x$ 　　(4) $y = 2 \sin \frac{1}{2}x$

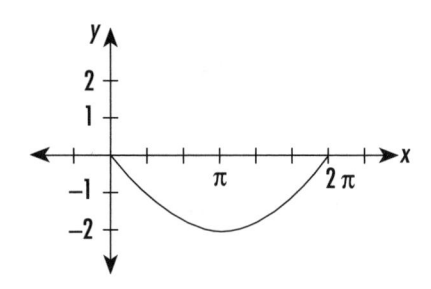

22. Expressed in $a + bi$ form, $\frac{5}{3+i}$ is equivalent to

(1) $\frac{15}{8} - \frac{5}{8}i$ 　　(3) $\frac{3}{2} - \frac{1}{2}i$

(2) $\frac{5}{3} - 5i$ 　　(4) $15 - 5i$

23. Gordon tosses a fair die six times. What is the probability that he will toss *exactly* two 5's?

(1) $_6C_5 \left(\frac{5}{6}\right)^2 \left(\frac{1}{6}\right)^4$ 　　(3) $_6C_5 \left(\frac{1}{6}\right)^2 \left(\frac{5}{6}\right)^4$

(2) $_6C_2 \left(\frac{5}{6}\right)^2 \left(\frac{1}{6}\right)^4$ 　　(4) $_6C_2 \left(\frac{1}{6}\right)^2 \left(\frac{5}{6}\right)^4$

24. If $\sin \theta$ is negative and $\cot \theta$ is positive, in which quadrant does θ terminate?
(1) I 　　(3) III
(2) II 　　(4) IV

25. The domain of the equation $y = \dfrac{1}{(x-1)^2}$ is all real numbers
    (1) greater than 1
    (2) except 1
    (3) less than 1
    (4) except 1 and –1

26. In the accompanying diagram, about 68% of the scores fall within the shaded area, which is symmetric about the mean, $\bar{x}$. The distribution is normal and the scores in the shaded area range from 50 to 80.

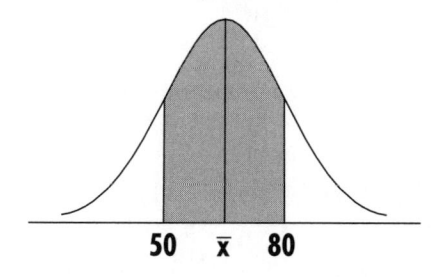

    What is the standard deviation of the scores in this distribution?
    (1) $7\dfrac{1}{2}$
    (2) 15
    (3) 30
    (4) 65

27. The expression 2 sin 30° cos 30° has the same value as
    (1) sin 15°
    (2) cos 60°
    (3) sin 60°
    (4) cos 15°

28. In the accompanying diagram of a unit circle, the ordered pair (x,y) represents the point where the terminal side of θ intersects the unit circle.

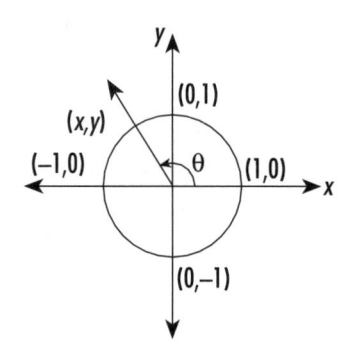

If m ∠θ = 120, what is the value of x in simplest form?

(1) $-\dfrac{\sqrt{3}}{2}$ (3) $-\dfrac{1}{2}$

(2) $\dfrac{\sqrt{3}}{2}$ (4) $\dfrac{1}{2}$

29. In △ABC, side a is twice as long as side b and m ∠C = 30. In terms of b, the area of △ ABC is
    (1) 0.25 b^2 (3) 0.866 b^2
    (2) 0.5 b^2 (4) b^2

30. Which quadratic equation has roots 3 + i and 3 − i?
    (1) $x^2 - 6x + 10 = 0$ (3) $x^2 - 6x + 8 = 0$
    (2) $x^2 + 6x - 10 = 0$ (4) $x^2 + 6x - 8 = 0$

31. Which is the fourth term in the expansion of $(\cos x + 3)^5$?
    (1) 90 $\cos^2 x$ (3) 90 $\cos^3 x$
    (2) 270 $\cos^2 x$ (4) 270 $\cos^3 x$

32. The graph of the equation $y = \dfrac{6}{x}$ forms
    (1) a hyperbola   (3) a parabola
    (2) an ellipse   (4) a straight line

33. The roots of the equation $-3x^2 = 5x + 4$ are
    (1) real, rational, and unequal
    (2) real, irrational, and unequal
    (3) real, rational, and equal
    (4) imaginary

34. Which equation does *not* represent a function?
    (1) $y = 4$ (3) $y = x - 4$
    (2) $y = x^2 - 4$ (4) $x^2 + y^2 = 4$

35. If the point (2, −5) is reflected in the line $y = x$, then the image is
    (1) (5, −2)   (3) (−5, 2)
    (2) (−2, 5)   (4) (−5, −2)

Part II

Answer four questions from this part. Clearly indicate the necessary steps, including appropriate formula substitutions, diagrams, graphs, charts, etc. Calculations that may be obtained by mental arithmetic or the calculator do not need to be shown.

36a. On the same set of axes, sketch and label the graphs of the equations $y = 2 \cos x$ and $y = \sin \frac{1}{2}x$ in the interval $-\pi \leq x \leq \pi$.

b. Using the graphs drawn in part *a*, determine the number of values in the interval $-\pi \leq x \leq \pi$ that satisfy the equation $\sin \frac{1}{2}x = 2 \cos x$.

37. In the accompanying diagram, isosceles triangle ABC is inscribed in circle O, and vertex angle BAC measures 40°. Tangent $\overline{PC}$, secant $\overline{PBA}$, and diameters $\overline{BD}$ and $\overline{AE}$ are drawn.

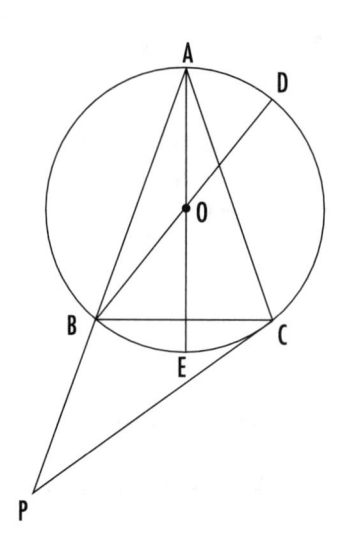

Find:

    a   m $\widehat{BC}$
    b   m $\angle ABD$
    c   m $\angle DOE$
    d   m $\angle P$
    e   m $\angle ACP$

38. Find, to the *nearest ten minutes* or *nearest tenth of a degree*, all values of x in the interval $0° \leq x < 360°$ that satisfy the equation $2 \sin 2x + \cos x = 0$.

39a. Find the standard deviation, to the *nearest hundredth*, for the following measurements:
24, 28, 29, 30, 30, 31, 32, 32, 32, 33, 35, 36.

b. A circle that is partitioned into five equal sectors has a spinner. The colors of the sectors are red, orange, yellow, blue, and green. If four spins are made, find the probability that the spinner will land in the green sector
(1) on *exactly* two spins
(2) on *at least* three spins

40a. Express in simplest form:
$$\frac{3y+15}{25-y^2} + \frac{2}{y-5}.$$

b. Solve for x and express the roots in simplest $a + bi$ form:
$$2 + \frac{5}{x^2} = \frac{6}{x}.$$

41. In $\triangle ABC$, $AB = 14$, $AC = 20$, and m$\angle CAB = 49$.

a. Find the length of $\overline{BC}$ to the *nearest tenth*.

b. Using the results from part a, find m$\angle C$ to the *nearest degree*.

42. Given: f $=\{(x,y) \mid y = \log_2 x\ \}$

a. On graph paper, sketch and label the graph of the function f.

b. Write a mathematical explanation of how to form the inverse of function f.

c. On the same set of axes, sketch and label the graph of the function f⁻¹, the inverse of f.

d. Write an equation for f⁻¹.

PRACTICE EXAM TWO **261**

ANSWER KEY

Part I

(1) $\dfrac{4\pi}{3}$
(2) 4
(3) 3
(4) −1
(5) $14i$
(6) −6, 1
(7) 4
(8) 5
(9) 150°
(10) $\dfrac{ab}{b+a}$
(11) $5\dfrac{1}{4}$
(12) IV
(13) 6
(14) 15
(15) −12
(16) 4
(17) 1
(18) 1
(19) 2
(20) 4
(21) 1
(22) 3
(23) 4
(24) 3
(25) 2
(26) 2
(27) 3
(28) 3
(29) 2
(30) 1
(31) 2
(32) 1
(33) 4
(34) 4
(35) 3

Part II

(36) *b*   2

(37) *a*   80
    b   20
    c   140
    d   30
    e   110

(38) 90°, 194.5°, 270°, 345.5°
    or
    90°, 194°30′, 270°, 345°30′

(39) *a*   3.06
    b   (1) $\dfrac{96}{625}$
        (2) $\dfrac{17}{625}$

(40) *a* $\dfrac{1}{5-y}$

(41)   b $\frac{3}{2} \pm \frac{1}{2}i$

(41)   a   15.1
        b   44

(42)   b   Reflect the funtion in $y = x$
             or
          Interchange the x's and y's
             or
          An equivalent statement
       d $y = 2^x$
          or
          $x = \log_2 y$

About the Author

David Kahn studied Applied Mathematics and Physics at the University of Wisconsin and has taught courses in calculus, precalculus, algebra, trigonometry, and geometry at the college and high-school level. He taught Princeton Review courses for the SAT I, SAT II, GRE, GMAT, and the LSAT, as well as trained other teachers in the same. He has been an educational consultant for many years and tutored more students in mathematics than he can count! (Actually, he can count them. Take a look at the acknowledgments.)

NOTES:

NOTES:

NOTES:

NOTES:

NOTES:

NOTES:

NOTES:

NOTES:

FIND US...

International

Hong Kong
4/F Sun Hung Kai Centre
30 Harbour Road, Wan Chai,
Hong Kong
Tel: (011)85-2-517-3016

Japan
Fuji Building 40, 15-14
Sakuragaokacho, Shibuya Ku,
Tokyo 150, Japan
Tel: (011)81-3-3463-1343

Korea
Tae Young Bldg, 944-24,
Daechi- Dong, Kangnam-Ku
The Princeton Review- ANC
Seoul, Korea 135-280,
South Korea
Tel: (011)82-2-554-7763

Mexico City
PR Mex S De RL De Cv
Guanajuato 228 Col. Roma
06700 Mexico D.F., Mexico
Tel: 525-564-9468

Montreal
666 Sherbrooke St.
West, Suite 202
Montreal, QC H3A 1E7 Canada
Tel: (514) 499-0870

Pakistan
1 Bawa Park - 90 Upper Mall
Lahore, Pakistan
Tel: (011)92-42-571-2315

Spain
Pza. Castilla, 3 - 5° A, 28046
Madrid, Spain
Tel: (011)341-323-4212

Taiwan
155 Chung Hsiao East Road
Section 4 - 4th Floor,
Taipei R.O.C., Taiwan
Tel: (011)886-2-751-1243

Thailand
Building One, 99 Wireless Road
Bangkok, Thailand 10330
Tel: (662) 256-7080

Toronto
1240 Bay Street, Suite 300
Toronto M5R 2A7 Canada
Tel: (800) 495-7737
Tel: (716) 839-4391

Vancouver
4212 University Way NE,
Suite 204
Seattle, WA 98105
Tel: (206) 548-1100

National (U.S.)

We have over 60 offices around the U.S. and run courses in over 400 sites. For courses and locations within the U.S. call 1 (800) 2/Review and you will be routed to the nearest office.

www.review.com

Expert Advice

Counselor-O-Matic

Pop Surveys

www.review.com

Paying for It

www.review.com

THE PRINCETON REVIEW

Getting In

Word du Jour

www.review.com

www.review.com

College Talk

Find-O-Rama College Search

www.review.com

Best Schools

MSN
The Microsoft Network
Includes FREE Offer

SAT Survival

www.review.com

Free!

Did you know that The Microsoft Network gives you one free month?

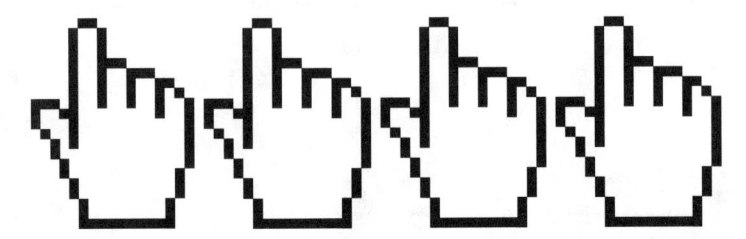

Call us at 1-800-FREE MSN. We'll send you a free CD to get you going.

Then, you can explore the World Wide Web for one month, free. Exchange e-mail with your family and friends. Play games, book airline tickets, handle finances, go car shopping, explore old hobbies and discover new ones. There's one big, useful online world out there. And for one month, it's a free world.

Call **1-800-FREE MSN**, Dept. 3197, for offer details or visit us at **www.msn.com**. Some restrictions apply.

Microsoft Where do you want to go today?®

MSn. The Microsoft Network

©1997 Microsoft Corporation. All rights reserved. Microsoft, MSN, and Where do you want to go today? are either registered trademarks or trademarks of Microsoft Corporation in the United States and/or other countries.